UNIVERSITY OF MASSACHUSETTS OCCASIONAL PAPERS 34

CURRENT ISSUES IN FIRST LANGUAGE ACQUISITION

2006

Edited by

Tanja Heizmann

Published by
GLSA
(Graduate Linguistic Student Association)
Department of Linguistics
South College
University of Massachusetts
Amherst, MA 01003-7130
U.S.A.

glsa@linguist.umass.edu
http://www.umass.edu/linguist/GLSA

Cover design: Jan Anderssen

ISBN: 1-4196-5076-9

A NOTE FROM THE EDITOR

This volume consists of a collection of papers from resident students and faculty, visiting researchers, visiting students and many fruitful collaborations among us. I would like to thank everybody who was, is and will be a part of the Language Acquisition Group at UMass Amherst. A special thanks goes to Jill de Villiers and the visiting researchers that she attracts. This always adds to a growing and ever evolving Language Acquisition Group. A grateful and special thanks goes to the director of the Language Acquisition Lab, Tom Roeper, who always has an open ear for students, visiting students and collaborating researchers alike. A special person who is always helpful in many ways is Barbara Zurer Pearson; thanks from everybody.

TABLE OF CONTENTS

Does every child produce "every" correctly?[*]

Emily Altreuter and Jill de Villiers

Smith College

1   Introduction

In this paper we will examine the classic phenomena associated with children's interpretation of "every," and present an experimental study that looks at production and comprehension in the same children. First, consider the sentence "Every cat has an apple," and the different simple stimulus arrays that have been used to test children's comprehension of the sentence.

> Type A: three cats each have an apple, and there is an extra apple. Adult answer: "yes."
> A common child error on Type A is to answer "no," due to the extra apple with no cat. This has also become known as the "spreading error," also "exhaustive pairing."

> Type B: three cats each have an apple and one cat has a banana. Adult answer: "no."
> An error on Type B would be to say "yes," misunderstanding "every." This is sometimes called an "underexhaustive search" error.

> Type C: three cats each have an apple and a dog has a banana. Adult answer "yes."
> An error on Type C, less studied, is to answer "no" because of the extra dog and banana. This has been called a "perfectionist" error.

[*] We would like to acknowledge the help of the children at the Smith College Campus school, their teachers and parents, and Cathy Yarnell for her patient help with our requests. Thanks are also due to Gabrielle Merchant, Clara Feldmanstern and Alison O'Connor for help testing and transcribing. We also thank the audience at the Fall 2005 UUSLAW for their helpful comments on an earlier version of this paper.

© 2006 by Emily Altreuter and Jill de Villiers
Tanja Heizmann (ed.): Current Issues in Acquisition. University of Massachusetts Occasional Papers in Linguistics 34, 1-19.
GLSA Amherst.

Type D: Four cats each have an apple. Adult answer "yes."
An error on Type D would suggest a failure to understand "every."

There are several distinct hypotheses that have been forwarded for these basic phenomena, particularly errors on Type A (from now on, we simply will call these "Type A errors"). Philip (2004) gives a very explicit comparison of two such theories, called the Event Quantificational Account (EQA, a revision of Philip 1995) and the Relevance Account (RA) a revision of the Presuppositionality Account of Drozd and van Loosbroek (2004). In addition, there is the Weak Quantifier Account (WQA) of Guerts (2003), and the Developmental Account (DA) of Roeper, Strauss and Pearson (this volume). There is no room to consider all the fine points of comparison but the major ones are reviewed to set up our experiment.

1.1   The Event Quantification Account

The EQA describes the child's semantic representation informally as follows:

> "Every minimal event which is a temporal subevent of a minimal cat-holding-apple event and in which a cat or an apple or both is a participant is a minimal event of a cat holding an apple."

In other words, if there is anything in the picture that is either cat or an apple, the child asks whether it is true that a cat is holding an apple. The child then sums across all such events to ask if is true that in every case, a cat is holding an apple. The EQA attributes to the child a semantic representation for "every" roughly equivalent to an adverbial quantifier such as "always" (see also Roeper & de Villiers, 1993). Since there are languages in the world that only have adverbial-type quantifiers, Philip asserts that the child is still following constraints on UG in positing such an interpretation. However, it is an immature representation for English. The consequence of such an interpretation is that a child would object to scenes in which, for example there was an additional apple, as in Type A. However, the EQA does not predict a mistake on Type C, where there is an extra dog holding a banana, since neither a dog nor a banana is a subevent of cat-holding-apple. As a result, errors on Type C are regarded by the EQA as a cognitive mistake of "perfectionism." In such a case a child has a processing failure of a much more basic kind, and cannot retain the lexical items called for in the representation. Similarly, underexhaustive responses (saying yes to Type B) are not given any linguistic account by the EQA, and are considered a separate cognitive error.

1.2   The Relevance Account

On this account, the child has full linguistic representation of the adult form. The particular problem manifest in exhaustive pairing is that the child imagines a fourth unseen object, say a cat missing from Type A. This happens because of symmetry requirements in the child's mental model. The child's verification process is non-adult like because s/he assumes that the missing cat is relevant to the verification of the sentence. Philip (2004) has demonstrated that this effect can be ameliorated in children by environments that discourage visual symmetry, and can be stimulated in adults by situations in which the missing agent is assumed relevant. Like with the EQA, Type B and Type C errors are considered different in kind from Type A and from each other. The RA then differs from the EQA in assuming full adult competence except for a pragmatic difficulty in determining relevance.

1.3   The Weak Quantifier Account

Geurts (2003) proposed that children construe the strong determiner as if it were *weak*. Children are said to adopt an interpretation of the quantifier as weak rather than strong because weak quantifiers are easier. He argues that the problem lies in the mapping between syntactic and semantic representations, namely a parsing problem, which is then "patched" by pragmatics. The adult interpretation (in Guerts' framework) of "every cat holds an apple" is:

(1)   <every> (x,y: cat (x) apple (y):x holds y]

However the child's semantic interpretation begins as this:

(2)   [...:....] <every> [x,y: cat(x), apple (y), x holds y.]

The front brackets contain an open variable for the domain of quantification. So, depending on the salience in the context, the child might interpret this as being about cats or about apples. In the case where the apples are in focus, the reading will be:

(3)   [y:apple(y)] <every> [x: cat(x), x holds y]

Thus the WQA accounts for Type A errors, because if there are apples without cats, the child will say "No", because every apple is not being held by a cat. Unlike the other theories, Geurts explains Type B or underexhaustive errors by the same mechanism: If there are cats without apples, the child might say "yes", because every apple *is* being held by a cat.

With some modification, WQA can also account for the Type C error, by arguing that the child quantifies over all animate objects, as if to say roughly "everything that is an animal is an animal holding an apple." As in the other accounts, in the WQA the Type C error is regarded as more serious than exhaustive pairing of Type A, and it resonates with the account in the EQA that the child making such an error fails to pay attention to the lexical items. However, Geurts emphasizes that more work is needed on Type C errors.

1.4   Developmental Account

Roeper, Strauss and Pearson (this volume) provide an account that considers closely the comparison of Type A and Type C errors, as well as Type B or underexhaustive responders who they class as "perseverators" or "yes-men." In a very large sample of children aged 4 through 9, they find a consistent age difference between the types of responders, with the Type B underexhaustive group being the youngest at 4;7, followed by Type C, then Type A, then target or adult-like children by age 8. However, responses of all types were found at all ages. They propose that children change in their semantic representations that are tied to the syntax of their quantifiers. At the start, children treat quantifiers adverbially, or via event quantification. At this stage, Type A and C errors will occur. At the next stage, the child assimilates "every" primarily to "each," which can "float" in the syntax in the adult language:

(4)   Each cat has an apple → Cats each have an apple

The claim is that at this stage a child can misconstrue this as quantifying over both subject and object:

(5)   Each cat has each apple

At this stage the quantifier is an NP-quantifier moved to the Focus phrase, where it can c-command elements in the VP. The child requires exhaustive pairing so commits Type A errors, but Type C errors should decline. What happens next on the DA story is the acquisition of the particular properties of quantifiers, e.g. whether they are in a DP, and if so, where. When the child discovers that *every* is not inherently distributive, i.e. it can also take a collective reading. Roeper et al argue that the child no longer raises it to the Focus position, and "every" instead gets fixed to the DP and no longer floats. As a result, the children will have adult like interpretations.

The advantage of the DA account is that it links semantic changes to syntactic developments and predicts a step-wise learning path that accommodates within the *grammar* three possible types of responses. However, it is at the cost of proposing non-adult-English grammatical options en route to the target form. Furthermore, it does not have an account of Type B underexhaustive readings. Children who give underexhaustive readings are said to perseverate on "yes" responses, which says nothing about their grammars.

In sum, the EQA and the RA consider only Type A exhaustive pairing of interest linguistically. In a careful comparison within studies designed to tease them apart, Philip (2004) favors the RA. Geurts' WQA predicts that Type A and Type B errors should co-occur as they are due to the same process. The DA predicts an ordered development, but considers Type B errors to be cognitive in origin.

The following chart attempts to capture which types of responses each theory captures or excludes:

Type of response:	EQA	RA	WQA	DA
Type B	Cognitive error	Cognitive error	Weak reading + salience	Cognitive error
Type C	Lexical error	Lexical error	Animate reading	Event quantification
Type A	Minimal event quantification	Symmetry + relevance failure	Weak quantifier + salience	Event quantification OR Floated NP quantification
Target	Event→ NP quantification	Adult pragmatics	Strong quantifier	DP quantification

How would the different accounts predict production of "every" by children? The DA most clearly would predict Type A and C errors in production, as it is the developing grammar that is being described. The EQA and the RA might predict Type B errors in production too, as those errors are attributed to cognitive mistakes. It is unclear whether the RA, EQA or WQA would expect Type C errors, as the lexical errors are meant to be processing problems that would be less likely in production. The EQA might predict Type A errors if the child's grammar allows them. However, since Philip attributes the error under the EQA to insufficient processing resources to maintain an adult LF, that could be taken to imply that the child would not have the same difficulty in production. The RA might also predict that Type A production errors should occur, since the same issues of symmetry and relevance would operate on production too. On both the RA and the EQA, the different error types have different causes, and so could presumably co-occur in the same child. The DA does not predict that, since the errors represent different stages of grammar. The exception is Type C errors, which should never appear without Type A, but Type A could occur without Type C.

The WQA is described as a processing account, so Geurts presumably would not predict parallel failures in production if the grammar is adult-like. Or would the child stumble over fixing the appropriate domain for the weakly construed quantifier even in producing such sentences? Guerts would at least need to predict Type A and Type B errors should co-occur, though none of the other theories predict this.

We are in a position to compare the various hypotheses against data from our own experiment that looks at both comprehension and production across the four types of scenario. In sum:

DA: Errors of different types should occur in different children, not in the same child. The different grammars should be consistent across comprehension and production. Underexhaustive or Type B errors are given no account, and might not be expected in production if they are simply "yes" perseveration. Type C errors should not occur alone.

EQA: No relationship is expected between Type A errors and other types. Type A errors should be consistent across production and comprehension. Different errors can co-occur in the same child but should not correlate as their sources are distinct.

RA: No relationship is expected between Type A errors and other types. Type A errors may not be found in production. Different errors can co-occur in the same child but should not correlate as their sources are distinct.

WQA: Type A and Type B errors should co-occur in comprehension and if they occur at all, in production too. Other errors should occur independently

There has to our knowledge been no work done to elicit production of "every" in an experimental setting of this sort. We designed a study to address the question of whether the error types A-D are restricted to comprehension. We also wanted to see if children knew that "every" had to be exhaustive, rather than just "plural," given the ambiguity of the ways in which children use "every" in spontaneous speech. Merchant (2005) searched the files of 18 CHILDES corpora and showed that children used "every" very rarely, with children under four or five almost never using it. When "every" was used, it was most often in the frozen forms such as "everyday" or "everybody," rather than "every toy" or "every apple." In fact, Merchant identified only 10 instances of "every N," all occurring late in the transcripts.

Of course there is a good reason why elicited production has not been tried, namely, how can a child be induced to use "every" if the context provided does not fit what the child's grammar demands? Following Chomsky (1965), we had to be cunning. We designed the stimuli to allow an alternative response that could be chosen by the child whose grammar did not allow the use of "every", but it required the child to choose something that had not been modeled. In this way, we could examine the child's resistance to the usual adult form.

2   Method

2.1   Subjects

Sixty-four children aged 5;0 to 7;11 were tested, with a mean age of 6;3. The subjects were in kindergarten, first or second grade at the Smith College Campus School. There were 26 boys and 38 girls.

2.2   Procedure

2.2.1   Comprehension

The children were taken one by one to the testing area, where a laptop computer presented the stimuli in a PowerPoint presentation that included the pre-recorded narration for each stimulus. The children all received the comprehension trials on one day, then the production trials on the second day. In this first study, we did not counterbalance the order. Children received a pretest slide with all the animals pictured, and we first ensured that they could easily identify the animals. Then the children were told that they would see some pictures on the computer with these animals in them, and hear the computer present a sentence for each picture. The children were warned that some of the sentences would be true, but others would not match the picture. The children were asked to say "yes" if they thought the sentence matched the picture and "no" if it did not.

Four stimulus conditions were presented. Consider the sentence "every cat has an apple" to illustrate what might be pictured in each stimulus type:

a) Type A, the source of the "spreading" error, in which there were three cats holding apples and a fourth apple on a table.
b) Type B, the "not-every" case as the source of perseveration or underexhaustive error, in which one cat held a different thing, say, a book.
c) Type C, the source of the "perfectionist" error, in which there were three cats holding apples and say, a sheep holding a book.
d) and Type D, the uncontroversial case, in which four cats are each holding an apple, that could provide the source for a "no"-bias error.

(See Appendix A and B for examples of each type of stimulus). Each randomization included five of each type of stimuli. The pictures were set up in line-ups, not randomly arranged, in such a way that they maximized symmetry. According to Philip (2004), that should also maximize the potential for spreading errors (also Rahklin, 2005).

There were two randomizations of the 20 stimuli, A and B, that were each given to half the children at each age. When the children had completed the 20 trials, they were thanked for their participation and told that they would return the next day for some further examples.

2.2.1 Production

The day after testing comprehension, the same children were tested again in production. Three children did not provide production data; in two cases they were absent and in one case the child refused to be recorded. The subjects were reminded that the day before, some of the computer sentences had not matched the pictures. They were told that we thought they could do a better job, and we liked having kids' voices on the computer, so today we would record them saying the sentences to get them right. The children were then shown a Powerpoint presentation of new pictures similar to the ones used in comprehension and told to make "a true sentence that starts with "Every…" The narrative that the child created was recorded on the same Powerpoint, a procedure used before with success and good recording fidelity (de Villiers, Cahillane & Altreuter, 2006). However, every session was also video-taped from behind the child so the stimulus was visible.

The production stimuli also had all stimulus types A-D represented, but a change was made so that the animals were all shown wearing hats or shoes. These items were not particularly salient, but the child would have a way to provide alternative true sentences for the array presented. This was necessary for Type B, where "every cat has an apple" was simply false. However, a child could say "every cat has a hat" and therefore make a true sentence. This option existed also for a child who was a classic "spreader" and therefore did not want to say that every cat had an apple if there was an apple on the table. That child also had the option of saying instead that "Every... cat has a hat" for Type D. The perfectionist could say "Every *animal* has a hat" for Type C. (See Appendix B for examples of stimuli.)

3   Results

3.1   Coding

All data were transcribed into a FileMaker Pro database. In the case of comprehension, the child's answers were tallied for correctness by type of stimulus A-D. Only in the case of Type B was a "no" answer considered correct. For production, all the children's responses were transcribed verbatim and then coded as below.

We first removed those children who made more than one mistake on Type D questions (these tended to be the "nay-sayers": children who answered "no" to everything). This removed 13 children: nine 5 year olds, three young 6 year olds and one young seven year old. This left 51 children. 5 of these children failed to do Production: one refused and 4 were absent, leaving 46 for production.

3.2   Comprehension

There was no major difference between the two randomizations so we ignored it in the analyses. We also tested for the effects of gender and found no difference in comprehension, so it also removed from consideration.

Table 1: Mean Number Correct/5 by Age and Type

	AGEGRP	Mean	Std. Deviation	N
TYPEA	5.00	4.75	.910	20
	6.00	4.41	1.064	17
	7.00	4.79	.579	14
TYPEB	5.00	4.05	1.877	20
	6.00	4.59	1.004	17
	7.00	4.93	.267	14
TYPEC	5.00	3.65	2.033	20
	6.00	3.65	1.618	17
	7.00	3.93	1.592	14
TYPED	5.00	5.00	.000	20
	6.00	5.00	.000	17
	7.00	5.00	.000	14

Table 1 shows the mean number correct out of 5 for each type for each age group. A repeated-measures analysis of variance was run on the number correct in comprehension, with age as the group variable and type of stimulus (A,B,C,D) as the repeated measure. There was a significant difference across types ($(F(3,48) =11.35$, $p< .001)$, but no significant effect of age nor interaction with age.

Table 2 shows the results of post-hoc paired samples t-test across type to locate which types were statistically different from each other. The asterisks indicate a significant difference between those question types.

Table 2: Paired Samples Test comparing performance across types of stimulus

| Compare: | Paired Differences | | t | df | Sig. (2-tailed) |
	Mean	Std. Deviation			
*Type D – Type B	.53	1.347	2.807	50	.007
*Type B – Type C	.75	2.448	2.173	50	.035
*Type D – Type A	.35	.890	2.831	50	.007
Type B – Type A	-.18	1.682	-.749	50	.457

The most difficult across age is Type C, with Type D being errorless. Type B and A are equally difficult.

To investigate the individual patterns more closely, we divided the children into five types of responders. It should be noted that these divisions were very easy to do: children were for the most part remarkably consistent in their responses for each type of stimuli. The majority of the data consists of 0s and 5s.

• "Target" children gave adult readings (allowing one error on any type).
• "Type A" children were the classic spreaders, saying more than one "no" just to Type A stimuli.
• "Type B" children answered "yes" across the board, even to Type B questions where the answer was clearly "no". It is possible that they allow "every" to mean "a lot of", i.e. non-exhaustive. However, it should be noted that this response could be a simple yes-bias as Roeper et al claim. The production data should help distinguish the alternatives.
• "Type C" children were the perfectionists, saying "no" more than once to Type C.
• "Type A & C" children made both types of error.

The first question is, are the types of children of different ages? The box–plot graph in Figure 1 below shows the mean age of each type and the spread of ages around it. It includes the excluded group who said "no" to everything. Type B children tended to be the youngest. There were only two Type A responders, intermediate ages. Type C kids are slightly younger on average than the target children. The Target children tend to be the oldest, but they have the greatest range. If the two Type A and the single Type A&C responders are removed, a univariate ANOVA with age as the dependent variable is statistically significant, with Type B < Type C <Target (F(2, 45)=3.79, p<.03).

Figure 1: Box plot of ages of children by each comprehension type

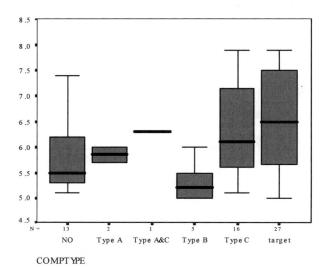

COMPTYPE

By seven years old, the majority of children (11 out of 15) were target responders. Without enough Type A children, the results are still not conclusive that there is a specific path of development that the DA alone would predict, since all the theories would concur that Type B is the most primitive error, and that Type C should precede adult-like responses.

Recall that the different theories make different predictions about co-occurrence of different errors. On the WQA, Types A and B should co-occur, but not the others as they are from independent sources. The correlations are in fact all very weak, with no sign of a significant correlation. This is what would be predicted under EQA, RA and DA. The DA predicts that Type C errors should not occur without Type A, but not vice versa. This is contradicted by the large number of Type C only children.

3.3 Production

Recall that the stimuli in production were designed to allow an escape hatch for children, in that they could choose to say something true about every animal if they wanted symmetry, such as "every cat has a hat." We thought that Type B stimuli would require this option. Instead, many children simply used negation, e.g. "every cat doesn't have an apple," even though this was never modeled. It was rare to choose the "hat" or "shoes" option below age seven, but the seven year olds took advantage of it, and sometimes used it for Type A and C stimuli as well as B stimuli. Only five responses mentioned the clothing for Type D, suggesting it was not salient. In contrast, 25 children constructed such sentences as "every cat has shoes" in the case of Type C. However, only 9 such responses used a general word such as "every animal has shoes", all from two children. There were 16 of the evasive kind for Type A.

If the child produced a response to either Type A or Type C that suggested that they were avoiding the standard answer, such as "Every animal has a hat," this was not counted as an error, but we took note of it in the coding. A statement counted as an *error* only if the child made a factually incorrect statement.

Evidence of Type A "spreading" in production was generally seen in negation, such as:

- "Every dog doesn't have an apple" (counted as an error)

but also may be evident in the following productions:

- "Every dog has an apple and one apple's on the table" (not counted as an error)
- "Wait a minute there's a balloon in midair! Every cat has shoes" (not counted as an error)

Production *error*s on Type B scenarios included "Not every elephant has a ball or a milkshake," and "Every dog has an apple." A type C *error* generally consisted of a negated statement. The following are some examples of what might be equivalent to Type C "spreading" in production:

- "Every sheep doesn't have a balloon"
- "Every cat has a watermelon and a hat and the elephant has a letter and a hat" (counted as correct)
- "Every dog has a watermelon but not the sheep. The sheep has a letter." (counted as correct)
- "Every elephant has a book except for the mouse" (counted as an error in quantifier scope)
- "Every animal has a hat" (counted as correct)

How do the errors correlate in production? To the extent that the WQA predicts production errors at all, it would presumably predict correlation of Types A and B, but this is not seen. And Type C errors do occur alone in three subjects, against the DA.

3.3   How do the two tasks relate?

We next tried to determine the relationship between response type in comprehension and production. Although some of the qualified production sentences above might be evidence that the child would reject *un*qualified sentences in comprehension, we cannot be sure. In the following analysis we only considered clear production errors for each stimulus type.

A series of one-way ANOVAs was conducted in which the grouping variable was not age but type of responder in comprehension, and the dependent measure was accuracy of production across each scene type A, B, C and D. The results in each case showed a significant match between the comprehension style of the child (Comp type) and the kinds of production errors made (See Table 3 for summary). The breakdown of the mean responses by type are shown by the following tables 4-6.

Table 3: Effect of comprehension error type on production errors of each type:

Production variable of:		df	Mean Square	F	Sig.	Partial Eta Squared	Observed Power
Type A	Comp type	4	6.128	176.551	.000	.945	1.000
Type B	Comp type	4	12.906	3.554	.014	.262	.825
Type C	Comp type	4	2.194	3.094	.026	.232	.764

Table 4 reveals that although there were only three Type A error children in comprehension (counting the one Type A&C child), their errors carry over into their production.

Table 4: Type A errors in production by comprehension error type

Comp type	Mean	Std. Deviation	N
Type A &C	**5.0**	.	1
Type B	0.0	0.0	5
Target	0.0	0.0	25
Type C	0.1	0.3	13
Type A	**0.5**	0.7	2

Table 5 reveals that the children who made Type B errors in comprehension (possibly taking "every" to mean "a lot of") did significantly worse at Type B questions in production than other types of responders. In other words, their errors in comprehension carried over into production. For these children, the fact that not every cat was holding an apple in the picture was not a problem: it was enough that most of them were, so they freely said, "every cat is holding an apple."

Table 5: Type B errors in production by comprehension error type

Comp type	Mean	Std. Deviation	N
Type A&C	0	.	1
Type B	**4.5**	1.0	4
Target	0.8	1.9	25
Type C	1.4	2.2	13
Type A	0.0	0.0	2

In Table 6, we see children who made Type C errors in comprehension (including the one Type A & C child) making significantly more Type C errors in production than other types of responders.

Table 6: Type C errors in production by comprehension error type

Comp type	Mean	Std. Deviation	N
Type A&C	**2.5**	.	1
Type B	0.0	0.0	5
Target	0.0	0.0	25
Type C	**0.6**	1.6	13
Type A	0.0	0.0	2

4 Discussion

Children in the age range five through seven years, the major population studied in quantifier comprehension testing, apparently do not have full adult competence in producing sentences containing "every." Their mistakes in comprehension carry over to their production.

Here we will review the results in light of the different models proposed in the introduction. Consider first the DA. It predicts that errors of different types should occur in different children, not in the same child. The fact that we had little trouble classifying the children suggest this is so, with one overlapping case of Type A and C, as the DA would predict. The different grammars should be consistent across comprehension and production, and they are. That is, the same kinds of errors get produced by the same children in production as in comprehension, though with lower frequency. Furthermore, the developmental ordering seems roughly correct. On the DA, Type C errors should not occur alone, but this is where the DA fails to predict the data as there are 13 such children.

As for the EQA, it predicts no relationship between exhaustive errors and other types, and that is true in the present data. Exhaustive errors should be consistent across production and comprehension, which they are. However, because they have different sources, different errors should be able to co-occur in the same child, but they rarely do in our data. They do not correlate as their sources are distinct in the EQA, which is confirmed. It is not clear that the EQA would predict the finding that the same errors occur in production as in comprehension for all types of error.

The RA also predicts no relationship between exhaustive errors and other types. It is not clear that exhaustive errors should be found in production, but they are found here. Again, the possibility that different errors can co-occur in the same child is not borne out, but they do not correlate, as predicted.

The WQA predicts that Type A and Type B errors should co-occur in comprehension and if they occur at all, in production too. Do these exhaustive and nonexhaustive errors pattern together? The answer is "no" - there is no correlation in comprehension and the errors are prevalent in different children at different ages. Nevertheless, it would be more clear if we had more Type A answers. Other errors should occur independently, and they do.

Roeper et al (this volume) argue for a comprehensive grammatical explanation (the DA) that would expect the errors to appear in production as well as comprehension. However, they propose a developmental progression beginning with both Type C and Type A errors, followed by only Type A. The very small number of classic Type A errors does not allow us to verify this claim. In addition, we found a significant number of children who made only Type C errors, which most of the literature would suggest is a somewhat unusual result. The DA predicts no stage at which Type C errors should occur in the absence of Type A errors, but we find 13 such responders. Although the DA cannot explain this fact, we look to a reason for why Type A and Type C did not *co*-occur more often.

We examine two potential explanations for this problem. First, there were 13 children who *did* make errors both on Type A and Type C, but because they also made errors on Type D, we excluded them as nay-sayers. Are we right in doing this, or should they count as representing the first stage in the DA?

One answer is that they are willful nay-sayers who do not have a logical reading for "every." If the children are really just *mindless* "nay-sayers," then they should be weak in *production* of Type B, where the adult answer really is "no," as well as the rest. In fact, they score very poorly in production of Type B. A univariate ANOVA shows this is a significant failure rate compared to the rest of the subjects ($F(1,54)=6.99$, $p<.01$)

A second answer about Type D errors is that it is a failure of accommodation or domain selection. One child gave us a possible explanation for the strategy when it came to production: he protested that you couldn't say "every cat" has an apple because in real life they don't. In other words, he judged the truth generically, and not with respect to the pictures.[1] Two children made consistent errors on Type D in production as well as saying no to them in comprehension. This phenomenon deserves more attention, as there is not only a logical requirement but also a pragmatic requirement in such experiments that the subject make an accommodation to the pictured context. However, this does not seem to be a consistent belief on the part of all the excluded children. The other eleven children excluded above because of Type D errors in comprehension nevertheless produced Type D correctly. It could be that they made an effort at compliance by the second day, when they came to realize that if they were to make the sentences, we meant them to focus only within the pictures. If this accommodation problem is *independent* of the other problems with quantifiers, then the 11 children who complied in production should show the same range of errors as the remainder of the group. However as we have seen, they do not: they make significantly more Type B errors.

Third, suppose that the children are really the kind who make Type A+Type C errors, because they are at that stage of the DA. The computer sentences would already violate their grammars 75% of the time, which might push them to find reasons to reject Type D as well. They then reject Type D for a somewhat unlikely reason such as the generic reading: cats don't all have apples in the world. This predicts that in production, these same children should be very prone to Type A and Type C errors. However, they do not make any more than the non-excluded children, in fact they do quite well (4.45/5 correct on each).

These facts lead us to reject the idea that the Type D nay-sayers are either accommodators-in-recovery or really Type A+Type C in disguise, and to admit that we do not know what these children think 'every' means. So we cannot count the nay-sayers as "lost" children from the first stage of the DA who make both Type A and Type C errors.

A second consideration is the fact that we found very few children who made classic Type A exhaustive paired answers, despite our attempts to a) sample the age range in which this has been reported as most prevalent and b) design stimuli that maximized attention to symmetry and c) provide little other pragmatic support and d) have no foils to break potential set effects (Philip, 2004; Rakhlin, 2005). In other words, we did everything that has been claimed might minimize the child's success and increase Type A errors, but without success. Why? Just possibly our stimuli might have broken symmetry by showing a table on which to rest the remaining object. Alternatively, perhaps our objects were just too small and non-salient to encourage the kind of refocusing that

---

[1] The fact that it was the younger children who did this suggests the error is a developmental one, not a smart-aleck response. One of us had a real-life experience with a precocious four year old that illustrates this point. She was trying to persuade the child to try sesame noodles, by using the argument that "Most people like them." The four year old responded quite seriously, "You haven't met most people."

Guerts and Philip predict leads to exhaustive pairing. Many such studies have included large animals as objects ("every boy rides on a horse") or sizeable inanimate objects (bikes, cars, ladders). However, Roeper & de Villiers (1993) had stimuli of boys drinking milkshakes, so it never occurred to us that the Type A error required large objects. If the presence of the table, and the size of the objects, are yet further contextual variables that influence the likelihood of Type A errors, this would have to be chalked up as a victory for the pragmatic side, i.e. RA or WQA, not the DA.

A significant number of children gave perfectionist or Type C errors. Those children who made spreading errors of either type in comprehension were likely to also make errors on the same stimuli in production. It cannot be estimated how many other true but qualified productions such as "well, every dog has an apple but one apple is on the table" might be due to the same discomfort with the unqualified "every" statements for Types A and C.

An unexpected group judged Type B sentences as true. These children might be rejected in comprehension studies as being "yes-bias" children, but our production results suggest at most of these same children are prone to the identical error in production: they use "every" for a majority but not an exhaustive group as in Type B. This is not an occasional error but a major form of response for these children. Prior work had suggested that children may consider "every" to be a plural, perhaps even a majority, but not necessarily an exhaustive majority. We contend that this be taken seriously as a stage in the development of the meaning of "every." The production data make it apparent that we should look with greater scrutiny at the concept of a "perseverator" whose data should be discarded. Geurts (2003) wrote "the determiner's lexical meaning is transparent enough, it is just the mapping from form to meaning that goes awry," but this may be too quick a conclusion.

In summary, these data are insufficient to decide among the different accounts, primarily because of the low number of Type A errors. The WQA is found wanting in respect of the clearly different nature of Type A and Type B errors. The DA made strong predictions that incorporated most response types under the grammar, instead of invoking other types of explanation for different responses. It correctly predicts the progression of stages, and the consistency of answers across comprehension and production, but it fails to account for the children who produce only Type C errors. We have suggested some "excuses" for this based on our stimuli, but those very excuses lean on the pragmatic factors that the RA and WQA invoke. So we cannot yet say with certainty whether our data support their developmental hypothesis. Furthermore, none of the different theories as they stand allow for either the "non-accommodators" or the "Type B/a lot of" children.

Like every researcher who embarks on a study of how children use "every," we now know every thing we wish we had done. However, we hope to have inspired researchers to take note of the potential for including production data in their models of how children learn "every" and other quantifiers.

References

Chomsky, N. (1965) *Aspects of the theory of syntax*. Cambridge, Ma: MIT press.

de Villiers, J.G., Cahillane, J & Altreuter, E. (2006). What can production tell us about Principle B? In B. Schwarz (ed) *Proceedings of the first GALANA conference, Hawaii*. U.Conn/MIT Working Papers in Linguistics.

Drozd, K & van Loosbroek, E. (2004). The effect of context on children's interpretation of universally quantified sentences. Ms.,University of Copenhagen.

Geurts, B. (2003). Quantifying kids. *Language Acquisition* 11: 197-218.

Merchant, G. (2005). Children's use of the quantifier "every". Lab report, Smith College.

Philip,W. (2005). *Event quantification in the acquisition of universal quantification*. Ph.D. dissertation, University of Massachusetts, Amherst, Ma.

Philip, W. (2004). Two theories of exhaustive pairing. Ms., Utrecht University.

Rakhlin, N. (2005) New forms of Quantifier-Spreading in Acquisition. Acquisition Laboratory meeting presentation, University of Massachusetts, Amherst.

Roeper, T. & de Villiers, J.G. (1993). The emergence of bound variable structures. In E. Reuland & W. Abraham (eds) *Knowledge and Language: Orwell's Problem and Plato's Problem*. Dordrecht: Kluwer.

Roeper,T. Strauss, U. & Pearson, B. (this volume) The acquisition path of the determiner quantifier every: Two kinds of spreading.

Appendix A

Type A: Every sheep has a banana.

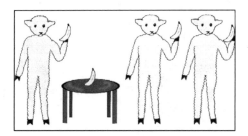

Type B: Every cat has a cookie.

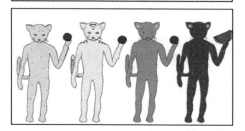

Type D: Every duck has an apple.

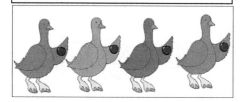

Appendix B

Type C in Production:
Every elephant has a book
OR
Every elephant has a hat
OR
Every animal has a hat

Type C in Production:
Every dog has a milkshake
OR
Every dog has a hat
OR
Every animal has a hat

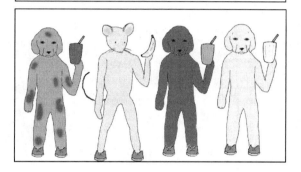

Box 6067
Smith College
Northampton
Ma 01063

ealtreut@smith.edu

Department of Psychology
Smith College
Northampton
Ma 01063

jdevil@smith.eu

Acquisition of Deontic and Epistemic Readings of *must* and *müssen**

Tanja Heizmann

University of Massachusetts, Amherst

1.   Introduction

This paper investigates the acquisition of deontic and epistemic readings of the English modal *must* and its German counterpart *müssen*. This paper proposes a syntactic analysis which assigns deontic and epistemic meanings in two structurally distinct positions. These positions are only divided by an adverb position which means that they are quite close in a phrase marker. This proposal has an impact on language acquisition. The hypothesis put forward here is that children perform poorly in deontic as well as epistemic instances when faced with comparing readings which are minimally distinct in structure.

This hypothesis is distinct from previous proposals made for the acquisition of deontic and epistemic readings of modals. Prior research and developmentalists, putting forward a Theory of Mind approach to the acquisition of modals, suggest that deontic readings are acquired first and epistemic readings do not emerge until later when children are cognitively mature enough to compute epistemic readings. This line of research proposes that deontic readings are easier for the cognitively less developed childe since these readings do not require a Theory of Mind ability from the child. This means that the child does not need to be able to attribute false beliefs and differing mental states to people in order to compute deontic meanings. However, Theory of Mind capabilities are needed to be able to compute epistemic readings since these involve more abstract concepts.

* This paper originates from work during my exchange year at UMass Amherst as an undergrad and a previous version ultimately resulted in a masters thesis. Thank you to Tom Roeper and Jill de Villiers for guidance and helpful comments. I am also grateful for input from Artemis Alexiadou, Andrea Cofalik, Kyle Johnson, Angelika Kratzer, Christine Lauenstein, Britta Sauereisen and Carola Trips. I would like to thank Jadranka Heizmann for help with the German study and Nikola Koch with the English study. Thanks also to my fellow students at UMass Amherst and the University of Stuttgart. A final thank to all the children, parents, teachers and care takers that made this study possible.

Tanja Heizmann (ed.): Current Issues in Acquisition. University of Massachusetts Occasional Papers in Linguistics 34, 21-49.
GLSA Amherst.

The Theory of Mind approach predicts children at around 3 to 4 years of age to perform significantly better on deontic tasks than epistemic tasks. Contrary to the Theory of Mind approach the hypothesis put forward in this paper predicts children to perform equally non-adult like in deontic as well as epistemic instances in cases of syntactically difficult environments.

This hypothesis was tested in an elicitation task with English and German children ranging in age from 3 to 5 years. The results of this study support the hypothesis put forward in this paper. The results also show that the Theory of Mind approach and other previous research have underestimated the role of the non-adult like syntactic system that children have partly by dividing deontic and epistemic instances into distinct acquisition tasks. This procedure does not force children to decide between closely competing structures thereby masking children's non-adult like syntactic abilities with modal verbs.

The reminder of this paper is structured in the following way. Section 2 introduces and discusses the different properties of English and German modal verbs, especially *must* and *müssen*. Section 3 summarizes and discusses previous research on the acquisition of modal verbs. Section 4 introduces and discusses the Theory of Mind approach and what prediction this kind of model makes for the experimental study presented in this paper. Section 5 lays out the theoretical assumptions made in this paper. Moreover the predictions of this model for the acquisition study are discussed. Finally, section 6 introduces the elicitation study and its results. This study was conducted in English and German to check the hypothesis put forward in this paper. Moreover, the results and its impact for further research is discussed in comparing the results crosslinguistically.

2.   Properties of Modals

Both English and German belong to the category of languages that take the same set of devices to express modality by using modal auxiliaries. Modal auxiliaries in English include *may, might, must, can, could, need, have (got) to, will, would, shall, ought to and should* [1]. In German, modal auxiliaries include *dürfen* 'to be allowed to', *sollen* 'have to', *müssen* 'must' and *können* 'can'. The set of English and German modals convey a broad cluster of meanings which are most commonly subsumed under deontic and epistemic modality. They play an important role in the domains of morality and law as well as in social conventions like expressions of politeness. Modal concepts are significant in theorizing and considering possible and hypothetical worlds. They influence planning, making predictions and expressing intentions and desires. Modal concepts reflect our ability to conceptualize parallel worlds.

---

[1] Taken from Greenbaum & Quirk (1990).

2.1   Semantic Properties

Deontic meaning involves notions of obligation, volition and permission. This kind of modality is concerned with the necessity or possibility of acts performed by morally responsible agents. The example in (1) represents a deontic interpretation of the modal *may*, more precisely one of permission.

(1)   You may go to the movies only after you have finished your homework.

Epistemic meaning involves the speaker's assumptions or judgments of possibilities or his conclusions about certain circumstances. Epistemic interpretations indicate the speaker's confidence or the lack of confidence in the truth of an expressed proposition. Understanding these kinds of structures means that the speaker is able to qualify propositions expressed, to judge their validity, truth or factuality. The example in (2) represents an epistemic interpretation of the modal *must*.

(2)   Mary must have missed the train.

In example (2) the only possible interpretation is an epistemic one, i.e. by all facts known to me, it must be the case that Mary has missed the train. The same interpretation holds for the equivalent examples in German.

(3)   Du darfst nur dann ins   Kino gehen, wenn du deine Hausaufgaben gemacht hast.
        you may only then to-the movies go   if   you your homework   done   have
        "You may go to the movies only after you have finished your homework."

(4)   Maria muss den Zug verpasst haben.
        Mary must the train missed   have
        "Mary must have missed the train."

Like the English example in (1), example (3) has a deontic interpretation, expressing permission. Sentence (4) has an epistemic interpretation like its English counterpart in (2), expressing a logical conclusion.

2.2   Syntactic Properties and Distribution

Modals in German can occur in a past tense construction (*musste*), they can have a German *Partizip* construction (*müssend*) [2], they have a distinct infinitival form (*müssen*), they show agreement properties (*muss, musst, müsst* etc.) and they can even function as full verbs like in (5) although the sentence is understood as containing in implicit verb, i.e. *I have to **go** to the bathroom.*

---

[2] Although native speakers do not agree on the acceptability of those constructions it is generally possible to have them. Some native speakers do not judge them as being perfectly good.

(5)   Ich muss aufs Klo.   ⇒   deontic
       I   must to-the toilet
       "I have to go to the bathroom."

In Modern English, modals do not show third person singular agreement as shown in example (6), they cannot be fronted in sentences, they do not have complement constructions with *to*, some modals do not have past tense constructions (e.g. *must, ought to*), or an infinitival form, and they are not marked with progressive tense as shown in example (7) [3].

(6)   No third person singular agreement: *He mays, musts, wills, cans, etc.

(7)   No progressive forms: *They are canning to do it

In short, German modals behave like full verbs, in English they do not. Modal verbs in Modern English syntactically behave like other auxiliary verbs. This divergence is due to different diachronic developments. In Old English modals behaved like German modals, therefore also exhibiting the same properties of full verbs.

2.2.1   Present Tense Differences in German and English

There are differences in the readings that can be assigned to German and English present and past tense structures. Since these were tested in the acquisition study discussed in section 6 the differences are exemplified here with the help of an actual test story. The stories were presented to children in form of a video with handpuppets much like *Sesame Street* stories. Consider the situation given in (8).

(8)   *We can see a house and within the milky window we can see Piglet's shadow
       eating a banana. In front of the house we see Bert (with a banana in his hands)
       and Cookie Monster.*
       Experimenter: "Look, there is Cookie Monster and there is Bert. Bert tells Cookie
       Monster: "You eat too many cookies and not enough fruit and vegetables. That's
       not healthy. So, you really have to eat a banana." *Throughout the story all three
       characters are visible. Although Piglet is behind a milky window he is clearly
       recognizable.*

In the context of (8) one character, *Cookie Monster*, is obliged to eat a banana because *Bert* ordered him to do so. We do not know whether *Cookie Monster* is really going to eat the banana or not. By deduction we know that *Piglet* is eating a banana right at that moment[4]. If we want to ask a question referring to *Cookie Monster* (deontic case of obligation), we would have to ask the question in (9).

---

[3]Examples (6) and (7) are taken from Roberts (1985: 21). See also for a diachronic analysis of English modal verbs.
[4]The children, and we for that matter, know that the shadow behind the milky window is Piglet because a picture of all participating characters is in front of the children throughout the story. Since there are only 3

(9)   Who must eat a banana?   ⇒   deontic

In English, (9) is clearly and exclusively deontic. An important issue is that the indefinite article *a* has to be used in English as well as in German to avoid confusion with the visible banana, i.e. the banana in *Bert*'s hands, as opposed to another banana that *Piglet* is eating. By using the definite article only one reading would be permissible based on pragmatic regulations, namely *the banana* would only mean the one visible. Since a biased setting is not desirable, the indefinite article is used to be as neutral as possible. The question for the epistemic/*Piglet* reading is as given in (10).

(10)   Who must *be* eat*ing* a banana?   ⇒   epistemic

As opposed to the deontic version of the question, the progressive *be* and ending *–ing* are added to the structure in the epistemic version.

       The context given in (8) applied to German, however, yields an ambiguous reading with respect to question structures[5] since German does not have a present progressive tense.

(11)   Wer muss 'ne Banane essen?   ⇒   ambiguous
        Who must a banana eat
        "Who must eat a banana? AND Who must be eating a banana?"

The German sentence (11) is ambiguous between the deontic/*Cookie Monster* reading and the epistemic/*Piglet* reading. The phonologically reduced form of the indefinite article *'ne* has to be used in German to avoid confusion with the cardinal number *one*. The indefinite article *a* in its non-reduced form (*eine*) is homophone with the cardinal number *one (eine)*, which would refer to the visible banana in *Bert*'s hands. Again, this is important to be able to maintain an 'as neutral as possible reading'.

2.2.2   Past Tense Differences in German and English

As mentioned in section 2.2 the past tense constructions of deontic and epistemic readings are also different in English and German. Again, the context in (8) is presupposed. The deontic version of the English question in the past tense is given in (12).

(12)   Who was supposed to eat the banana?   ⇒   deontic

---

participating characters and two of them, Bert and the Cookie Monster, are clearly visible, the third character must be Piglet.
[5] Some German native speakers seem to prefer the deontic reading and classify the epistemic reading as being marginal. Since this preference does not influence the line of reasoning in this paper, I will not go in further details here.

This question form necessarily has to use a form other than *must* since must does not have a past tense form that conveys a deontic meaning. In order to be able to ask a deontic question in the past tense one has to resort to *be supposed to* as in (12) or *have to* as in (13).

(13)   Who had to eat a banana?   ⇒   deontic

Both questions, (12) and (13), yield the deontic/*Cookie Monster* reading. The epistemic/*Piglet* reading though can be constructed with *must* as in (14).

(14)   Who must have eaten a banana?   ⇒   epistemic

In German both readings, deontic and epistemic, can be composed with *müssen* in the past tense. The deontic question is given in (15) and the epistemic question is given in (16).

(15)   Wer hat 'ne Banane essen müssen?   ⇒   deontic
        Who has a banana eat must
        "Who had to eat a banana?"

(16)   Wer muss 'ne Banane gegessen haben?   ⇒   epistemic
        Who must a banana eat   has
        "Who must have eaten a banana?"

In (15) we have a deontic/*Cookie Monster* reading, in (16) an epistemic/*Piglet* reading. The difference between English and German seems to be due to contrasting properties of modals since German modals behave like full verbs whereas in English modal verbs have the distribution of auxiliary verbs. Furthermore *must* has the odd property of not having a deontic past tense construction[6]. German *müssen* has no quirks like the English counterpart. It shares regular properties with other modal verbs.

The syntactic distribution observed so far has the implication that while in German modal verbs are base-generated within the VP system like other main verbs, modal verbs in English are base-generated higher in the IP system like other auxiliary verbs.

3.   Previous Research on Acquisition of Modal Verbs

In this section an overview of literature on the acquisition of deontic and epistemic interpretations of modals is given. One can always approach the course of acquisition

---

[6] Moreover, *must* in combination with negation also has the odd property of not conveying the semantic negation of the positive sentence. Compare i) and ii).
i) John must eat a banana.
ii) John must not eat a banana.
Modals in combination with negation is an interesting topic but it cannot be included in the current paper due to space limitations. Interestingly no acquisition study so far has looked at this interaction.

from two angles, observational and experimental. It is very important to examine insights gained from both perspectives in order to avoid the potential pitfall of looking only at a fragment of a whole puzzle. A more complete picture of the development of modals is certainly more desirable. A very well known fact, for example, is that production data always lags behind the competence of children[7]. Therefore both perspectives are needed to get the complete picture of what is going on in child speech. First I will give an overview of naturalistic data and later I will turn to experimental data.

3.1   Natural Production Data

In general, all studies on natural speech data taken together produce a quite consistent pattern of the early development of modals[8]. Shatz & Wilcox (1991), Hirst & Weil (1982) and Noveck et al. (1996) have good summaries of the assembled data on natural speech production of modals. The following summary can be reviewed in detail in their papers.

2 to 3 years: Kuczaj (1975), Kuczaj & Maratsos (1982) and Kuczaj & Maratsos (1983) assembled evidence that modals appear in child speech as early as 2;6 years of age. Although deontic concepts like those of permission were used quite frequently by young children, epistemic concepts of possibility did not appear frequently until around 3;3. Wells (1979) and Perkins (1983) yielded similar findings as those by Kuczaj.

It seems as if the growth in modal meanings is far more rapid than the change in syntactic contexts in which the modals appear. Kuczaj & Maratsos (1983) observed that children seem to be restricted in syntactic productivity at the onset of modal acquisition. Modals occurred earliest in declaratives and some months later in yes-no questions. This patterns with the observation made by Shatz et al. (1986) that confirms the early predominance of modals in declaratives. Later on more syntactic structures are used. Another consistent observation in all production data is the fact that deontic meanings of modals appear earlier in child language than epistemic readings.

3 to 4 years: The age between 3 and 4 seems to show a significant increase in the number of modals used to express different, predominantly deontic, meanings. The use of epistemic uses of modals is rarely attested in natural speech at this age but they do occur.

4 to 5 years: Around the age of 4;5 to 5 the use of notions of necessity and possibility, i.e. epistemic meanings, increase. Opposed to Kuczaj's findings, Wells (1985) observes that epistemic meanings are not produced very frequently yet during that period. However, the observed epistemic notions involve inference or certainty, Kuczaj's epistemic notions, on the other hand, involve possibilities. Wells' findings indicate that deontic meanings are in place by the age of 3;3. Epistemic meanings conveying certainty appeared later and with a lower frequency. And finally, epistemic meanings involving inferences appeared even later than those of certainty.

---

[7] The same observation can be made in L2 acquisition.
[8] Unfortunately, most of the studies, naturalistic and experimental, are restricted to English data.

3.2   Experimental Data

One of the earlier studies in the acquisition of modal verbs has been conducted by Hirst an Weil (1982). Their study contained two different elicitation tasks with children aged 3 to 6. One for deontic interpretations, the other for epistemic interpretations. In the deontic condition two teachers each gave one statement about what room a puppet should go to. These two statements were evaluated by the children, i.e. the children had to tell where the puppet would go. For example children had to choose between (i) *You must go to the green room* and (ii) *You may go to the red room*. The epistemic condition tested the propositions concerning the location of a peanut, i.e. the children had to choose where the peanut was. For example the children had to choose between (i) *The peanut should be under the box* and (ii) *The peanut must be under the cup*. In both tasks children had to choose between two utterances containing modals or the factive *is* of varying strength where the strength was supposed to decrease in the following order.

(17)   is > *must* > *should* > *may*

The results show that the greater the difference in strength between the modals was, the earlier this difference was acquired. In other words the difference between *must* and *may* was acquired before the difference of *should* and *may*. Moreover their findings seem to suggest that epistemic interpretations are acquired earlier than deontic interpretations. Hirst and Weil themselves put forward that these results may have been influenced by performance factors rather than reflecting the competence of children. That might have been the case because the children had to evaluate some sort of authority of the two teachers issuing commands to a puppet as well as the puppet's compliance in the deontic task therefore making it more demanding overall.

A study conducted by Noveck et al. (1996) replicates parts of the Hirst & Weil (1982) study with 5-year-olds exclusively. Moreover they address the question as to whether feedback influences the performance of children on the relative force of modals. In a second task Noveck et al. aimed to determine the influence of logical reasoning to a greater extent than the original Hirst & Weil study. The results from the first task, the modified replication of the Hirst & Weil study, shows that even without feedback children obey the relative force hierarchy, i.e. removing the feedback does not seem to influence their performance. This seems to support Noveck et al.'s hypothesis that logic meaning is already present in 5-year-olds "[O]r at least an awareness of what is contextually appropriate for their use .." (Noveck et al. 1996: 641) and that relative force is not the only factor in the development of modals. Experiment 2 was a truth-value judgment task which included children aged 5 to 7 years. They presented two statements to the children, one true and one false statement. The two statements were uttered by two puppets (each puppet a different one). Then the children were asked to determine which one of the statements is correct, i.e. the children were asked *Which puppet is right?*. The two statements were presented in a context that determined that only one statement was logically correct, i.e. the children were told beforehand that only one puppet can be right. If children would solely rely on the relative force of modals, they were expected to agree with the statement containing the stronger modal even if this statement was established to be false. If on the other hand the children have an understanding of logical meaning they are expected to ignore relative force contrasts and rely on truth values. The results show that the relative force influence can be muted. The results from the second task shows that 5-year-olds employ the logically correct modal statement. Even if the two statements contained the same modal, the logically correct statement was chosen significantly more often. If relative force were the only influence, it would predict a chance responding. The results also show an increase in performance with age. 5-year-olds agree with some regularity with the logically correct statement (and not the more forceful modal), 7-year-olds systematically agree with the logically correct statement and 9-year-olds show an adult like performance on the task. This means that even the younger children do not consider relative force at the expense of logical considerations. Unfortunately this study did not include children under the age of 5. As we have seen in section 3.1 the emergence of the modal system is critical between the ages of around 3 years of age and 5 years. We will also see in the next section that this age is critical for the emergence of the Theory of Mind.

Interestingly, mental verbs seem to develop parallely to what is known about the acquisition of modal verbs, cf. Moore et al. (1989) and Moore & Furrow (1989). Both, mental verbs and epistemic readings of modals can be linked to the development of metacognitive abilities which are impacted by the development of the Theory of Mind, cf. Miller (2004).

4.   Theory of Mind

This section discusses the Theory of Mind (henceforth ToM) approach to the acquisition of deontic and epistemic readings and its implications and predictions for the acquisition study described in section 6. ToM   approaches to the acquisition of modals, e.g. Papafragou (1998) and (2001), emphasize the importance of cognitive development of children. Prior to a certain developmental stage epistemic meanings are supposed to be harder to grasp as a model for the child as opposed to deontic meanings. This approach predicts that deontic meanings are acquired before epistemic readings since deontic meanings are congitively less demanding for the child. However, I suggest that the ToM approach underestimates the syntactic demands which a child faces. If deontic meanings are earlier in place according to ToM, younger children should perform better and more stable on deontic readings in elicitation tasks than on epistemic tasks. This prediction is not borne out completely as the acquisition study in section 6 shows. Cognitive demands might well influence the early development of modals, however, as I show in subsequent sections, when children are faced with a difficult syntactic decision, they perform equally unstable on deontic as well as epistemic tasks. These results are not expected according to ToM.

4.1 Introduction to the Theory of Mind

An influential topic for cognitive developmentalists has been the Theory of Mind Hypothesis[9]. Essentially, the ToM supposes that the cognitive abilities of younger children are different from those of older children and adults. These different cognitive abilities are important for the acquisition of modal verbs. To be able to pass ToM tasks one needs the understanding that people have mental states, for example beliefs and desires, that can differ from one's own. To have a ToM also means that one has the ability to predict and explain people's behavior based on their, possibly false, belief states. Within the framework of ToM deontic readings are supposed to be easier for cognitive reasons since epistemic readings represent more abstract concepts than deontic readings, i.e *It is messy here, you must clean up your room* (deontic) is less demanding on children's cognitive abilities than *Daddy must have left work earlier because he caught the 5 o'clock train* (epistemic). As we have seen in the preceding section children as young as 3;3 produce epistemic readings of modals although deontic readings are attested earlier and more frequent and stable in natural production data.

Papafragou (1998) defines this hypothesis as given in (18). However, this is not a complete definition that entails all implications.

(18)   On one of its central interpretations, this hypothesis entails that part of
        [the] human cognitive mechanism is the ability to know one's own
        mind as such, i.e. to reflect on one's mental contents and processes and
        to accommodate the results in a coherent commonsense theory about
        the mental world.   (Papafragou 1998: 382)

In the prestage of the period described above the child's mind is a container that is nothing more than a storage place for representations of reality. These representations are taken to be accurate. They are directly induced by external stimuli and children are unable to produce representations that are not identical to reality. In a later stage when ToM kicks in, the mind starts to function as an active processing unit that forms and processes representations of reality and not only reality itself. By doing that this unit is also able to detect instances of false belief, different sources of evidence and to calculate possibilities.

Researches presupposing the Theory of Mind Hypothesis predict that children understand deontic interpretations of modals earlier than epistemic ones because they are limited cognitively from doing otherwise and are therefore constrained in acquiring these modal interpretations. The central question then is how do concepts of knowledge state and evidence arise?

According to Papafragou 'epistemic uses of modals mark operations on mental representations' (Papafragou 1998: 373). As mentioned earlier, the interpretation of epistemic modals is a reflection on the knowledge of a mental state. In other words the

---

[9] For a more detailed exposition of the Theory of Mind Hypothesis see e.g. Wellman (1990).

ability to differentiate between reality and hypothetical worlds and the **awareness** of doing so. In literature on child development this kind of reflection is rarely attributed to children under 4 years of age. Such a metacognitive ability presupposes a deduction on an abstract content of beliefs of speakers, i.e. of the type *'this is reality/a hypothetical world I am thinking about'*, in order for them to arrive at a valid conclusion about a proposition.

Early structures involving volition and permission, i.e. *can, will* etc., seem to reflect the egocentricity which is also a feature attributed to children in a stage prior to the one needed for more abstract, i.e. epistemic, interpretations. This is supported by the observation that modals surface initially in first person usage, i.e. with self-reference, cf. Fletcher (1979). This subjectivity can be directly connected to the egocentricity issue.

There some debate about to which specific age period the different stages of ToM can be attributed to, cf. Papafragou (1998). The ability to contrast a belief or a dream against reality are attributed to children around 2;8, but 2-year-olds are not able yet to grasp desires and perceptions in an adult form. Desires are conceived as a drive towards objects and not as inner urges, and perceptions are conceived as awareness of objects, i.e. by visual contact and not as the knowledge of things still continuing to exist even when out of the visual range. At this stage children seem to establish causal links between the mind and the world. Even for 3-year-olds belief contents are taken to reflect the world directly and they are still incapable of recognizing that beliefs may have different sources. Finally between 4 and 5 years of age children seem to have established a representational model of mind. They are now able to conceive mental contents as representations distinct from reality. And since epistemic modality represents the ability to assess one's judgment of beliefs, and to consider the reliability of these judgments, it makes sense to believe that the developing ToM of children may influence the course of acquisition of modal interpretations. In other words, deontic meanings of modals do not require a fully fledged ToM from the child in order to understand them. To summarize, researchers such as Papafragou (1998) assume that ToM develops before language can map onto it.

Opposing developmentalists such as Papafragou (1998) are researchers stating that ToM is dependent on certain linguistic abilities, e.g. de Villiers and de Villiers (2000), de Villiers and Pyers (2002) and Miller (2001) and (2004). These accounts suggest that a specific syntactic structure, namely complementation, is necessary to be able to compute false beliefs, a component of ToM. This is so because complementation structures provide the representational structure for embedded propositions. Consider sentence (19).

(19)   [$_{mc}$ Mary thinks [$_{ec}$ that the chocolate is in the box.]]

In example (19) the truth value of the matrix clause, *mc*, can be different from the truth value of the embedded clause, *ec*. In other words, it is not important whether the chocolate is actually in the box or not, Mary can still think that the chocolate is in the box even that belief is false.

The ability to compute a false belief within a ToM task is usually tested according to the blueprint given in (20).

(20)   Displacement Task:
       A puppet sees a toy hidden in location A and then leaves the scene. While the puppet is gone, the object is moved from location A to location B. The child is then asked where the puppet will look for the toy upon returning.
       Question to the child: *Where does X think the toy is?*

For the situation described in (20) the correct adult response is that the puppet mistakenly thinks the toy is in location A since the puppet has a false belief about the toy's location, i.e. the puppet has no knowledge of the displacement. However, children of around 3;5 - 4;0 years of age and younger answer non-adult like by stating that the puppet thinks that the toy is in location B. As we can see from the question in (20) it involves complementation just as in example (19).

4.2   Predictions

If the Theory of Mind Hypothesis is right in assuming that ToM ability develops prior to language structures mapping onto it, children should have no problems with deontic tasks by the age of 4 since their cognitive abilities are capable of computing these. Children in that age range should however have problems with epistemic tasks since their cognitive capabilities are not developed enough yet.

According to the research of de Villiers et. al and Miller, children's non-adult like syntactic abilities could cause them to have trouble once they are faced with structures they have not acquired yet. This account claims the opposite of the Theory of Mind Hypothesis since certain language structures have to be in place before ToM maps onto that. The current paper supports this line of research. I propose that performance on both, deontic as well as epistemic, structures is impaired once the child is faced with a syntactic problem. Independent from a connection to ToM like de Villiers et al. and Miller's work, this prediction has not been examined in the literature on the acquisition on modals yet. This prediction however is supported by the experiment discussed in section 6. Before we can look at the actual experimental task we have to establish the theoretical assumptions underlying the current line of research and look at all structures that were tested in the experimental task.

5.   Towards a Syntactic Approach of Deontic vs. Epistemic Readings

This section provides a syntactic approach to account for the difference between deontic and epistemic readings. I propose that there is not only a semantic difference between the two readings but moreover that the two different readings occupy two different structural positions. To my knowledge, a syntactic approach to these differences has not been explored in the literature yet. The claim in acquisition terms is that while ToM does partly influence the acquisition of modals the syntactic difficulties that the child faces must not be underestimated. When the child faces the acquisition of the two different readings but these distinct readings are encoded in a syntactic structure which differs minimally, the child has more trouble in acquiring the two readings than in a situation where the two readings are encoded in syntactic structure which does not differ minimally. In the latter case the child has more success in detecting and acquiring the structure because there are more differences, e.g. two different lexical items in the case of the deontic past tense structure in English.

5.1   Two Syntactic Positions for Two Readings

As we have seen in the previous sections, linguists approach modal meanings on various levels: semantic, pragmatic and on the level of cognitive development of children. For example, the hypothesis that deontic meanings are the source of modal understanding does not seem to be confirmed as the findings of Hirst & Weil (1982) suggest[10]. Thus it seems plausible that the development of epistemic modals does not hinge on that of deontic ones[11]. Of course they belong to the same set of linguistic devices used to express modality and therefore they are not two completely distinct concepts and linguistic items. The question now is, how do they differ and does that difference influence the order of acquisition? One possibility to account for the difference is to say that both meanings of modals, deontic and epistemic, have the same syntactic distribution but that children will still be able to recognize a difference. This argument is known as the Principle of Contrast[12]. Children recognize a difference in meaning without necessarily knowing what those meanings are when they first encounter them. This awareness could alert the children to pay attention to those differences.

There are two problems with this account. First this principle by itself does not really do any explanatory work because it does not make any predictions about why deontic meaning would come in first, followed by epistemic meanings. The second problem is that there might well be a syntactic difference in the different meanings of modals. Up to now the syntactic aspect of the acquisition of modals has been neglected.

I approach deontic and epistemic readings from a syntactically based position, which has not been done before. First we have to establish that there is a structural difference between the two possible readings. Consider the context in (21) and the different interpretations in (22) and (23)[13].

(21)   *Peter* is ordered to go to the icebox every day to get the food out (deontic interpretation, because *Peter* is obliged to do that). He has small hands. But on the icebox only handprints from huge hands can be seen. Since *John* is the only other person in the house and he has very big hands, he must be the only one really

---

[10] For a more thorough discussion of advantages and disadvantages of polysemous approaches vs. monosemous approaches see Papafragou (1997) and Papafragou (1998).
[11] For example, Papafragou (1998) emphasizes that the emergence of the modal system can be predicted solely on grounds different from a polysemous account.
[12] For a longer discussion of this topic see Shatz & Wilcox (1991).
[13] Thanks to Tom Roeper and Jill de Villiers for English judgments.

going to the icebox (epistemic interpretation because of a conclusion based on handprints).

(22)   He always must go to the icebox.   ⇒   deontic

(23)   He must always go to the icebox.   ⇒   epistemic

Given the context in (21), example (22) has a deontic interpretation. *Peter* is the only person supposed to go to the icebox. Example (23) has an epistemic interpretation. *John* is the only person who is really going to the icebox. This interpretation is based on the evidence that only handprints from huge hands are on the icebox. Since *Peter* has small hands, *John* is the person whose handprints are on the icebox.

If we leave out the adverb *always* in sentences (22) and (23), the surface strings look identical. Moreover that structure then is ambiguous as we can see in the example in (24).

(24)   He must go to the icebox.   ⇒ ambiguous

The difference between the possible epistemic example in (24) and the exclusively epistemic example in (10) is that (24) has a habitual reading and (10) has a situational reading, hence the present progressive. An example like the one in (10) would not be appropriate in the context of (21) since the situation is not currently ongoing. This difference is discussed in more detail in section 5.2.

As the data in (21) through (23) shows, deontic and epistemic readings may not have the same underlying structure. The crucial examples get disambiguated by an adverb. This observation leads to the assumption that the modal interpretation, i.e. the deontic or epistemic meaning, is assigned to modal auxiliaries within the I-system. Based on the examples in (22) and (23) I propose the structure in (25). There is reason to believe that there are two different modal positions within the IP system. One encodes deontic meaning, the other epistemic meaning. Based on (22) the deontic modal position is the lower one. Based on (23) the epistemic modal position is higher in the hierarchy given that the adverb position is fixed [14].

---

[14] This observation can only be made with *always*-type adverbs based on Cinque (1999) and not with any kind of adverbs. Of course, Cinque uses different examples and the original Cinque phrase marker involving modals is more complex since it proposes several distinct positions for the different interpretations of deontic cases. For simplicity's sake this complex structure is omitted here.

(25)   Two Modal Positions

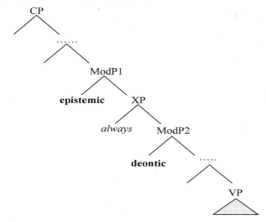

Since German is a V2 language the deontic/epistemic interpretation is assigned a bit differently. As we have seen in example (11) in section 2.2.1 the German present tense question is ambiguous. Since German modals have properties of main verbs it is reasonable to assume that they are base-generated in VP, then they move to CP via the IP system. While passing through the IP system, the modal gets assigned either a deontic or an epistemic meaning in the respective positions exemplified in (25). The adverb *immer* (always) cannot disambiguate the structure as in English since always type adverbs have a fixed position within the IP system which is lower than the surface position of the verb, cf. Cinque (1999). This is exemplified in sentence (26). Since, in German, the modal occupies a position higher than the IP in the surface string, the adverb cannot intervene between the two positions yielding disambiguation as in the English cases.

(26)   [CP Er muss [IP immer an den Gefrierschrank gehen.]]   ⇒   ambiguous
              He must   always to the   icebox   go
          "He must always go to the icebox AND He always must go to the icebox."

For the German past tense deontic construction I assume that the modal meaning is checks off its feature at LF since the modal appears in the VP, as seen in (15) repeated here as (27). In other words, the modal moves to the ModP2 position at LF to get interpreted.

(27)   Wer hat 'ne Banane essen müssen?   ⇒   deontic
          Who has a   banana eat   must
          "Who had to eat a banana?"

As we can see from the structure in (25), the distinction between the structural position for deontic versus the epistemic position is quite delicate. This subtle difference in positions is quite a challenge in acquisition terms. More so since the disambiguation for the English cases is quite rare, i.e. only *always* type adverbs. In German, pragmatic particles can support the disambiguation process as we can see in examples (28) and (29).

(28)   Er muss wohl   immer an den Gefrierschrank gehen.   ⇒ epistemic

      He must modal-particle always to the icebox   go
      "Indeed, it must be him who must always go to the icebox."

(29)   Er muss eigentlich   immer an den Gefrierschrank gehen.   ⇒ deontic
      He must modal-particle always to the icebox   go
      "Necessarily, he always must go to the icebox."

These modal particles, *wohl* in (28) and *eigentlich* in (29) have no lexical meaning and do not contribute anything to the propositional content of the sentence, cf. Bussmann (1996). This kind of disambiguation is more frequent in German than the disambiguation possibility for English.

To keep the acquisition task as syntactically minimal as possible these pragmatic helps were not included on purpose.

5.2   Implications and Predictions for Language Acquisition and Set Up of Task

In section 4.2 we have seen that the ToM approach predicts children to perform quite well on deontic cases at latest by the age of 3;5 and quite poor on epistemic cases possibly up until the age of 5;0. However, I propose that the non-adult like syntactic capabilities of children will cause then to have trouble in syntactically difficult situations, deontic as well as epistemic. This proposal does not claim that ToM does not play an important role in the acquisition of modals. Nevertheless the ToM approach underestimates the importance of syntax in the acquisition of modals.

This section points out and summarizes the cases for English and German that are crucial in the acquisition task that checked the hypothesis that children have trouble with deontic as well as epistemic cases in the case of a syntactically difficult environment.

5.2.1 Situational Conditions

As we have seen in section 2.2.1 the English present tense presents the child with the following minimal pair. As we can see the deontic form in (30) differs only minimally from the epistemic form in (31) making this a minimal but crucial distinction which needs to be acquired.

(30)   Who must eat a banana?   ⇒   deontic

(31)   Who must *be* eat*ing* a banana?   ⇒   epistemic

In the situation described in (8) we can see that both possibilities, deontic/*Piglet* and epistemic/*Cookie Monster*, are present in one and the same story. This is an important departure from previous experiments which divided deontic readings and epistemic readings into separate tasks. However, in order to be able to check my hypothesis that children have trouble in syntactically difficult situations, it is crucial that both syntactic structures are an option to the child in one and the same task. This way the child is forced to consider all characters, i.e. structures, and if the child is indeed having trouble in the area of syntax we expect the child to perform poorly no matter whether the question is a deontic one or an epistemic one.

The hypothesis here is that opposed to the minimal difference in the present tense, the deontic/epistemic distinction in the past tense in English is easier to acquire for children because it does not involve a syntactically minimal pair but different lexical items. This is exemplified in examples (12) through (14) repeated here for convenience.

(32)   Who was supposed to eat the banana?   ⇒   deontic

(33)   Who had to eat a banana?   ⇒   deontic

(34)   Who must have eaten a banana?   ⇒   epistemic

As we can see, the child can acquire the difference between deontic and epistemic readings in the past via different lexical items.

For German there is a minimal pair in past tense constructions. Again, I hypothesize that children have difficulties acquiring these structures since they are minimal. And as in the English example, both possibilities, deontic/*Piglet* and epistemic/*Cookie Monster*, are options in one and the same story.

(35)   Wer hat 'ne Banane essen müssen?   ⇒   deontic
        Who has a banana eat must
        "Who had to eat a banana?"

(36)   Wer muss 'ne Banane gegessen haben?   ⇒   epistemic
        Who must a banana eat   has
        "Who must have eaten a banana?"

On the other hand the difficulty that English children face for the present tense is not a problem in German since the structure of (31) is not present in English, i.e. there is no present progressive in German. As we have seen in section 2.2.1 the German present tense is ambiguous between the deontic and the epistemic reading[15].

---

[15] Of course the acquisition of an ambiguous structure presents a different kind of complexity. This aspect has not been tested yet and I will not test this acquisition in the current paper.

(37)   Wer muss 'ne Banane essen?   ⇒   ambiguous
        Who must a   banana eat
        "Who must eat a banana?"

5.2.2 Habitual Condition

In addition to the situational conditions described in section 5.2.1 another condition was tested in the acquisition task. All of the conditions described in the previous section are situational. In other words the can be used in ongoing situations for the present tense or just finished situations, for the past tense cases. Another possibility is to compare habitual cases which were briefly introduced in section 5.1. The habitual examples were introduced into the task to be able to observe children's responses when both, deontic and epistemic, were possible and correct answers. This condition can tell us how the children in this study do compared to the Hirst and Weil (1982) and Noveck et al. (1996) which both used separate tasks for deontic and epistemic readings. In the habitual cases there is no possible wrong answer. This means that there is no forced choice between a correct answer, deontic or epistemic, and a competing syntactic structure representing the other reading. Thereby children do not get into trouble syntactically.

Consider the example in 0. Again, this is an actual test story which was used in the acquisition study.

(38)

Picture 1: See this man? His little girl is having a birthday party tomorrow and she says that every kid has to have his own special cake and her dad has to bake them all.

Picture 2: See this man? He likes to lie on the beach and read.

Picture 3: See this man? He owns this bakery and people love his cakes.
Question: Who must bake a lot of cakes?

The question that follows the pictures is ambiguous, i.e. 'the daddy' (deontic) and 'the baker' (epistemic) are correct answers to this question. The same holds for German, both answers, deontic and epistemic, are correct adult responses. As opposed to the Banana story situation in example (8) and the questions in (30) through (37) the example in 0 is not situational but habitual. This difference is reflected in the fact that the progressive present tense epistemic question cannot be asked here, i.e. Who must be baking a lot of cakes?.

    To make difference between situational and habitual easy to grasp for the children the situational examples were presented in an animated video story format and the situational examples were presented in non-animated still picture format to the children.

6.   Acquisition Study

6.1   The English Study

For the English study the following conditions were tested. According to my hypothesis children should have trouble when pitting example (30) the deontic/*Piglet* reading against (31) the epistemic/*Cookie Monster* reading. Since the number of token was limited, the children already had two trial days each, only question (30) was asked. If the child mistakenly answered with the epistemic character we know that the she is misinterpreting the question with the epistemic meaning since children had to point to a character of their choice. Furthermore a neutral setting and a biased setting was introduced into the task. The Banana story that we have seen in previous sections had all three participating characters visible at all times. This setting was considered a neutral setting. In the biased setting the children were biased towards the non-adult epistemic interpretation by having the character representing the epistemic reading be present exclusively in the last frame. For the Banana story this would have meant to have *Piglet* alone in the last frame when the story ended. This biased setting was introduced to check whether children would fall for the lure of the immediate present and thereby being influenced towards an epistemic reading.

Furthermore past tense constructions with *must* were checked. As we have seen in the previous section it is predicted that children do not have a problem interpreting this structure since it does not compete with another minimally different structure. This is not expected under the ToM approach since this reading is epistemic.

The last condition that was tested in English were the ambiguous habitual conditions described in the previous section.

6.1.1   Procedure

Subjects: 28 children from 3 to 5 years. A control group of 6 adults. The children were not all monolingual but it was made sure that their English abilities met standard English abilities expected at this age. All children were considered to be developing normally and were not language impaired or had any perceptual impairment, for example hearing loss. Since a pilot study did not show any difference in performance of male and female children a balance in sex was not required.

Task: After a warm-up session, where the characters and the tasks were introduced, the children saw stories on a laptop from a CD ROM but without sound. While showing the video the experimenters told the corresponding story live[16]. Before each story a picture of the characters that were involved in the particular story were laid on the table before the child. After the story the child was asked either a deontic or an epistemic question.

---

[16] We tried to have native speakers of English as experimenters but this was not possible for the whole experiment. Thanks to Jill de Villiers' students Marissa Fond and Kathy D'Amato for helping us out.

In a second task the children saw a sequence of three pictures with a corresponding description of the content of these pictures. This task was used for the ambiguous questions exclusively. This condition included one picture compatible with a deontic reading, one picture compatible with an epistemic reading and one picture that functioned as a distractor. The 3 pictures were changed for sequence for each child. Afterwards the children were asked an ambiguous question, i.e. two answers, deontic and epistemic, were possible and correct answers.

Throughout the stories *have to* was used. As observations in Papafragou (1998) show, children perform better with items that are more colloquial to them. Therefore, the more colloquial form *have to* is used for English. The question that followed the stories, however, contains *must*. This replacement should not pose a problem for the task. On the contrary, possible effects from 'the lure of the immediate present' can be reduced. This is so because *is* and *have to* are farther apart than *is* and *must* in the relative force hierarchy.

Token: 8 stories per day (2 neutral present tense, 2 biased present tense, 2 past tense and 2 ambiguous). With 2 test days it made up a total of 16 stories per child. The token were evenly distributed and there were distractors included that were not related to the structure.

6.1.2 Results and Discussion

Table 1: 3-year-olds

	Correct		Wrong		Total
Deontic	16	(47%)	18	(53%)	34
Epistemic	21	(87%)	3	(13%)	24
	Deontic		Epistemic		
Ambiguous	18	(82%)	4	(18%)	22

Table 2: 4-year-olds

	Correct		Wrong		Total
Deontic	13	(33%)	26	(67%)	39
Epistemic	18	(86%)	3	(14%)	21
	Deontic		Epistemic		
Ambiguous	13	(57%)	10	(43%)	23

Table 3: 5-year-olds

	Correct		Wrong		Total
Deontic	13	(32%)	28	(68%)	41
Epistemic	23	(92 %)	2	(8%)	25
	Deontic		**Epistemic**		
Ambiguous	12	(41%)	17	(59%)	29

As we can see in Table 1 through Table 3 children do have trouble in answering the deontic question. This confirms the prediction that when there is a competing syntactic structure children do have problems because of their non-adult like syntactic abilities. If the ToM approach were correct children should have performed that much better on this task. As we can see there is no significant improvement in performance within the age groups. As for the difference within the deontic task in the neutral versus the biased condition it was observable the there was no significant difference between the two subconditions for the 3-year-olds. For the 4 and 5-year olds there was an effect observable. These age groups did indeed fall for the biased setting since the results show a slight above chance response for the non-adult epistemic reading as opposed to the neutral setting[17].

Moreover as we can see in Table 1 through Table 3 children of all age groups performed quite well on the past tense epistemic condition which did not compete with a minimally different syntactic structure. This finding is expected under the hypothesis put forward in the previous section. However, this result is not expected under a ToM approach. If the ToM were correct at least the younger age groups should have performed significantly worse in the epistemic task. As we can see there is no significant increase in performance within the age groups.

Finally the habitual ambiguous condition in which both, deontic and epistemic, were correct adult responses we can see that 3-year-olds prefer deontic readings, 4-year-olds have no preference for either reading and 5-year-olds have a slight preference for epistemic readings. This finding is compatible with the current hypothesis as well as the ToM approach. Children do indeed seem to start out with deontic readings and then develop a better understanding of epistemic readings.

Summarizing these findings I conclude that the ToM approach might well play its part in the acquisition of deontic and epistemic readings as the habitual ambiguous condition shows. However, research so far has underestimated the role of children's non-adult like syntactic abilities. This underestimation might have also been caused by the fact that experimental tasks so far have separated deontic from epistemic tasks thereby not forcing children to choose between two closely related syntactic structures.

---

[17] In the interest of space limitations only the most important results are given here. Please contact the author for specific details.

6.2   The German Study

For the German study the following conditions were tested. According to my hypothesis German children should have trouble in past tense constructions pitting example (35) against (36) which is a syntactic minimal pair. Both question types, i.e. (35) and (36) were asked. Moreover the biased and neutral subcondition was maintained just as described in section 6.1 for the English study.

For German there are two ambiguous conditions, the present tense situational condition in the video task, i.e. example (37), and the present tense habitual condition in the picture task.

6.2.1   Procedure

Subjects: 26 children from 3 to 5 years. A control group of 5 adults. The children were monolingual. All children were considered to be developing normally and were not language impaired or had any perceptual impairment, for example hearing loss. Since all previous studies did not show any difference in performance of male and female children a balance in sex was not required.

Task: After a warm-up session, where the characters and the tasks were introduced, the children saw stories on a laptop from a CD ROM but without sound. While showing the video the experimenter told the corresponding story live. Before each story a picture of the characters, that were involved in the particular story, were laid on the table before the child. After the story the child was asked either a deontic or an epistemic question in the past tense condition or an ambiguous question in the present tense conditions.

In a second task the children saw a sequence of three pictures with a corresponding description of the content of these pictures. This task was used for the ambiguous questions exclusively. This condition included one picture compatible with a deontic reading, one picture compatible with an epistemic reading and one picture that functioned as a distractor. The 3 pictures were changed for sequence for each child. Afterwards the children were asked an ambiguous question, i.e. two answers (deontic and epistemic) were possible and correct answers.

Token: 8 stories per day. Day 1: 1 neutral present tense, 2 biased present tense, 3 past tense and 2 ambiguous. Day 2: 2 neutral present tense, 1 biased present tense, 3 past tense and 2 ambiguous. The questions for the past tense condition were evenly distributed for deontic and epistemic token. The various token were evenly distributed and there were distractors included that were not related to the structure.

6.2.2   Results and Discussion

Table 4: 3-year-olds

	Correct		Wrong		Total
Deontic	16	(67%)	8	(33%)	24
Epistemic	12	(50%)	12	(50%)	24
	Deontic		Epistemic		
Ambiguous (situational)	36	(80%)	9	(20%)	45
Ambiguous (habitual)	22	(69%)	10	(31%)	32

Table 5: 4-year-olds

	Correct		Wrong		Total
Deontic	14	(58%)	10	(42%)	24
Epistemic	6	(25%)	18	(75%)	24
	Deontic		Epistemic		
Ambiguous (situational)	28	(58%)	20	(42%)	48
Ambiguous (habitual)	16	(48%)	17	(52%)	33

Table 6: 5-year-olds

	Correct		Wrong		Total
Deontic	18	(60%)	12	(40%)	30
Epistemic	8	(27%)	22	(73%)	30
	Deontic		Epistemic		
Ambiguous (situational)	36	(75%)	12	(25%)	48
Ambiguous (habitual)	6	(19%)	26	(81%)	32

As we can see in Table 3 through Table 6 children did have trouble with the past tense condition as predicted. Children of all age groups performed equally on the deontic conditions, i.e. no increase in performance was detectable. However as we can see in Table 3 3-year-olds performed better on the epistemic condition than the older age groups but these responses are by chance responses as the numbers show. The 4 and 5-year-olds performed better on the deontic than the epistemic condition. This finding is compatible with the current hypothesis as well as partly with the ToM approach. However, under the ToM approach we would have expected the children of all age groups to perform significantly better in the deontic condition which is not the case here. An explanation for the worse performance in the epistemic conditions of 4 and 5-year-olds could be that they start to realize that there is indeed an epistemic reading but that they still mistakenly assign a non-adult deontic structure to the sentence.

This explanation is supported by the fact that the numbers for the ambiguous condition show an increase in epistemic readings when we compare the 3, 4 and 5-year-olds. Again, this finding is compatible with the current hypothesis as well as the ToM approach.

Furthermore there was no difference detectable for any age group for the biased versus the neutral subcondition in the situational ambiguous condition in any of the age groups.

6.3   Comparing the English and the German Study

As predicted in section 5.2 English and German children exhibited problems with deontic as well as epistemic readings when these structures were syntactically closely related, i.e. minimally different. This means that English children indeed showed trouble in the present tense (deontic) versus the present progressive (epistemic) condition. Furthermore, as predicted even the youngest English children did not have trouble in the past tense condition although it was an epistemic condition since this structure was syntactically not competing with closely related structures. As predicted, German children had trouble in the past tense condition no matter whether it was deontic or epistemic since these structures are a syntactic minimal pair.

For English as well as German children it was observable that in the habitual ambiguous condition, children seem to start out with a preference for deontic readings and acquire more epistemic readings later as the preference for epistemic readings in the 5-year-olds in both languages shows.

An additional interesting conclusion can be drawn by comparing English and German children with regard to the biased and neutral settings. As we have seen the biased subcondition does have an effect on the older English age groups. However it does not effect any of the German age groups. The biased setting does have an impact exactly in the case where children are having difficulties syntactically, i.e. the English children. It does not have an effect when there is no syntactically precarious situation to begin with, i.e. no trouble for the German children.

These results support the hypothesis that children's non-adult like syntactic abilities in deontic as well as epistemic readings has a quite important impact on their performance. These findings combined show that the ToM approach as well as previous studies have underestimated the role of syntax in children's acquisition of modals. Furthermore these findings support researchers like de Villiers et al. and Miller in their view that certain syntactic structures might be necessary for a Theory of Mind to develop in the first place.

7.   Conclusion

This paper has put forward a syntactic approach to deontic and epistemic readings of modals such as *must* and *müssen* by proposing that deontic and epistemic readings are assigned to modals in two distinct syntactic positions. This analysis supports a monosemous semantic approach to modals over a polysemous approach since a polysemous approach would most likely map both readings onto one syntactic position. The two distinct syntactic positions for the two meanings also have an impact on how children's acquisition of these meanings might be guided. The difference in syntactic positions is quite subtle and therefore it is expected that the acquisition of this difference is quite complicated. This proposal however does not predict which of the two readings emerges first. The Theory of Mind predicts that a deontic meaning emerges first. The Theory of Mind is no doubt a part of the acquisition of modals. Nonetheless its importance in the acquisition of modals might have been overestimated.

The experimental part of this paper put forward the hypothesis that although the Theory of Mind has a part in the path of acquisition of modals the syntactic influence must not be underestimated. The Theory of Mind approach as well as previous experimental studies underestimated the impact that a non-adult like syntactic grammar has on the acquisition of modals.

The hypothesis put forward in this paper predicted that if children are put in a situation were they have to compare two minimally distinct syntactic structures their performance is equally impaired in deontic as well as epistemic instances. This prediction was borne out by the English as well as the German data. A subpart of the data in both languages also confirms previous studies that showed that if children are not in a syntactically minimal environment, deontic readings emerge prior to epistemic readings.

This study investigated only a subpart of modals in English and German. More studies including more modals are certainly desirable to complete the picture. However, the general hypothesis should be transferable to other modals and languages.

References

Bussmann, H. (1996). *Routledge Dictionary of Language and Linguistics*. London: Rutledge.

Choi, S. (1995). The Development of Epistemic Sentence-ending Modal Forms and Functions in Korean Children. In: J. Bybee and S. Fleischman (Eds.), *Modality in Grammar and Discourse*. Amsterdam: Benjamins, 165-204.

Cinque, G. (1999). *Adverbs and Functional Heads*. Oxford: OUP.

Coates, J. (1987). The acquisition of the meanings of modality in children aged eight and twelve. In: *Journal of Child Language* 15 (2), 425-434.

de Villiers, J. G. and de Villiers, P. A.. (2000). Linguistic Determinism and the Understanding of False Beliefs. In: P. Mitchell and K. Riggs (eds), *Children's Reasoning and the Mind*. Hove: Psychology Press, 191–228.

de Villiers, J.G. and Pyers, J.E. (2002). Complements to Cognition: a Longitudinal Study of the Relationship Between Complex Syntax and False-belief-understanding. *Cognitive Development* 17, 1037–1060.

Greenbaum, S. & R. Quirk. (1990). *A Student's Grammar of the English Language*. Harlow: Longman.

Hirst, W. & J. Weil. (1982). Acquisition of Epistemic and Deontic Meaning of Modals. In: *Journal of Child Language* 9(3), 659-666.

Kuczaj, S.A. & M.P. Maratsos. (1975). What children can say before they will. In: MPQ 21, 89-111.

Kuczaj, S.A. & M.P. Maratsos. (1983). Initial verbs of yes-no questions: A different kind of general grammatical category. In: *Developmental Psychology* 19, 440-444.

Miller, C. A. (2001). False Belief Understanding in Children with Specific Language Impairment. In: *Journal of Communication Disorders*,34, 73–86.

Miller, C.A. (2004). False Belief and Sentence Complement Performance in Children with Specific Language Impairment. In: International Journal of Language & Communication Disorders 39(2), 191-213.

Moore, C., D. Bryant & D. Furrow. (1989). Mental terms and the development of certainty. In: *Child Development* 60, 167-171.

Moore, C. & J. Davidge. (1989). The development of mental terms: Semantics or pragmatics?. In: *Journal of Child Language* 16, 633-641.

Noveck, I. A., S. Ho & M. Sera. (1996). Children's Understanding of Epistemic Modals. In: *Journal of Child Language* 23(3), 621-643.

Papafragou, A. (1997). Inference and word meaning: The case of modal auxiliaries. In: *Lingua* 105, 1-47.

Papafragou, A. (1998). The Acquisition of Modality: Implications for Theories on Semantic Representation. In: *Mind & Language* 13(3). 370-399.

Papafragou, A. (2001). Linking Early Linguistic and Conceptual Capacities: The Role of Theory of Mind. In: A.Cienki, B. Luka & M.Smith (eds) *Conceptual and Discourse Factors in Linguistic Structure*. Stanford: CSLI Publications, 169 -184.

Palmer, R. F.. (1998). *Mood and Modality*. Cambridge: CUP.

Perkins, M. (1983). *Modal Expressions in English*. London: Frances Pinter.

Roberts, I. (1985). Agreement Parameters And The Development Of English Modal Auxiliaries. In: *NLLT* 3(1), 21-58.

Shatz, M., Billman D. & Yaniv, I. (1986). *Early occurrences of auxiliaries in children's speech*. Unpublished manuscript. University of Michigan, Ann Arbor.

Shatz, M. & S. A. Wilcox. (1991). Constraints on the Acquisition of English Modals. In: S. A. Gelman & J. P. Byrnes (Eds.). *Perspectives on Language and Thought: Interrelations in Development*. Cambridge: CUP, 319-353.

Wellman, H. (1990). *The Child's Theory of Mind*. Cambridge: MIT Press.

Wells, G. (1979). Learning and Using the Auxiliary Verb in English. In: V. Lee (Ed.) *Cognitive Development: Language And Thinking from Birth to Adolescence*. London: Croom Helm.

Appendix A – Situational Condition

Questions are not given after the stories since they differed for German versus English and they were psudorandomized for each child. Each question type is compatible with each story.

1. Banana

We can see a house and within the milky window we can see Piglets shadow eating a banana. In front of the house we can see Bert and Cookie Monster. Look, there is Cookie Monster and there is Bert. Bert tells Cookie Monster: "You eat too many cookies and not enough fruit and vegetables. That's not healthy. So, you really have to eat a banana." *Throughout the story all three characters are visible.*

2. Tires

We can see a house and in front of the house there are Eey-ore, Piglet and a car. Look, there are Eey-ore and Piglet. Eey-ore tells Piglet: "Our car has a flat tire. So, before we go to Tigger's house I'll buy a present for him. But you really have to change the tire." *(New scene) Eey-ore and Piglet are gone but Mickey Mouse's big ears are visible behind the car. Note that only the ears are visible not the whole puppet.* Uh, look!

3. Dishes

Kitchen scene is set up. The kitchen looks messy. Look, there is Ernie and there is Elmo. Ernie tells Elmo: "Look at the mess you made. This is terrible. You really have to wash the dishes before Bert comes home." *(New scene) Ernie and Elmo are gone. Through a window we can see a pair of blue arms washing dishes.* Oh, look.

NOTE: Elmo is red, Cookie Monster is blue!

4. Spinach

Kitchen scene is set up. Winnie the Pooh is behind the stove. Tigger sits at a table. Look, there is Tigger and there is Winnie the Pooh. And here comes Eey-ore. Tigger says: "Can I go outside and play with Eey-ore?" Winnie the Pooh says: "Sure, but first you have to eat all your spinach. *We can hear a phone ringing.* Winnie the Pooh says: "Oh, the telephone." *Winnie the Pooh leaves.* Tigger says: "I really don't like spinach." *Fade out and fade in. Winnie the Pooh enters the scene.* Now, Winnie the Pooh is back. He says: "Oh, the spinach is all gone. Good, Tigger, now you can go outside." Oh, look at Eey-ore! *We can see that Eey-ore face is smudged with spinach.*

5. Shelving

Grocery store scene set up. Look, there is Bert and there is Ernie. Ernie works for Bert in the grocery store. See the cash register and all the shelves. Bert says: "Look at all these cans on the floor. The customers can't walk through here and they can't push their shopping carts down the aisle. *Behind one of the shelves we can see a pair of red hands piling up cans. Note that only the hands are visible not the whole puppet.* They'll get angry and complain. You really have to put the cans on the shelf." "Okay," says Ernie, "I'll do it right away."

6. Ball

There are no props at all. We can see Ernie and Cookie Monster. Bert comes in with a ball. Look, there is Cookie Monster and there is Ernie. Ernie says: "Cookie Monster, do you want to play ball?" "Yeah, sure," says Cookie Monster. "Well, first I have to get a ball. Because without a ball we can't play."

7. Banana Buying/ Birthday Cake

Kitchen scene is set up. Look, there is Minnie Mouse. She wants to bake a banana cake for Mickey Mouse because it is his birthday. She reads the recipe and says: "Let's see: I need flour, I have flour. I need a banana, ... oh no, I don't have any bananas. I'd better go to the grocery store because I have to buy a banana." *(New scene) Minnie Mouse is gone. A grocery store from outside and through a milky window we can see shadows moving. The shadows can clearly be identified as Bert and Winnie the Pooh. Winnie the Pooh is behind the cash register and Bert has a banana in his hands.* Look, here is the grocery store. See the sign for Stop & Shop? *We can hear a bing from the cash register.*

8.Trumpet

Kitchen scene is set up. In the rightmost corner of the scene there is a wall with a milky window. Look there are Winnie the Pooh and Eey-ore. Winnie the Pooh tells Eey-ore: "Eey-ore, you have to play your trumpet because your concert is tomorrow." Look, there is Piglet. He says: "Yey, I just got a trumpet." *Piglet vanishes behind the wall then reappears as a shadow in the milky window with the trumpet at his mouth. We can hear trumpet sounds. Winnie the Pooh and Eey-ore are still in the kitchen.*

9. Jam

Kitchen scene is set up. Look, there is Elmo and there is Ernie. Ernie says: "Hmm, I really want toast with jam for breakfast." "Me too", says Elmo. "But look, the jar is empty." Ernie says: "Oh no, what should we do?" Elmo says: "Well, we have to buy some jam. So let's go to the grocery store." *(New scene) A grocery store.* Look, there they are in the grocery store. Ernie says: "Oh no, Elmo. There is no jam left. The store is all sold out." Elmo says: "Well, what should we do? Should we have toast with honey instead?" Ernie says: "That's okay with me. So let's go home." *(New scene) Back in the kitchen. Bert sits at a table having a toast with jam in his hand.* And now they're back at home. "Oh", says Elmo, "Look, what Bert has for breakfast!"

10. Drinking

Kitchen scene is set up. We can see Mickey Mouse with a basket full of groceries. Look, there is Mickey Mouse. Oh, he has some groceries. Mickey Mouse says: "I am so thirsty. I really have to drink something. But first I should bring in the rest of the groceries." *(New scene) A house. In front of the house we can see a car and Mickey Mouse. In a milky window of the house we can see the shadow of Bert with a bottle at his mouth.* Look, there he is at the car with the rest of the groceries.

11. Sandbox

A house. In front of the house we can see a sandbox. Look, there are Cookie Monster and Ernie in the sandbox. Cookie Monster says: "I don't really want to play anymore. I'm kind of tired. I guess I'll go inside and take a nap." "Okay," says Ernie, "That's fine." Cookie Monster says: "I cleaned up last time. So, could you clean up this time?" "Okay then," says Ernie. And Cookie Monster goes inside. *Fade out, fade in. Same set up. In front of the house we can see Cookie Monster's shoes. Ernie has finished cleaning up.* Look, Ernie put away all the toys. And now he is ready to go inside. *Bert enters the scene.* But look, there is Bert and he says: "Ernie, don't go inside with your sandy shoes. I cleaned the whole house this morning and if you go inside with your sandy shoes it'll get all dirty. So, you really have to take off your shoes. Look, somebody already did it."

12. Apple-picking

We can see a tree with a lot of red apples. Look, there is Piglet and there is Winnie the Pooh. And Winnie the Pooh says: "I'll get some honey, but you really have to pick apples so that we'll have enough food for the winter." Piglet says: "Okay." *Winnie the Pooh leaves the scene.* Piglet tries to reach the apples, but he realizes that he is too small. He says: "I think I'd better get a ladder." *Piglet leaves the scene. Fade out, fade in. A basket with apples is under the tree and the feet and parts of Bert's face are visible in the tree.* Look, I think there is someone up in the tree. I think I can see a foot and a face.

Appendix B – Ambiguous Condition [18]

1. Burgers

Picture 1: See this little boy? He is so skinny his mother is trying to get him to eat more. So she says he can't go out until he finishes all these burgers. Phew!

Picture 2: See this guy? He is so big he can hardly fit through the door of McDonald's. I guess he eats plenty.

Picture 3: See this man? He is trying to catch a fish.

Who must eat a lot of burgers?

2. Heavy

Picture 1: See this man? He is eating some corn.

Picture 2: See this man (*man has weights in his hands*)? He's got lots of muscles! I guess he works out in the gym.

Picture 3: This boy can't go and play today because his family is moving, and he has the job of moving all these big boxes.

Who must lift a lot of heavy things?

3. Bake

Picture 1: See this man? His little girl is having a birthday party tomorrow and she says that every kid has to have his own special cake and her dad has to bake them all.

Picture 2: See this man? He likes to lie on the beach and read.

Picture 3: See this man? He owns this bakery and people love his cakes.

Who must bake a lot of cakes?

4. Ice-Cream

Picture 1: See this woman? She works in the ice-cream store – what a nice job – YUM! She tries every flavor and loves them!

Picture 2: This woman can't remember which of these boxes has vanilla ice cream in it, so she's gonna have to try them all.

Picture 3: See this woman? She is having a nice nap.

Who must taste a lot of ice cream?

Tanja Heizmann
Department of Linguistics
South College
Box 37130
University of Massachusetts
Amherst, MA 01003-7130

tanja@linguist.umass.edu

---

[18] Thank you to Jill de Villiers and her students at Smith College for providing the stories as well as the terrific pictures for these test questions.

Children's interpretation of particle verbs and aspect: A pilot study[*]

Liane Jeschull

University of Massachusetts, Amherst

1.   Introduction

The goal of this pilot study is twofold: it introduces a new proposal explaining the nature of aspectual entailments of particle verbs and tests the validity of the two major claims of the proposal in an experimental study of children's interpretations of particle verbs. The proposal I am advocating comprises two hypotheses:

(1)   H1 (preliminary):
There is a fundamental difference between what I will call particle telicity (e.g. *eat the pizza up*, *drink the coke up*) and what has been called compositional telicity (e.g. *eat the pizza*, *drink the coke*) in the way they are structurally manifested.

(2)   H2 (preliminary):
Telicity entailments of particle verbs do not necessarily have to coincide with completion (cf. *eat up*, *drink up* vs. *doze off*, *nod off*).

The proposal raises two central questions for acquisition:

(3)   Acquisition question Q1:
Are children able to differentiate particle telicity and compositional telicity?

(4)   Acquisition question Q2:
Are children able to interpret particle verbs as telic even in the absence of completion information?

Assuming the proposal is correct and assuming, further, continuity between child and adult grammars, the answer to both acquisition questions will be yes. Sections 1.1 and 1.3

[*] The research reported here has been funded by a doctoral fellowship of the German Academic Exchange Service (DAAD).

Tanja Heizmann (ed.): Current Issues in Acquisition. University of Massachusetts Occasional Papers in Linguistics 34, 51-75.
GLSA Amherst.

will spell out the new proposal in more detail. 1.2 and 1.4 will explain the two acquisition questions. Section 2 will introduce a novel experimental design to implement the proposal; section 3 gives the results of the experiment; section 4 discusses the implications of the results; and section 5 draws conclusions for this pilot study.

1.1   Particle telicity and compositional telicity

Telicity associated with transitive simplex verbs of creation or consumption with an incremental theme as direct internal argument (e.g. *eat the pizza, drink the coke*) has received a good deal of attention in the literature studying telicity in English and other Germanic languages. However, Verkuyl (1972) in his pioneering work on the compositional nature of aspect as well as Dowty (1979) inter alia observed that telicity arises in a compositional manner in more than just this one type of predicate. Despite the insights of those earlier studies, a lot of the subsequent work has focused on the role of the direct object for the composition of telicity in Germanic (Krifka 1989, 1992; Tenny 1994; Borer 1994, 1998, 2005; van Hout 1996 inter alia). Relevant acquisition work, in particular, has equated 'compositional telicity' with transitivity (cf. van Hout 2001; Schulz & Penner 2002)[1].

Approaches assuming that event structure is encoded syntactically generally agree that telicity arises via spec-head relationship between verb and object in a functional projection above VP. As to the label and precise nature of this projection, various suggestions have been offered ranging from AspP (Borer 1994, 1998, 2005) and AgrOP (van Hout 1996) to delimiting FP (Ritter & Rosen 1998). For the sake of simplicity, let's call it FP. Regardless of the discussion on the precise nature of FP, the impression emerges that languages choose one type of telicity and a single environment that gives rise to it. This picture is oversimplified. Instead, I suggest that the actual picture is more complex.

I propose that particle verbs, like *eat up* and *drink up*, are another major type of predicate that gives rise to aspectual entailments in a regular fashion across Germanic languages, yet in a fundamentally different way. Let's call the telicity entailments of particle verbs 'particle telicity'[2]. For the sake of the present argumentation, let's also keep the term 'compositional telicity' for telicity associated with transitivity, following previous acquisition studies (van Hout 2001, Schulz & Penner 2002). Preserving the assumption that telicity is encoded in syntactic structure, I argue that particle telicity and compositional telicity emerge in different places in the phrase marker and via different syntactic mechanisms. Preserving moreover the assumption that compositional telicity arises via spec-head relationship of object and verb in FP, it is interpreted in a moved

---

[1] For a somewhat different approach to telicity see Schulz et al. (2001, 2002) and Penner et al. (2003).
[2] In fact, not all particle verbs are telic. Some may be atelic, such as those with *on* and *along* and some with *away*. Examples are *ramble on, slave away* and possibly also those of the type *drink the night away* discussed by Jackendoff (1997, 2002). But note that these examples do not contradict the present argumentation, since atelicity here still emerges as an aspectual entailment after all. Atelic particle verbs will not be discussed here, however.

position after (overt or covert) movement of verb and direct object DP to that projection. A partial tree is given in (5):

(5)   compositional telicity

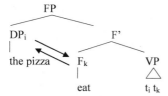

Particle telicity, in contrast, is instantiated lower down in the tree, directly on the verb. Hence it is interpreted in its base position. I will follow the Abstract Clitic hypothesis of Keyser & Roeper (1992) and Roeper & Snyder (2005) in assuming that aspect in particle verbs is associated with an Abstract Clitic Position (ACP) on the verb. Particle telicity then arises whenever the ACP is projected. Whether or not a direct object is involved and verb and DP move (overtly or covertly) to a higher functional projection is irrelevant for particle verbs to be interpreted as telic. A partial representation adapted from Keyser & Roeper (1992) is given in (6)[3]:

(6)   particle telicity

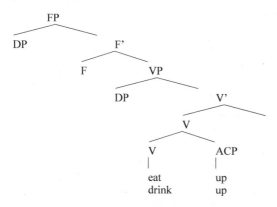

This way, the difference in structure between compositional telicity and particle telicity is spelled out in a clear-cut way. It predicts different acquisition patterns for the two types

---

[3] The literature on particle verbs is rich in analyses of how the structure of particle verbs should be represented. A comprehensive overview can be found in Dehé (2002). For the purpose of the present discussion, namely representing how aspect is associated with particle verbs, I will simply assume the structure in (6).

of telicity. Tenny (1994: 36) assumes that verb particles merely "enforce" telicity if telicity is already associated with transitivity, as in the examples discussed here. Van Hout (1998b) suggests that they are simply more "overt and transparent indicators of telicity" (98). I argue that particle verbs do more than that: particle telicity is fundamentally different from compositional telicity.

As a consequence of the suggested analysis, the two different instantiations of telicity should bear different interpretations. As we will see in section 1.3, aspectual entailments of particle verbs are not limited to completion, but can assume a wider range of aspectual meanings. Compositional telicity, however, is restricted to interpretations of completion. Moreover, when completion entailments of particle verbs and those of corresponding transitive simplex verbs are compared, the suggested analysis predicts a more complex set of syntactic operations involved in the interpretation of compositional telicity. This will have implications for the acquisition of telicity.

Hypothesis H1 can now be summarized as follows:

(7)   Hypothesis H1 (final):
        There is a fundamental difference between particle telicity (e.g. *eat the pizza up*, *drink the coke up*) and compositional telicity (e.g. *eat the pizza*, *drink the coke*) in the way they are structurally encoded. Particle telicity is inherent to the particle within the VP and arises whenever the particle position is projected. Compositional telicity emerges via spec-head relationship in FP, a functional projection above VP, after (overt or covert) movement of verb and direct object DP to that projection.

1.2   Acquisition of particle telicity and compositional telicity

The analysis proposed here raises questions for our study of the acquisition of telicity in English. Assuming that particle telicity (e.g. *eat the pizza up*) differs fundamentally from compositional telicity (e.g. *eat the pizza*) in its structural manifestation in the adult English target grammar, are children able to differentiate the two types of telicity (Q1)? The Continuity Hypothesis in a broad sense predicts that they are. What consequences does this prediction bear for production and comprehension? The complexity involved in the derivation of compositional telicity suggests that children might fail to project FP and/or fail to move verb and/or object (whether overt or covert). In case they fail on any one of these operations, compositional telicity will be absent from their grammar altogether. Yet particle telicity will be present once the ACP is in place. Under the strictest assumption of continuity between child and adult grammar, however, children will successfully produce and understand both types of telicity.

Previous studies of children's comprehension of particle telicity and compositional telicity have shown that children between the ages of 3 and 6 associate particle verbs with telicity consistently more often than transitivity (van Hout 1998a,b, 2001 for English and Dutch; Schulz & Penner 2002 for German). Yet so do the adults in those studies. Now this finding is not at all surprising assuming our proposal, but is even predicted by it. Thus, in addition, our analysis offers an explanation for the findings of previous studies that they neither predicted nor could account for. Our experimental study, in contrast, builds on the assumption of a structural difference between particle telicity and compositional telicity.

1.3   Aspectual types of particle verbs

The literature on particle verbs has long noted that particle verbs do not form a semantically homogeneous group, but can assume a variety of meanings. Based on their primary lexical meanings, three categories have been discussed at least since Emonds (1972): directional, idiomatic and purely aspectual particle verbs. Bolinger (1971: 96ff.) notes that particle verbs are aspectual in nature regardless of their literal meanings. Thus in addition to the variety of primary lexical meanings, we find various aspectual meanings associated with particle verbs. Moreover, there is no one-to-one relationship between particular particles and specific lexical or aspectual meanings.

To clarify the proposal, let's first assume that telicity is not merely a property of a subgroup of particles, such as those commonly labeled 'aspectual' or 'completive', like *up*. Instead it is a general characteristic of particle verbs that they inherently entail telicity. Let's further assume that telicity entailments of particle verbs arise in addition to their lexical meanings proper. One way to implement this idea would be to assume that telicity is derived from the structural position of the particle[4]. Such reasoning is compatible with hypothesis H1 in that particle telicity is manifested inherently by the presence of the particle position in the structure of the VP.

Second, particle verbs can convey more fine-grained and diverse telic qualities than telicity associated with transitivity. While compositional telicity is restricted to entailments of completion, particle verbs may very well pick out other parts of an event. Particle telicity may focus on the completion or inherent final boundary of an event, but also on the inception or beginning of an event. Let's call the former 'completive' and the latter 'inceptive' particle verbs. The most prominent examples of completive particle verbs in English are those with *up*. Although the group of inceptive particle verbs is much more limited and less frequent in English, it is predominantly comprised of particle verbs with *off*, as in *doze off*, and *away*, as in *sail away*. Consequently, particle verbs can pick out particular parts of events in a way that compositional telicity cannot.

Finally, as Bolinger (1971: 98) and Brinton (1985, 1988: 168ff) have argued, particle verbs convey telicity, i.e. lexical aspect / situation aspect / *Aktionsart*, rather than perfectivity, i.e. grammatical aspect / viewpoint aspect / aspect per se. This assumption is in line with the distinction made by Comrie (1976) and Smith (1991). Brinton (1985: 160, 1988: 168) offers a number of arguments and linguistic evidence in favor of analyzing

---

[4] This is not to say, however, that all particle verbs must have lexical meanings in addition to aspect and that aspectual entailments surface on top of those. In the case of *eat up* and *drink up* the particle denotes nothing but telicity. Yet in the case of, say, *throw the garbage out*, the particle *out* both adds to the lexical meaning of the simplex verb *throw* and entails telicity.

particle verbs as telic, rather than perfective (see also the formal tests in Dowty 1979). Note that completion then is only implied when telic predicates, such as completive particle verbs, are also marked with perfective morphology and the events they denote are presented from a perfective viewpoint. This will become crucial for our predictions for children's understanding or non-understanding of various aspectual types of particle verbs.

Hypothesis H2 can now be summarized as follows:

(8)   H2 (final):   There is a variety of telic qualities that particle verbs can entail, including completion entailments of completive PVs, which pick out the final boundary of an event (e.g. *eat up*, *drink up*), and inception entailments of inceptive PVs, which pick out the initial boundary of an event (e.g. *doze off*, *nod off*) inter alia.

1.4   Acquisition of different aspectual types of particle verbs

Our hypothesis H2 raises an entirely new set of questions for our acquisition study. Assuming that children's knowledge of lexical aspect, grammatical aspect and tense is initially limited to a subset of features, as claimed by various versions of the so-called 'Aspect Hypothesis' or 'Aspect First Hypothesis', are children able to interpret particle verbs as telic even if telicity does not coincide with completion (Q2)? Will they equally well associate inceptive particle verbs and completive particle verbs with telicity? Moreover, will they be able to retrieve telicity entailments in the absence of a perfective viewpoint on events and in the absence of perfective morphology in the verbal stimuli, i.e. in the absence of completion in the visual and verbal information? Under the further assumption of continuity between child and adult grammar, the predicted answer to this set of questions will be yes.

A broader problem behind all these questions is whether children are able to understand features of lexical aspect (or situation aspect), such as telicity, independently of features of grammatical aspect (or viewpoint aspect), such as perfectivity. This broader question is pertinent in the literature on the acquisition of aspect. Versions of the Aspect Hypothesis or Aspect First Hypothesis have suggested various analyses according to which children's grammar is initially restricted to a subset of the lexical aspect, grammatical aspect and tense features of the adult grammar. The different analyses make varying predictions for children's comprehension of completive and inceptive particle verbs.

The two main versions of the Aspect Hypothesis may be labeled 'Lexical Aspect First' and 'Grammatical Aspect First'.[5] The 'Lexical Aspect First' or 'Primacy of Aspect'

---

[5] The terminology I am using here goes back to van Hout (2001). The label 'Lexical Aspect First', which comprises both the 'Lexical Aspect Before Tense' hypothesis and the 'Lexical Aspect Before Grammatical Aspect' hypothesis, parallels Slabakova's (2002) 'Primacy of Aspect' (POA), a term which goes back to Shirai & Andersen (1995) and Andersen & Shirai (1996), with its 'Early POA' ('Lexical Aspect Before Tense') and 'Later POA' ('Lexical Aspect Before Grammatical Aspect') correlates.

hypothesis is based on findings that suggest lexical aspect initially determines the use of tense ('Lexical Aspect Before Tense') and those that suggest it initially restricts the use of grammatical aspect to particular categories ('Lexical Aspect Before Grammatical Aspect'). Representatives of what I call 'Lexical Aspect before Tense'[6] (Bronckart & Sinclair 1973; Antinucci & Miller 1976; Bloom et al. 1980 inter alia) argue quite generally that children restrict their early tense marking according to particular lexical aspect categories, e.g. past tense to telic predicates and present tense to atelic predicates. As prime representatives of what I call 'Lexical Aspect before Grammatical Aspect'[7], Olsen & Weinberg (1999), but also Shirai & Andersen (1995) and Andersen & Shirai (1996), propose that it is particular grammatical aspect morphemes that children initially restrict to particular lexical aspect categories, thus English perfective *–ed* to telic verbs (e.g. *fixed*) and *–ing* to durative verbs (e.g. *carrying*), as Olsen & Weinberg suggest, or to atelic verbs (e.g. *dancing*), as Shirai & Andersen (1995) suggest[8].

Slabakova (2002: 176) correctly points out that most of the early studies in the 1970s and 1980s looked at English and the Romance languages only, but these languages often conflate tense and grammatical aspect.[9] For example, the English past tense morpheme *–ed* has often been claimed to express perfectivity (cf. also Klein 1992). Note further that both analyses of the observed initial mapping are based on production data, whether spontaneous or elicited. As a consequence, they were only able to look at grammatical aspect morphology, but not at viewpoint aspect in the sense of Smith (1991). Therefore, I abstract away from the distinction between tense and grammatical aspect morphology for the sake of the present argumentation and subsume both versions of the mapping under the 'Lexical Aspect First' hypothesis.

The 'Grammatical Aspect First' hypothesis (Wagner 2001) claims the exact opposite. It claims that grammatical aspect influences tense in early child grammar. Crucially, Wagner's hypothesis pertains to children's understanding, rather than production, of tense and aspect. She conducted a controlled comprehension experiment in order to test children's interpretation of tense morphology in the presence or absence of grammatical aspect information. Thus she manipulated scenes as to whether they were completed or not and asked questions about them in either past tense or present tense, while she held grammatical aspect morphology constant by using progressive *–ing* in both tenses. She found that young children were only able to correctly understand tense morphology if temporal information correlated with completion information. Thus they were only able to correctly understand the past tense of a predicate if the event it denoted was also completed. Therefore, she concluded in favor of 'Grammatical Aspect First'.

The diverging findings of the earlier studies supporting the 'Lexical Aspect First' hypothesis and those of more recent studies, like Wagner's, supporting the 'Grammatical

---

[6] 'Lexical Aspect Before Tense' has also been labeled more generally 'Aspect Before Tense', which goes back to Bloom et al. (1980).

[7] Olsen & Weinberg's (1999) exact wording is 'Acquisition of Grammatical Aspect via Lexical Aspect'.

[8] As a further complication, these authors restrict their generalization to the lexical aspect of verbs alone, rather than the entire predicate.

[9] Weist et al.'s (1984) study on Polish is an exception among those earlier studies.

Aspect First' hypothesis may very well turn out to follow from the difference between production and comprehension. Again, the earlier studies of the 1970s and 1980s were exclusively concerned with children's production, whereas more recent research has found its way into testing children's comprehension of aspect. As an additional factor, the age of the children investigated crucially depends on the type of study and is not necessarily an indicator for age of acquisition. As documented in studies of spontaneous child data, children start producing aspectual categories well before the age of three, while experiments testing the comprehension of different features of aspect demand a rather elaborate design, such that it is rarely successful with children of that age. Not surprisingly then, the different types of studies came to different conclusions. Assuming hypothetically for the purpose of this study that both major versions of the Aspect Hypothesis are equally valid for production and comprehension and may account for both types of data, what repercussions do they have for our study?

Returning to our question Q2 (Are children able to interpret particle verbs as telic even if telicity does not coincide with completion?), the acquisition task consists in figuring out that particle verbs may, beside completion, entail inception, and other aspectual qualities. The main point is to acquire different categories of lexical aspect, as they relate to parts of the internal structure of events such as a possible initial boundary or final boundary. It extends to finding out what particles and particle verbs entail what lexical aspect quality. For the purpose of this study, we are primarily interested in completive and inceptive particle verbs.

The acquisition task also involves figuring out that telic particle verbs carry telicity (i.e. lexical aspect) entailments independently of grammatical aspect and tense. While lexical aspect (Smith's (1991) situation aspect) gives information about the internal structure of events, grammatical aspect refers to the perspective taken onto events (in the sense of Smith's viewpoint aspect) and the morphological or lexical markers used to denote that perspective (aspect per se in its traditional and more narrow construal). Completive particle verbs entail that an event has an inherent goal or final boundary even if the event is incomplete. The actual completion of an event is entailed compositionally only when a perfective viewpoint and a perfectivity marker, such as past tense -ed, operate on the telic predicate. Thus even completive particle verbs only entail the actual completion of an event if telicity coincides with perfectivity.

The two versions of the Aspect Hypothesis make opposite predictions for children's success in the acquisition task. If children's knowledge of aspect is initially restricted to lexical aspect ('Lexical Aspect First'), they will understand particle telicity (lexical aspect) independently of perfectivity (grammatical aspect). They will understand both completive and inceptive particle verbs, and they will do so even in the absence of a perfective viewpoint on events and perfective morphology on verbal stimuli. If, on the other hand, children's knowledge of aspect is initially restricted to grammatical aspect ('Grammatical Aspect First'), they will have problems understanding particle telicity independently of perfectivity. They will need completion clues, such as a perfective viewpoint and perfective morphology, in order to understand completive particle verbs as telic. They will interpret inceptive particle verbs as telic less often than completive particle verbs.

Our approach spells out the relationship between particle verbs and aspect more clearly than previous acquisition studies have done. The pioneering studies of van Hout (1998a,b, 2001) and Schulz & Penner (2002) found that 3-to-6-year old children acquiring English, Dutch or German as their first language understand telicity associated with particle verb from early on. However, they relied exclusively on completive particle verbs with *up*, viz. *eat up* and *drink up*, in English or the corresponding *aufessen* ('eat up') and *austrinken* ('drink up') in German. They restricted the perspective from which events were to be interpreted to a completed viewpoint by presenting the resultant states of the events. They also restricted tense and aspectual morphology used in the trigger questions to perfective. This way, lexical aspect was conflated with grammatical aspect and telicity with perfectivity. Our study, however, aims at avoiding these complications.

We implement our proposal in a novel experimental design. It contrasts two different types of telic particle verbs: completive particle verbs, like *eat up* and *drink up*, and inceptive particle verbs, like *send off* and *carry off*. It avoids completion information as given by either a perfective viewpoint on events, which implies completion, or perfective morphology, viz. the morpheme *-ed* in English. Instead, subjects are asked to make predictions about the future outcome of events by use of questions in future tense starting: *What do you think: Who's gonna ...?* In these points, the experiment reported on here, differs crucially from previous experiments. The innovations provide for a more thorough investigation into the precise aspectual nature of particle verbs.

To summarize the main points of this introduction, the literature on children's acquisition of aspect and tense has shown that their early aspectual systems are highly restrictive, while the aspectual system of the adult target grammar may be fairly complex. At the same time, the intertwined relationship between particle verbs and aspect has not received sufficient attention in discussions of the acquisition of aspect and calls for more fine-grained distinctions. On the one hand, particle telicity and compositional telicity need to be delineated more clearly. On the other hand, different lexical aspect categories need to be distinguished, while lexical aspect needs to be distinguished from grammatical aspect in a more principled fashion. Our study aims at accommodating these needs. It contrasts entailments of completive particle verbs like *eat up* and *drink up* with those associated with transitivity and inceptive particle verbs like *send off* and *carry off* with verbs of motion with a goal PP.

2.   Method

2.1   Materials

The present experiment used a nested hierarchical design. In order to test hypothesis H1 and investigate acquisition question Q1 (Are children able to differentiate particle telicity and compositional telicity?), materials were designed to match telic particle verbs in one condition and compositionally telic structures in another condition. In order to test hypothesis H2 and explore acquisition question Q2 (Are children able to interpret particle verbs as telic even if telicity does not coincide with completion?), completive and inceptive particle verbs were further assigned to two different conditions. The two particle verb type conditions with two matching control conditions make four conditions. Examples for each of the four conditions are given in (9):

(9)   A.   **eat** the apples **up**
        B.   eat the apples
        C.   **send** a letter **off** to Mickey
        D.   send a letter to Mickey

Completive particle verbs (condition A) were matched with corresponding transitive simplex verbs of creation or consumption and incremental theme argument (condition B), e.g. *eat the apples* **up** (A) and *eat the apples* (B). Inceptive particle verbs (condition C) were matched with corresponding simplex verbs with a goal PP (condition D), e.g. **send** *a letter* **off** *to Mickey* (C) and *send a letter to Mickey* (D). Thus conditions A and B, on the one hand, and conditions C and D, on the other hand, differ only in the presence or absence of the particle. The particle verb conditions A and C differ in the type of telicity they mark: condition A yields completives and condition C inceptives. All conditions are meant to be telic.

Condition A was matched with condition B to compare particle telicity and the object-marking mechanism for telicity, viz. *eat DP up* with *eat DP* and *drink DP up* with *drink DP*. The items in condition C were matched with the items in condition D by choosing verbs that can appear with a particle to form inceptive predicates and as simplex verbs with a goal PP, viz. *send* as in *send off* and *send to DP* and *carry* as in *carry off* and *carry to DP*. In order to keep the difference between the two conditions as minimal as possible and avoid further syntactic or semantic differences as possible confounding factors, both the particle verbs and the simplex verbs appeared with goal PPs, e.g. *to Mickey* in *send a letter off to Mickey* (C) and *send a letter to Mickey* (D).[10] This way, the items in the test conditions and the control conditions differed only in the presence or absence of the particle.

In order to control for the other point that plays into acquisition question Q2, perfective aspect was avoided altogether. This pertains to both the perspective from which events were presented and aspectual morphology used on verbs. First, the events were not presented as finished or completed until subjects answered the respective test questions. A possible conflation of presence of a goal in the sense of beginning or end point and the actual attainment of that goal was thus avoided from the very beginning. Second, the stimuli were presented in future tense, using *is gonna VP*, instead of the simple past, which was used in previous studies. As the English simple past morpheme – *ed* is often assumed to bear perfective entailments in the absence of perfective aspect morphology proper (cf. Klein 1992), it has, in fact, been taken for granted as a marker of

---

[10] As we will see in the results, the choice of particle verb with goal PP in condition C, in fact, turned out to be problematic. See section 4.

perfectivity in much of the literature on the acquisition of aspect. Telic predicates presented in perfective aspect will inevitably yield completion information. In the present experiment, a possible conflation of telicity as entailed by the uninflected predicate and perfectivity as marked by inflectional morphology was thus prevented from the outset.

There were four different events across eight different stories, thus two stories per event. Every story was followed by exactly one question. Thus there were two questions per event, one each in a particle verb condition and one in a simplex verb condition. The events included eating, drinking, sending and carrying something. Each of the eight video stories comprised two parallel subplots, one of which priming an event as such or mere activity and the other one priming its completion in case of eating and drinking or its inception in case of sending and carrying something. The expectation was that particle verbs should map onto the completion and inception sub-plots more often than the corresponding transitive simplex verbs. Thus *eat up* and *drink up* should link to the context aimed at completion, while *send off* and *carry off* should link to the one for inception. The transitive simplex verbs should be equally likely to map onto the entire telic event or the completion and inception sub-plots.

The two contexts were contrasted by showing two characters, say Cookie Monster and Tigger, as about to engage in the same type of event, say eating apples, but quite obviously to varying degrees. Tigger has a huge pile of apples and will not possibly be able to finish all of them. Cookie Monster, in contrast, has only two apples and might very well be able to finish both of them. Thus Tigger is likely to *eat his apples*, but unlikely to *eat his apples up*. For Cookie Monster, both statements are felicitous in the given context: He might very well *eat his apples* and also *eat his apples up*. The two characters were thus portrayed as differing in their ability or likelihood to finish their apples due to the different sizes of the two sets of objects. This set-up invites participants to make judgments about who might be able and more likely to finish his apples if they understand the predicate in the relevant question as entailing telicity.

In addition, the second sub-plot, here acted out by Cookie Monster, was set up as a distracter from the completion (or inception) orientation to invite an alternative interpretation. On the one hand, presupposed knowledge about the characters and their habits was integrated. The fact that Cookie Monster loves eating makes it seem even more likely that he is gonna eat his apples up. For Tigger, this is not the case. On the other hand, Tigger is shown as grabbing an apple out of his huge pile, whereas Cookie Monster is actually grabbing a chocolate bar instead of one of his two apples. Thus only Tigger is about to eat his apples, while Cookie Monster is about to eat a chocolate bar. Both of them want to or are about to *eat something*, but none of them is about to *eat it up*. Thus the second sub-plot is set up to distract from the completion context and invite participants to make judgments about who is more likely to engage in an apple-eating event as such.

Now let us look at how the simplex verb frame *eat his apples* and the particle verb frame *eat his apples up* map onto these events. The SV question *Who's gonna eat his apples?* can be construed as either *Who's about to eat his apples?* or *Who's gonna be able to eat all his apples?* Under the first interpretation, it is felicitous to say *Tigger is gonna eat his apples* (because he is grabbing one of them), but possibly also *Cookie Monster is gonna eat his apples* (because he might eat them after finishing the chocolate bar he is grabbing). Under the latter, ability interpretation, it seems only true that *Cookie Monster is gonna eat his apples*, but *Tigger is NOT gonna eat his apples*. Thus the SV question may be interpreted as referring to the completion context or to the context without completion.

The PV question *Who's gonna eat his apples up?* can only be construed as *Who's gonna be able to eat his apples up?* because none of the characters is about to eat his apples up or has even started eating. Therefore *only Cookie Monster is gonna eat his apples up* (because he has fewer apples). An utterance like *Tigger is gonna eat his apples up* will not match the truth conditions for the ability interpretation, and it would be pragmatically odd if it was to capture the alternative interpretation (*Who's about to eat his apples up?*). The SV condition thus invites two possible interpretations, one that focuses on the telicity of the predicate and one that suppresses telicity. The PV condition, on the contrary, offers only one interpretation, namely the telic one.

While subjects were shown the videos, they were simultaneously told what was going on in them. The example story for the above situation, as narrated in the experiment, is given in (10):

(10)   Look. Here's Tigger. He has a huge pile of apples, see? [Tigger is shown as grabbing one of his apples.] And here's Cookie Monster. He has only two apples and also a chocolate bar, see? [Cookie Monster is shown as grabbing the chocolate bar.]

      a.   Now what do you think: Who's gonna eat his apples?
          or
      b.   Now what do you think: Who's gonna eat his apples up?

The expected response pattern is summarized in (11):

(11)   a.   Who's gonna eat his apples up?
         ➤ Cookie Monster

      b.   Who's gonna eat his apples?
         ➤ Tigger, possibly also Cookie Monster

The PV question (a) and the SV question (b) here correspond to our test conditions A and B with completive particle verbs in (a).

An example story facilitating the use of an inceptive particle verb is illustrated in (12) below. The PV question (a) corresponds to test condition C with the inceptive particle verb *send off* and the SV question (b) to test condition D.

(12)   Look. Here's Minnie. She's waiting for a letter, see? And here's Mickey. [Standing in front of a mail box.] He has a huge letter and wants to drop it into the mailbox. And here's Tigger. [Also standing in front of the mail box.] He has a small letter. And he also wants to drop it into the mail box.

    a.   Now what do you think: Who's gonna send his letter off to Minnie?
        or
    b.   Now what do you think: Who's gonna send his letter to Minnie?

The expected response pattern for this example is given in (13):

(13)   a.   Who's gonna send his letter off to Minnie?
        ➢ Tigger

    b.   Who's gonna send his letter to Minnie?
        ➢ Mickey, possibly also Tigger

The distracter here obviously is that Mickey is more likely to send a letter to Minnie. Yet his letter is too big to fit into the mail box, so that he is not gonna be able to send his letter off. Tigger, who is completely unrelated to Minnie, is less likely to send his letter to her, although he might very well do so. Yet his letter will sure fit into the mail box, so that he is gonna be able to send his letter off. Thus *Mickey is gonna send his letter to Minnie*, but *Tigger is gonna send his letter **off** to Minnie.*

In sum, great care was taken that the content of each video story was counterbalanced as to the likelihood of an event to take place altogether or to be completed (in the case of *eat up* and *drink up*) or started (in the case of *send off* and *carry off*). Thus for the eating event, Tigger was assumed to be more likely to *eat his apples*, as he was shown to be reaching out for one apple from the huge pile in front of him. Yet Cookie Monster was assumed to be more likely to *eat his apples up*, although he is shown to be reaching out for a chocolate bar instead, but he has only two apples in front of him. For the sending event, Mickey was assumed to be more likely *to send his letter to Minnie*, but Tigger to *send his letter **off** to Minnie* because Mickey's letter is too huge to fit into the mailbox. The same counterbalancing strategy was applied to all eight stories.

Each of the four events was deliberately used twice and in a parallel fashion, but employed different characters and objects. This way, every event could be asked about in both the PV condition and the SV condition, without prompting two questions per story. Fillers were not used, so that the PV and SV conditions would be contrasted. There was no reason to veil the target structures of the experiment. On the contrary, the task of differentiating the PV and SV conditions depends on a direct contrast between them. Establishing a contrast without directly priming responses was the intention behind the experimental design.

2.2   Subjects

10 children between the ages of 3 and 5 (M=4;6, SD=0;7, range=3;5-5;4) participated in
the study. There were two 3-year olds, five 4-year olds and three 5-year olds. All subjects
were tested individually. The children were tested in day-care centers in Amherst,
Massachusetts. All of the children passed the training, which was administered to ensure
that they understood the task. One child had to be excluded from later analysis because he
failed on more questions than he gave appropriate answers.

2.3   Procedure

The children who participated in the study were first shown the real puppets and asked
for each puppet's name, all of them well-known Disney and Sesame Street characters.
They were told they would see short self-made movies involving these puppets. Then
they were trained on the types of stories that would be told and the types of questions that
would be asked in the test. The first training item was acted out live in front of the
children in order to concentrate on the actual task. Another one used a movie just like the
test items in order to familiarize children with the technique. Immediately following the
training, subjects were administered the eight test items and asked questions according to
the design described in 2.1 above. They were instructed to answer verbally or by pointing
at the characters in the movies. Children's responses were recorded by hand and by
videotape. The hand-written responses were later checked against the video recordings
for further clues children might have given by commenting on the stories.

Children were shown short movies without sound on a laptop using MS
PowerPoint. Each movie consisted of two parts: one that introduced the event and one
that showed the further course of the event. Subjects saw the first part of the movie twice
in order to first familiarize themselves with the stories and to then make a prediction
about the further course of the event. During the first part, they were simultaneously told
what happened to the puppets and objects in the movies, in line with examples (10) and
(12) in section 2.1 above. While the experimenter told the stories depicted in the movies,
she emphasized the size of the objects and pointed to objects and characters in order to
prime subjects for both possible interpretations.

Then children were asked to make predictions about the further course of events.
Predictions were prompted by questions including a test item in one of the four
conditions that started: *What do you think: Who's gonna ...?*. Only after they made their
predictions, subjects were shown the second part of the movie, which displayed the actual
outcome of the event.

2.4   Predictions

(14)   Prediction for acquisition question Q1:
        Children will understand particle telicity differently from compositional telicity
        from early on. They will map particle telicity onto the completion and inception
        parts of events more often than compositional telictiy.

Based on hypothesis H1, I predicted an effect of verb frame as reflected in a difference between conditions A and B, on the one hand, and conditions C and D, on the other hand. If particle verbs indeed yield telic interpretations different from compositionally telic structures, subjects should assign different interpretations to the stimuli in conditions A vs. B and conditions C vs. B respectively. They should map the particle verbs in conditions A and C onto the completion and inception parts of events more often than the corresponding transitive simplex verbs in conditions B and D.

(15) Prediction for acquisition question Q2:
 If children understand telicity entailments of particle verbs in an adult-like manner, they will interpret both completive and inceptive particle verbs as telic, and they will do so even in the absence of completion information.

Note that the same prediction will hold even if children's interpretation of particle verbs is initially restricted to features of lexical aspect and precludes those of grammatical aspect. (15) predicts that there will be no effect of particle verb type.

(16) Alternative prediction for acquisition question Q2:
 If children's interpretation of telic particle verbs is initially bound to the presence of completion information, they will interpret completive particle verbs as telic more often than they will inceptive particle verbs.

In contrast to (15) above, (16) predicts a main effect of particle verb type. Children might understand only completive particle verbs as telic because completion information of whatever kind might figure more prominently in their grammar if grammatical aspect was the driving force.

Recall that grammatical aspect was controlled for in the present experiment. Due to the lack of perfective viewpoint and perfective morphology, one might predict that children will not understand inceptive particle verbs at all and may not even understand completive particle verbs as telic if their comprehension indeed depended on grammatical aspect features. However, if completion information of some sort was indispensable for children to identify telicity, intended completion instead of the actual attainment of a resultant state might be sufficient. If this was so, the difference between inceptive and completive particle verbs predicted in (16) makes sense even when perfectivity is controlled for.

With (16) above in mind, I further predict an interaction between PV type (completive or inceptive) and verb frame (PV or SV). Children will be less likely to understand inceptive PVs (condition C) as telic than they will completive PVs (condition A) and transitive simplex verbs (conditions B and D), since all of the latter three conditions can be construed as aimed at completion, while inceptives cannot. If, however, intended completion is not sufficient for children to project telicity onto, they will be equally likely or unlikely to understand inceptive particle verbs, completive particle verbs and compositional telicity and perform at chance level.

3.   Results

Responses were coded in a threefold way: as referring to the inception or completion part of an event only, to the process or event as such or to both. If, in response to the question *Who's gonna ...?*, subjects chose the character who might indeed be able to begin or finish what he is about to do, because the size or amount of his object was smaller, the response was taken to refer to inception or completion only. If they instead picked the character who could impossibly begin or finish his event, because the size or amount of his object was too large, this was taken to mean a preference for the process interpretation, which defocuses telicity. If subjects chose both, the response was naturally taken to include both types of mappings. For statistical analysis the responses referring to inception and completion interpretations received a score of 1, all others a score of 0.

3.1   Analysis of verb frame

I first performed a univariate Analysis of Variance ($F(3,76)=.124$, $p=.345$). Post Hoc Tukey F test showed that, consistent with the non-significant F-value, none of the pairwise comparisons was significant.

As hypothesis H1 only addressed the difference between the overall verb frame types PV (particle verbs) and SV (simplex verbs) and the difference between inceptive and completive particle verbs did not play a role at this point, the two particle verb (PV) conditions A and C were collapsed, as were the two simplex verb (SV) control conditions B and D. Since only 10 children participated in the study and the responses of one child had to be excluded from further analysis, all children were analyzed as one age group. Table 1 and figure 1 display the overall distribution of responses.

Table 1	Distribution of responses by verb frame		
verb frame	inception or completion	process	both
particle verb	43%	31%	26%
simplex verb	44%	28%	28%

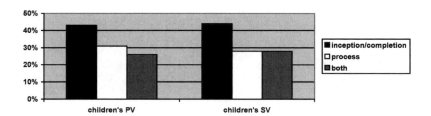

Figure 1   Distribution of responses by verb frame

Children do not seem to treat particle verbs and simplex verbs differently from one another. They seem to have a slight preference for the inception/completion readings in both verb frames alike. However, they also assign process interpretations to the particle verb frames and the simplex verb frames alike. Thus children seem to be easily distracted by the events that are impossible on an inception / completion interpretation, yet offer a more plausible alternative. The results of the ANOVA did not show a difference between the PV and SV condition ($F(1,78)=.239$, $p=.626$). Thus the results do not seem to support our prediction for hypothesis H1.

3.2 Analysis of telicity type

In order to test hypotheses H2, children's responses to questions with completive particle verbs in condition A and those with inceptive particle verbs in condition C were analyzed separately in comparison with their respective control conditions B and D. Table 2 and figure 2 display the responses in terms of telicity type chosen for the two particle verb conditions A and C.

Table 2   Distribution of responses by telicity type

PV type	inception or completion	process	both
inceptive	28%	36%	36%
completive	56%	33%	11%

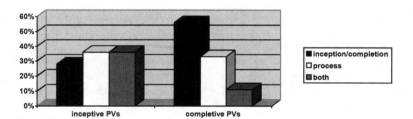

Figure 2   Distribution of responses by telicity type

Children associate completive particle verbs with completion more often than they associate inceptive particle verbs with inception. The ANOVA also yielded the comparison of greatest interest between conditions A (completive PVs) and C (inceptive PVs). In this case, the mean for condition A was .27 higher than the mean for condition C, which is suggestive but, in the context of this experiment, not reliable. The suggestive difference between completive and inceptive particle verbs acts against our prediction for hypothesis H2.

Despite the non-significant results of the Post Hoc Tukey, the above results suggest an interaction between verb frame and telicity type. Table 3 and figure 3 exhibit the distribution of responses by both verb frame and telicity type.

Table 3   Distribution of responses by verb frame and telicity type

	telicity type	inception or process completion	process	both
particle verbs	completive	56%	33%	11%
	inceptive	28%	36%	36%
simplex verbs	SV + DP	44%	28%	28%
	SV + PP	44%	28%	28%

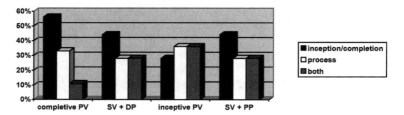

Figure 3   Distribution of responses by telicity type and verb frame

Note, first of all, that the responses in the two compositionally telic simplex verb conditions mirror each other. Children preferably choose the completion/inception interpretation for both transitive simplex verbs with incremental theme DP and transitive simplex verbs with goal PPs. Note next that they pick the completive interpretation for completive PVs more often than they consider the process interpretation. For inceptive PVs, finally, they choose the inception interpretation less often than the process or event as such. In this respect, the results show a difference between the inceptive particle verbs and all other conditions, in line with the alternative prediction for hypothesis H2. What the other three conditions have in common is that their telicity can be construed as intended completion, whereby completion does not necessarily have to be attained. The crucial point is that they indicate an intention or attempt at completing the event, rather than its beginning or any other subpart. Thus completion information of some sort seems to play a role in children's understanding of telicity. This supports the alternative prediction for hypothesis H2.

4.   Discussion

One goal of the present experiment was to test whether children differentiate particle telicity and compositional telicity (Q1). The initial analysis of responses seemed to show that children do not understand particle telicity and compositional telicity differently. However, a closer look at the two different particle verb types integrated in the present experiment, completives and inceptives, reveals that children indeed interpret the two of them differently from their respective controls. Thus they associate inceptive PVs with inception less often than the compositionally telic control sentences containing simplex verbs with goal PPs. In contrast, they map completive particle verbs onto completion more often than their compositionally telic control sentences comprising simplex verbs with incremental theme arguments.

The asymmetry found here, in fact, does not fully conform to the prediction for Q1 that children would map the two particle verb types in conditions A and C onto the completion and inception more often than the corresponding transitive simplex verbs in conditions B and D. The prediction is only borne out for the completive particle verbs in condition A. The initial analysis, which collapsed conditions A (completive PVs) and C (inceptive PVs), did not catch this difference. Separate comparisons of conditions A and B, on the one hand, and C and D, on the other hand, however, revealed differences between particle telicity and compositional telicity.

The findings for Q1 eventually support our hypothesis H1 that particle telicity and compositional telicity arise from a structural difference in the target grammar and children are aware of it from early on. Thus the difference between the two is not only shown to have substance, but, at the same time, may explain the findings of previous acquisition studies. Recall that earlier studies tested only completive particle verbs and for those found the same results as this experiment found for completives. I suggest that the difference between the two types of telicity found in earlier studies may be attributed to the structural difference in the target grammar, rather than a developmental delay. It would also explain why not only children, but also adults treated the two structures differently in the experiments of van Hout (1998a,b, 2001) and Schulz & Penner (2002). In this respect, all studies prove continuity between child and adult grammars in the comprehension of particle telicity and compositional telicity.

In contrast to the previous studies, the specific contribution of the experiment reported here is that it aimed not only at detecting a possible difference between particle telicity and compositional telicity, but more specifically at identifying what particular interpretations children assign to telic structures. The experiment offered three types of responses: one that maps the stimulus onto that part of an event that identifies telicity proper, one that maps it onto the telic event as such without focus on telicity and one that includes both. Children allowed all three types of interpretations, with only a slight preference for the inception / completion interpretations, for both telic structures alike. Considerations of what story character will be (un)able to start or finish the respective event he is involved in and, hence, the boundedness of events do not seem to play a much more important role for children than possible alternative interpretations. I suggest that the reason for this response pattern is more likely to be a pragmatic one rooted in the experimental design than one based on grammar. It may have to do with the distracter contexts they were provided with.

The second aim of the present study was to test whether children interpret both completive and inceptive particle verbs as telic and whether they do so even in the absence of completion information (Q2). It touches upon the issue of whether children's choice of aspectual interpretations they associate with particle verbs might be constrained by more general restrictions on their early aspectual systems. The two versions of the Aspect Hypothesis proposed in the acquisition literature make opposing predictions in this regard, as we saw in 2.4 above). We predicted, however, that children would understand telicity entailments of particle verbs in an adult-like manner and interpret both types of particle verbs tested here as telic. The same would be the case if only lexical aspect was available to children, while the opposite would be the case if they only had access to grammatical aspect.

The design of the experiment was able to detect a suggestive preference with regard to what part of an event children map their particle verbs onto. They are more likely to associate completive particle verbs with completion interpretations (56% of cases) than inceptive particle verbs with inception interpretations (28% of cases). Thus they chose the telic interpretations for completive particle verbs twice as often as for inceptive particle verbs. Even though children did not treat inceptives along the same lines as completives, they interpreted both particle verb types differently from their corresponding compositionally telic controls. They have some understanding that completive particle verbs with *up* are unacceptable to refer to an event that can impossibly be finished, while the corresponding compositionally telic structure might very well be coerced to mean something like that. Thus they indeed understand telicity associated with particle verbs, even in the absence of information about the actual completion of events. This supports our prediction in (15) above for Q2.

Alternatively, the findings suggest that completion information of some sort nevertheless plays an important role for children in their understanding of telicity. This could likewise account for children's preference of the intended completion interpretations for completive particle verbs as opposed to their lack of preference of the intended inception interpretations for inceptive particle verbs. Mere intention of completion seems to be enough, however, to associate the completive particle verbs with that type of interpretation, as information about the actual completion of the relevant events was not available at the moment of interpretation. If intended completion rather than the presence of a perfective viewpoint or perfective morphology per se were taken to mean that completion influences children's understanding of telicity after all, this would support the alternative prediction for Q2 in (16) above. However, this scenario seems far fetched, especially since the mere presence of an inherent boundary rather than completion itself is precisely what telicity means.

While children's differing treatment of inceptive and completive particle verbs may be explained by some version of the Aspect Hypothesis, the interaction between verb frame and telicity type deserves further explanation. Therefore, let's look at the possible interpretations for the four experimental conditions in more detail. Out of the four telic constructions tested altogether, completive particle verbs were most likely to be associated with telicity, while inceptive particle verbs were least likely to be. The range of possible interpretations is shown given in (17):

(17)   A: eat the apples up
           ➢ completive
       B: eat the apples
           ➢ completive or non-completive
       C: send a letter off to Mickey
           ➢ inceptive or completive
       D: send a letter to Mickey
           ➢ completive or possibly non-completive

Theoretically, all four conditions could be associated with a completion interpretation to the same extent. In the two compositionally telic control conditions B and D, completion is mapped onto the event by the final boundary of the object of the eating and drinking events in B (transitive simplex verb frame) and the goal of the path of the sending and carrying events in D (transitive simplex verb of motion with a goal PP). For the completive particle verbs with *up* in condition A, I claimed that the completion interpretation is, in fact, the only one possible. Condition C parallels its control condition D in that the goal of the path denoted by the PP in both conditions may add a final boundary to the event referred to by the particle verbs in C and the simplex verbs of motion in D. Yet, in contrast to all other conditions, only the inceptive particle verbs in condition C can also be associated with inception.

The picture of possible responses that emerges from the predicted interpretations provide for a third explanation. It reflects the following pattern: The completive particle verbs in A, by hypothesis, must be unambiguously interpreted as telic in the sense of completion. The two compositionally telic control conditions may or may not be associated with completion and, hence, are ambiguous. They crucially depend on how many speakers indeed find that measuring out the entire object or the entire path in question is necessarily entailed by the compositionally telic structures. From previous studies we know that the transitive simplex verb frame (condition B) is not always interpreted as telic, but can instead be associated with partial measuring out.

By means of the distracter contexts integrated into the video stories, the two compositionally telic control conditions B and D were, in addition, ambiguous between a reading that focuses on the completion part of the event and an alternative interpretation that takes into account the event as such and defocuses completion. The inceptive particle verbs in condition C allowed for the inceptive interpretation entailed by the particle *off* and the completion interpretation intended by the goal PP. Thus all conditions but the completive particle verbs in condition A were ambiguous and allowed for alternative interpretations beside the possible completion interpretations common to all of them. This may have caused a higher proportion of completive answers in condition A relative to all other conditions, where more than one reading was possible.

What remains to be explained at this point is why children did worst at identifying inceptive particle verbs with inception. I suggest three possible reasons. As already suggested, completion information of some kind may be indispensable for children to understand telicity. While completive particle verbs may be interpreted to mean intended completion, children might be at loss with inceptive particle verbs. Second, the results for the inceptive particle verbs may be attributed to a problem with the stimuli in condition C, so that they did not invite inceptive interpretations as much as they were expected to. Thus the criteria used for matching conditions C and D, such that they would differ only with respect to the presence or absence of the particle and exclude additional semantic and syntactic differences, might turn out to be too strict. As a third explanation for the observed results, the statistical analysis suggested that there was too much variability in the data because of the small number of observations. Therefore, more experiments with a larger number of subjects, for which this study served as a pilot, are necessary in order to draw final conclusions about children's aspectual interpretations of particle verbs.

A factor that was not a test condition in the experiment produced an additional interesting finding. The concern that children's comprehension of telic particle verbs might be influenced by perfectivity was incorporated into the experimental design by fully controlling for it. In contrast to previous experiments testing children's comprehension of telicity, information about the actual completion of events as entailed by a perfective viewpoint and perfective morphology was avoided and cannot possibly have influenced interpretations. Commensurate with our prediction for question Q2 and contrary to the alternative prediction, children are very well able to understand particle verbs as telic even in the absence of completion information. This supports the Lexical Aspect First hypothesis, even if only partially. Yet the finding that children most often associate completive particle verbs with telic interpretations suggests that completion, nevertheless, plays a role, even if not entailed by a perfective viewpoint or perfective morphology. If completion information is more broadly construed as intended or attempted completion, then children's preference for completion over inception provides evidence against Lexical Aspect First, although it does not necessarily support the Grammatical Aspect First hypothesis.

The novel experimental design evoked one further, very important finding, even though it was not a main question of the study. It was able to show that children's understanding of telicity is not constrained by cognitive limitations. They are very well able to make predictions about whether an event is likely to be completed or not, based on the size and the final boundary of objects and events they map onto. The particular linguistic structures of the predicates did not affect children's understanding of the boundedness of objects and events as much as their fascination with the story characters. Their knowledge of the habits of the story characters tended to distract their interpretations away from telicity. Therefore, it is safe to conclude that children understand the concept of telicity.

5.   Conclusion

The aim of the present study was twofold. On the one hand, it tested the hypothesis that particle telicity differs structurally from compositional telicity and that children are sensitive to the difference. The results of the study eventually confirmed the hypothesis, although our specific predictions are not borne out for all types of telic particle verbs alike. Only completive particle verbs produced a higher number of responses that focused on the telic part of the event, here its completion, than their compositionally telic controls. The same does not hold true for inceptive particle verbs. Moreover, completive particle verbs like *eat the pizza up* and corresponding transitive simplex verbs of the type *eat the pizza* were precisely the two types of telic verb frames that were tested in previous acquisition studies and produced the same results in children and adults alike. Therefore, the results of the present study as well as those of previous studies provide evidence for a structural difference between particle telicity and compositional telictiy and support our hypothesis H1.

The other aim of the study was to test the hypothesis that telicity entailments of particle verbs do not necessarily have to coincide with completion. The experiment explored whether children are able to interpret particle verbs as telic even in the absence of visual and verbal completion information. The results showed that children are very well able to understand telicity (lexical aspect) in the absence of information about the actual completion of events, as given by as given by a perfective viewpoint or perfective morphology (grammatical aspect). Yet the finding that they do more so for completive than for inceptive particle verbs might suggest a bias for completion in children's construal of telicity. The first finding is in line with the English target grammar and predicted under the assumption of continuity. The same is predicted by the Lexical Aspect First hypothesis. The latter finding is predicted by the Grammatical Aspect First hypothesis. Although not the main question of the study, none of the versions of the Aspect Hypothesis proposed in the acquisition literature can account for the results of the experiment. The picture that emerges from our study is far more complex and demands further investigation.

In conclude that children between the ages of 3 and 5 understand the aspectual entailments of particle verbs. The suggested novel experimental design is able to capture the difference between particle telicity and compositional telicity, as manifest in the target grammar. It is also on the right track to incorporate telic particle verbs other beyond completives and avoid suggestive completion information. Future research will have to test whether children indeed have a conceptual bias for completion interpretations and difficulty in identifying inception interpretations or whether the differing results for completive and inceptive particle verbs found in the present study can be attributed to the specific material used in the experiment.

References

Andersen, R. & Y. Shirai. 1996. Primacy of aspect in first and second language acquisition: The pidgin/creole connection. In *Handbook of second language acquisition*, eds. W. C. Ritchie & T. K. Bhatia, 527-570. San Diego et al.: Academic Press.

Antinucci, F. & R. Miller. 1976. How children talk about what happened. *Journal of child language* 3, 167-189.

Bloom, L. et al. 1980. Semantics of verbs and the development of verb inflection in child language. *Language* 56(2), 386-412.

Bolinger, D. 1971. *The phrasal verb in English*. Cambridge, MA: Harvard UP.

Borer, H. 1994. The projection of arguments. In *Functional categories*, eds. E. Benedicto & J. Runner, UMOP 17, 19-47. Amherst, MA: GLSA.

Borer, H. 1998. Deriving passive without theta roles. In *Morphology and its relation to phonology and syntax*, eds. S.G. Lapointe et al., 60-99.

Borer, H. 2005. *Structuring sense: The normal course of events*. Vol. II. Oxford: OUP.

Brinton, L.J. 1985. Verb particles in English: Aspect or aktionsart? *Studia linguistica* 39, 157-68.

Brinton, L.J. 1988. *The development of English aspectual systems*. Cambridge: CUP.

Bronckart, J. P. & H. Sinclair. 1973. Time, tense and aspect. *Cognition* 2(1), 107-130.

Dehé, N. 2002. *Particle verbs in English: Syntax, information structure, and intonation*. Amsterdam: Benjamins.

Dowty, D. 1979. *Word meaning and Montague grammar: The semantics of verbs and times in Generative Semantics and in Montague's PTQ*. Dordrecht: Reidel.

Emonds, J. 1972. Evidence that indirect object movement is a structure-preserving rule. *Foundations of language* 8, 546-61.

Jackendoff, R. 1997. Twistin' the night away. *Language* 73(3), 534-559.

Jackendoff, R. 2002. English particle constructions, the lexicon, and the autonomy of syntax. In *Verb-particle explorations*, eds. N. Dehé et al., 67-94.

Keyser, S.J. & T. Roeper. 1992. Re: The abstract clitic hypothesis. *Linguistic Inquiry* 23(1), 89-125.

Klein, W. 1992. Tempus, Aspekt und Zeitadverbien. *Kognitionswissenschaft* 2, 107-118.

Krifka, M. 1989. Nominal reference, temporal constitution, and quantification in event semantics. In *Semantics and contextual expression*, eds. R. Bartsch et al., 75-115. Dordrecht: Foris.

Krifka, M. 1992. Thematic relations as links between nominal reference and temporal constitution. In *Lexical Matters*, eds. I. Sag & A. Szabolcsi, 29-53. Stanford & Chicago: CSLI & Chicago UP.

Olsen, M. & A. Weinberg. 1999. Innateness and the acquisition of grammatical aspect via lexical aspect. In *BUCLD 23*, eds. A. Greenhill et al., 529-540.

Penner, Z. et al. 2003. *Linguistics* 41(2), 289-319.

Ritter, E. & S.T. Rosen. 1998. Delimiting events in syntax. In *The projection of arguments: Lexical and compositional factors*, eds. M. Butt & W. Geuder, 135-164.

Roeper, T. & W. Snyder. 2005. Language learnability and the forms of recursion. In *UG and external systems: Language, brain and computation*, eds. A.M. DiScullio & R. Delmonte, 155-169. Amsterdam: Benjamins.

Schulz, P. et al. 2001. The early acquisition of verb meaning in German by normally developing and language impaired children. *Brain and Language* 77, 407-418.

Schulz, P. et al. 2002. Comprehension of resultative verbs in normally developing and language impaired children. In *Investigations in clinical phonetics and linguistics*, eds. F. Windsor et al., 115-129. Mahwah: Erlbaum.

Schulz, P. & Z. Penner. 2002. How you can eat the apple and have it too: Evidence from the acquisition of telicity in German. In *Proceedings of the GALA 2001 conference on language acquisition*, eds. J. Costa & M.J. Freitas, 239-246.

Shirai, Y. & R. W. Andersen. 1995. The acquisition of tense-aspect morphology: A prototype account. *Language* 71, 743-762.

Slabakova, R. 2002. Recent research on the acquisition of aspect: an embarrassment of riches? *Second language research* 18(2), 172-1888.

Smith, C. 1991. *The parameter of aspect*. Dordrecht et al.: Kluwer.

Tenny, C. 1994. *Aspectual roles and the syntax-semantics interface*. Dordrecht et al.: Kluwer.

van Hout, A. 1996. *Event semantics of verb frame alternations: A case study of Dutch and its acquisition*. Tilburg: TILDIL.

van Hout, A. 1998a. The role of direct objects and particles in learning telicity in Dutch and Englisch. In *BUCLD 22 Proceedings*, eds. A. Geenhill et al., 397-408. Somerville, MA: Cascadilla.

van Hout, A. 1998b. On learning the role of direct objects for telicity in Dutch and English. In *New perspectives on language acquisition*, ed. B. Hollebrandse, 87-104. UMass Occasional Papers 22. Amherst: GLSA.

van Hout, A. 2001. Acquiring telicity cross-linguistically: On the acquistion of telicity entailments associated with transitivity. In press in *Crosslinguistic perspectives on argument structure: Implications for learnability*, eds. M. Bowerman & P. Brown. Erlbaum.

Verkuyl, H. J. 1972. *On the compositional nature of the aspects*. Dordrecht: Reidel.

Wagner, L. 2001. Aspectual influences on early tense comprehension. *Journal of child language* 28, 661-681.

Department of Linguistics
South College
University of Massachusetts
Amherst, MA 01003

jeschull@linguist.umass.edu

Direct *versus* indirect *wh*-scope marking strategies in French child grammar

Magda Oiry

University of Nantes

This paper presents some new data on the acquisition of long-distance questions in French L1. These results are consistent with the previous study, presented in Oiry & Demirdache (in press): French child grammar involves *wh*-scope marking strategies.

I.   Previous study: Evidence from French L1 Acquisition.

This section presents a summary of the main hypothesis based on French data originally presented in Oiry (2002) and analysed in Oiry & Demirdache (in press).

Oiry & Demirdache (in press) argued for the existence of two *wh*-scope marking strategies in French L1, namely a direct *versus* an indirect strategy. The former involves a partially moved *wh*-phrase bound by a non-lexical Q morpheme. The latter exhibits two *wh*-phrases, which move overtly or covertly to each CP.

1.1   Partial movement in French L1: a direct dependency analysis.

In Oiry & Demirdache (in press), henceforth O&D, empirical evidence were presented for a *direct dependency* strategy in the French first language grammar. Look first at the sentence in (1).

(1)   L1 French (Oiry 2002)[1]

Tu   penses   **quoi** # que # Tinky Winky   l'adore ?
you think   what   C°   Tinky Winky   CL-loves
'What do you think that Tinky Winky likes?'

Although the example in (1) is not grammatical in the French adult grammar, the strategy is productive in children's answers. The *wh*-phrase *quoi* (*what*) in (1) moves from its original position, namely the object of the verb *adorer* (love), to the intermediate Spec CP, which bears the features [-wh]. Hence, no lexical scope marker appears in the matrix

---

[1] The symbol # indicates a phonological pause.

© 2006 by Magda Oiry
Tanja Heizmann (ed.): Current Issues in Acquisition. University of Massachusetts Occasional Papers in Linguistics 34, 77-95.
GLSA Amherst.

CP. In this respect, French children's questions differ from their English counterparts, as illustrated in (2).

(2)   L1 English (Thornton 1990: 246)
        What do you think which Smurf really has roller skates?

Wh-Scope Marking strategies in English L1 are conformed to the German partial movement, see (3).

(3)   German Adult Grammar (Mc Daniel 1989: 569).
        Was$_i$ glaubt Hans mit wem$_i$ Jakob jetzt t$_i$ spricht?
        what believes H.   with who   J.   now   talk.to
        'With whom does Hans believe that Jacob is now talking?'

The matrix verb *believe* in (3) selects a [-*wh*] complement. Partial movement of the embedded *wh*-phrase to the intermediate [-*wh*] Spec CP position thus violates the *Wh*-criterion (Rizzi 1996, among others) which requires that every *wh*-phrase shows up in the specifier of a [+*wh*] C°. The sentence in (3) would be ungrammatical if the German *wh*-phrase *was* (what) in the matrix [+*wh*] Spec CP was omitted. The latter is analyzed as a base-generated dummy *wh*-phrase acting as a scope marker, that is, signaling where the medial *wh*-phrase is to be interpreted.

McDaniel (1989) suggests that the scope marker (in scope marking structures involving partial movement) is directly coindexed with the contentful medial *wh*-phrase with which it is associated. It is a kind of expletive *wh*-phrase forming a *wh*-chain with the *wh*-phrase whose scope it marks in the overt syntax and replaced by the latter at LF.

Since the syntax of the exceptional questions in (2) parallels the syntax of partial *wh*-movement in (3), Thornton (1990) concludes that children produce questions involving partial *wh*-movement. *What* in (2) is thus analyzed as a base-generated scope marker indicating the (matrix) scope of the intermediate *wh*-phrase.

Thornton (1990) and Crain & Thornton (1998) conclude that the non-adult long-distance (henceforth LD) questions illustrated in (2), are determined by principles of Universal Grammar. That is, children produce questions that, although not well-formed in the target language (English), are nonetheless well-formed in other languages (e.g. German). This is expected under the Continuity Hypothesis according to which children's developing grammars can differ only in the way adult grammars can differ from each other.

The French L1 questions differ crucially from their English counterparts, lacking an overt scope marker. O&D postulate the existence of a non-lexical Q morpheme in the French L1 grammar, which fullfills at least three functions: it marks the matrix clause as interrogative, checks the strong Q features of CP1 and binds the partially moved *wh*-phrase.[2] The structure for the French L1 question in (1) is illustrated below in (4).

(4)   Partial *wh*-movement (at Spell-out & LF)
        [$_{CP}$ [$\mathbf{Q_i}$ Tu   penses   [$_{CP}$ **quoi** $_i$ # que # Tinky Winky   l'adore t$_i$?
                you   think   what   C°   Tinky Winky CL-loves
        'What do you think that Tinky Winky likes?'

In sum, once we adopt the proposal that French children's L1 grammar has a non-lexical Q morpheme, then the syntax of partial *wh*-movement is no longer surprising.

This proposal is further supported by the fact that partial *wh*-movement structures without an overt scope marker are attested cross-linguistically in languages such as, Quechua (5), Bahasa Indonesia (6) or Kitharaka (7). We analyze these partial movement structures as involving a null Q morpheme signaling where the medial-*wh* is to be interpreted at LF.

(5)   Ancash Quechua (Cole and Hermon 1994: 240)
        Ø   Jose   munan   **may-man**   Maria   away-na-n-ta ?
            Jose   wants   where-to   Maria   go-NOM-3-ACC
        'Where does Jose want Maria to go?'

(6)   Bahasa Indonesia (Saddy 1991: 189)
        Ø   Bill   tahu   **siapa**   yang   Tom   cintai ?
            Bill   knows   who   FOC   Tom   loves
        'Who does Bill know that Tom loves?'

(7)   Kitharaka (Muriungi 2004: 10)
        Ø   U -   ri-thugania   ati   **n-uu**   John   a- ring-ir- e- t ?
            2ndSG-T°-think   that   FOC-who   J.   SUBJ-beat-T°-FINALVOWEL
        'Who do you think that John beat?'

Furthermore, following Cheng & Rooryck (2000) and Matthieu (1999), French *wh*-in situ is licensed by a Q morpheme:

(8)   *Wh*-in situ
        [$_{CP}$ [$\mathbf{Q_i}$] il mange **quoi**$_i$?]
                Q   he eat   what
        'What does he eat?'

Under this proposal, the syntax of partial *wh*-movement in French L1 parallels the syntax of *wh*-in situ. In both (4) and (8), a non-lexical Q morpheme is merged in the matrix [+*wh*] Spec CP in the syntax.

---

[2] Based on Mathieu (1999), Cheng & Rooryck (2000); see O&D for details.

Both partial *wh*-movement in French L1 and *wh*-in situ in child/adult French are *wh*-scope marking constructions involving a scope marker generated in a *non-argument/operator position* in the matrix clause (Spec CP) and *directly associated* (via binding) with a lower *wh*-phrase, itself either in situ or stranded in the specifier of [-*wh*] C°.

O&D do not assume that the scope marker licensing both partial *wh*-movement in the child grammar of French and *wh*-in situ (be it in the child or adult grammar) is a semantically vacuous element subject to expletive replacement at LF, for at least three reasons. First, LF-raising of the associate (i.e. the contentful *wh*-phrase) to the expletive position is argued not to be conceptually motivated in Chomsky (1998); that is, expletives do not attract and need not be replaced. The associate simply does not move. Moreover, as Fanselow & Mahajan (2000) point out, merging an expletive into Spec CP is in fact no longer even an available option in the Minimalist framework. Second, O&D do not take the scope marker base-generated in the matrix Spec CP and licensing partial *wh*-movement/*wh*-in situ in child/adult French to be semantically vacuous, but rather to be a full-fledged Q morpheme serving three functions. It marks the matrix clause as interrogative, binds the medial/in-situ *wh*-phrase and checks the latter's *wh*/Q feature via Agree (see the discussion below). Thirdly, this proposal allows to draw a principled distinction between the grammar of overt long movement in French on the one hand, and that of *wh*-in situ and partial movement on the other, as illustrated in (4) and (8).[3]

O&D leave open the question of whether this null Q morpheme is phonological or not. Following Cheng & Rooryck (2000) intonation plays a certain role in French *wh*-in situ. Previous acoustic studies seem to suggest that the rising contour that Cheng & Rooryck argued for, is not the only intonative pattern of French *wh*-in situ. This is still an open question.

The question then is how to compositionally assign matrix scope to the medial/in situ *wh*-phrases in (4), without further (covert) movement. There are at least two well-defined semantic mechanisms available in the literature for encoding scope without movement. (i) Unselective Binding as in Pesetsky (1987) and Nishigauchi (1990): the lower *wh*-phrase is analyzed as an indefinite introducing an individual variable subject to existentially closure, and the matrix Q provides the existential binder (see Fanselow & Mahajan (2000) for an analysis of partial movement in German along these lines). (ii) A choice function analysis (Reinhart 1997): the lower *wh*-phrase is analyzed as an indefinite introducing a variable over choice functions, and the matrix Q provides the existential quantifier binding this variable (see Brandner (2000) for an analysis of partial movement in German along these lines).

---

[3] Fanselow (to appear) draw a correlation between languages with simple partial *wh*-movement (i.e. without an overt scope marker) with the availability of both in situ strategy and long-distance movement. This generalization is consistent with our data.

1.2   Wh-scope marking in French L1: an indirect dependency analysis.

O&D also provided empirical arguments for an indirect dependency strategy in French L1.

The *wh*-scope marking construction in Hindi is illustrated in (9), from Dayal (2000: 160-162). Notice that two *wh*-phrases appear in (9): *kyaa* ('what') appears in the object position of the main clause, and *kisse* ('who') in the object position of the embedded verb *talk*.

(9)   Jaun   **kyaa**   soctaa hai   ki   Merii   **kis-se**   baat karegii?
       John   what   think-PR   that   Mary   who-INS   talk do-FUT
       'Who does John think Mary will talk to?'
(10)   Jaun   **kyaa**   soctaa hai?
       John   what   think-PR
       'What does John think?

Dayal (2000) argues that the *wh*-scope marker *kyaa* (what) occurring in the matrix clause is crucially not a non-referential (expletive) scope marker. Rather, it is an ordinary *wh*-phrase appearing in its base argument position. Dayal thus draws a parallel between the matrix clause in (9) and the independent clause in (10). In both (9) and (10), the object *wh*-phrase *kyaa* occurs in the internal argument position of the verb 'think' and is used to indicate a question over the set of propositions that John thinks about, i.e., the set of propositions p such that John thinks p.

In (9), we thus have two clauses, each containing a contentful *wh*-phrase, each interpreted as a *wh*-question in its own right. The matrix (CP1) is a question over propositions, and the subordinate clause (CP2), syntactically analyzed as an appositive clause adjoined to the matrix, is a question over individuals.

The LF for (9) is given in (11). The in situ *wh*-phrases each move to CP specifier position, yielding two local *wh*-dependencies. The connection between the two clauses is established *indirectly* by coindexing the matrix *wh*-phrase and the subordinate *wh*-question.

(11)   Covert syntax of *wh*-scope marking in Hindi
       [$_{CP1}$ **kyaa**$_i$ [Jaun **t**$_i$ soctaa hai] [$_{CP2i}$ **kis-se**$_j$ ki   Merii   **t**$_j$ baat karegii]
              what   John   think-PR   who-INS   that   Mary   talk do-F
       'Who does John think Mary will talk to?'

We found in the French data some questions involving an indirect dependency, illustrated below.

(12)   *Wh*-Scope Marking in French L1 (Oiry 2002)
a.   Tu   crois   **quoi** # lala elle aime   bien **quoi** ?
         you   believe **what**   L.   she   likes well **what**
         'What do you believe Lala likes?'

b.   **Qu'est-ce que** tu   crois   **qu'est-ce** caché dans le sac ?
         what-is-it that you believe what-is-it hidden   in the bag
         'What do you think that is hidden in the bag?'

The French data exhibit either the LF or Spell-out structure of Hindi's *wh*-scope marking: in (12a), each *wh*-phrase appears in situ whereas in (12b), the two *wh*-phrases move covertly to each CP. Syntactically, we have two juxtaposed/adjoined matrix questions. Semantically, the *wh*-phrase *que/KESK* in CP1 is a quantifier over propositions restricted by the *wh*-question with which it is coindexed (CP2).

The proposal that the French L1 questions illustrated in (12) are *wh*-scope marking structures instantiating indirect dependency explains the seemingly ungrammatical syntax of these non-adult questions. In particular, the syntax of these questions involves two root questions with a *wh*-phrase occurring in both the matrix and the subordinate clause. Both *wh*'s can either remain in situ or be fronted in the overt syntax. The *wh*-phrase occurring in the first clause can be any of the *wh*-phrases used to quantify over propositions in French: that is, either *quoi*, *que/KESK* or (*ce*) *que*. Indirect dependency straightforwardly explains how these two root questions combine semantically to yield the meaning of a long distance question.

Furthermore, Dayal (2000) draws a parallel between *wh*-scope marking in Hindi and sequential questions in English. She takes sequential questions to have properties characteristic of scope marking. In (13a), the *wh*-phrase occurring in CP2 is construed as taking scope outside its syntactic domain as the possible answers to (13a) show: the answer in (13b) embeds the proposition corresponding to CP2 as a complement to the verb in CP1, supplying a value for the variable in CP2. The sentence in (13a) is assigned the LF structure in (13c). Syntactically, the two independent clauses are adjoined. Semantically, the *wh*-phrase in CP1 is a quantifier over propositions restricted by the *wh*-question with which it is coindexed (CP2).

(13)
a.   What do you think? Who will Mary see?
b.   I think Mary will see Tom.
c.   LF: $[[_{CP1}$ what$_i$ do you think t$_i]$ $[[_{CP2i}$ who$_j$ t$_j$ will Mary see]

In conclusion, O&D clearly identified two classes of *wh*-scope marking strategies: *indirect* vs. *direct* dependency. The direct dependency strategy yields both partial *wh*-movement and *wh*-in-situ: the matrix non-lexical Q morpheme is merged in the matrix clause in an operator/A' position and *directly associated* (via binding) with the lower *wh*-phrase, itself either in situ or stranded in the specifier of [-*wh*] C° at Spell-out. The indirect dependency strategy (in the sense of Dayal 2000) involves two clauses, each containing a contentful *wh*-phrase, and interpreted as a *wh*-question in its own right. Both *wh*'s can simultaneously appear at Spell-out either in situ or else fronted to the specifier position of the CP in which they occur. The *wh*-phrase in the matrix is *not directly associated* with the *wh*-phrase in the subordinate clause; rather, it is associated (coindexed) with the CP containing the latter.

II   2005 study: Task, Participants & Results

2.1   Production Task

This experiment was adapted from Crain & Thornton's (1998) protocol to induce long distance questions. Two experimenters were involved and acted out different situations with props and toys to lead the child to ask questions. A lead-in to a subject LD question is presented below in (14).

(14)   LD Subject extraction (original version and translated)

> <u>Exp 1.</u> : Koko, on a caché trois objets, on va voir si tu devines où est caché chaque objet. *Koko n'entend pas. Parler à voix basse à l'enfant.*
> On sait où chaque chose est cachée. Le chat est dans le lit, le pistolet est sous le chapeau et l'indien est sous le pot de yaourt. On va voir si Koko peut deviner où on a caché chaque objet. On commence par le lit, d'accord ?
> On sait que le chat est dans le lit, mais demande à Koko ce qu'il pense.
> 2.a (*Question sujet*) Enfant : ...
> *S'il ne répond pas ou seulement une question racine : demande à Koko ce qu'il pense qui est caché sous le lit.*
> <u>Koko</u> : euh...Le chat !

> <u>Exp 1</u>: Koko, we have hidden three objects; we will see whether you can guess where they are hidden.
> *Talk to the child with a low voice, and then, Koko can't hear:*
> Both of us know where each object is hidden. The cat is in the bed, the weapon is below the hat and the Indian character is hide below the jar of yoghurt. ; we will see whether Koko can guess. Let's begin with the bed, ok?
> We know that the cat is hide in the bed, but ask koko what he thinks.
> 2.a. child answer:...
> If he doesn't answer or only a matrix question: ask Koko what he thinks is hide in the bed.
> <u>Koko</u>: hum...the cat?

2.2   Participants

Nine children were involved int his study: 6 boys and 3 girls, aged between 3.08 and 5.09.[4]

The two experimenters induced 14 questions from each child. Two controls were part of this protocol. When the child produce a matrix question or a LD yes-no question, we prompteagain by repeating the lead-in. This technique was used for eliciting subject (5), object (5) and adjunct (2) LD *wh*-questions with bare *wh*-phrases.

The types of target questions elicited are shown in (15) below.

(15)   Expected Answers
a.   (*control*)
Tu veux jouer avec nous ? / Est-ce que tu as envie de jouer avec nous ? /
'Do you want to play with us?' / 'Do you feel/wish to play with us?' /
Veux-tu jouer ?
'Do you want to play?'

b.   (*subject-animate*)
Qui est-ce que tu penses qui est caché dans le lit ?
'Who do you think is hidden in the bed?'

c.   (*subject-inanimate*)
Qu'est-ce que tu penses qui est caché sous le chapeau ?
'What do you think is hidden below the hat?'

d.   (*subject-animate*)
Qui est-ce que tu penses qui est caché sous le pot de yaourt ?
'Who do you think is hidden below the jar of yoghourt?'

e.   (*control*)
Tu as faim? Est-ce que tu as faim ? As-tu faim ?
'Are you hungry?'

f.   (*object- inanimate*)
Qu'est-ce que tu penses que le policier mange ?
'What do you think the policeman is eating?'

g.   (*object- inanimate*)
Qu'est-ce que tu penses que l'indien mange ?
'What do you think the policeman is eating?'

---

[4] They were originally 11 but two three years old were eliminated because they didn't produce any LD questions, but answered them.

h.   (*object-inanimate*)
Qu'est-ce que tu penses que le cow-boy mange ?
'What do you think the policeman is eating?'

i.   (*adjunct- inanimate*)
Où est-ce que tu penses que l'assiette est cachée ?
'Where do you think the plate is hidden?'

j.   (*subject- inanimate*)
Qu'est-ce que tu penses qui est caché sous le tabouret ?
'Who do you think is hidden below the stool?'

k.   (*subject- inanimate*)
Qu'est-ce que tu penses qui est caché dans le lit ?
'Who do you think is hidden in the bed?'

l.   (*object- inanimate*)
 Qu'est-ce que tu penses que l'infirmière a caché ?
'What do you think that the nurse hid?'

m.   (*object- inanimate*)
Qu'est-ce que tu penses que le policier a caché ?
'What do you think that the policeman hid?'

n.   (*adjunct*)
Comment est-ce que tu penses qu'ils rentrent chez eux ?
'How do you think they come back home?'

2.4   General Results

See table 1 below which shows the general results of the experiment.

Table 1- Typology of questions produced

Wh- scope marking	39[5]	(36%)
Fronted-*wh* LD / adult form	23	(21%)
Matrix questions	22	(20%)
Yes-no LD	12	(11%)
Other	12	(11%)
Total	108	

---

[5] 20 produced at first elicitation, 19 more after the second elicitation.

The most striking result is that the preferred structure is the *wh*-scope marking strategy (36%). The adult strategy is the second most produced (21%), almost equal to the root question strategy (20%).

Table 2: General results.

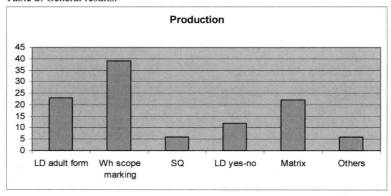

The results show that most subjects, i.e. 7/9 (78%), produced w*h*-scope marking structures.

In contrast, only 4 children (44%) volunteered adult LD questions. None of the children produced in situ LD questions. Each question type is illustrated below.

(16)   **Scope Marking**[6]
a.   Tu penses où   elle   est cachée l'assiette ?
        you think where it-FEM is   hidden the-plate
        'Where do you think the plate is hidden?'

b.   Est-ce que tu   penses qu'est-ce qui est caché dans le   lit ?
        ESK   you think   what   is hidden in   the bed?
        'What do you think is hidden in the bed?'

c.   Est-ce que tu penses qu'est ce qui   est caché en d'ssous le chapeau ?
        ESK   you think KES/ K +C° is hidden below   the hat
        'What do you think is hidden below tha hat?'

d.   Qu'est-ce que tu penses l'assiette où   elle   est cachée ?
        what-is-it that you think the-plate where it-FEM is   hidden
        'Where do you think the plate is hidden?'

---

[6] What-is-DEM-that = KESK. Realize as KESKi when a *wh*-subject is extracted.

(17) **Fronted-*wh* LD / adult form**
a.   Qu'est-ce que   tu   penses que le   policier mange ?
         what-is-it that you   think   that the policeman eats
         'What do you think the policeman is eating?

b.   Qu'est-ce que tu penses   que l'infirmière elle a   caché en d'ssous le   pot ?
         what-is-it-that you think   that the-nurse   she has hidden below   the jar ?
         'What do you think that the nurse hide below the jar of yogourt?'

c.   Où   est-ce que tu penses   que   l'assiette est cachée ?
         Where ESK   you think   that   the-plate is   hidden
         'Where do you think the plate is hidden?'

d.   Qu'est-ce que   tu   penses, koko, qu'il mange le facteur ?
         what-is-it-that you think   K.   that-he eats the postman
         'What do you think the postman is eating?'

(18) **Yes-no LD[7]**
a.   Est-ce que tu penses que l'assiette que l'assiette elle   est cachée en d'ssous
         ESK   you think that the-plate that the-plate it-FEM ·is hidden   below
         du   tabouret ?
         DE+LE   stool
         'Do you think the plate is hidden below the stool?'

b.   Est-ce que tu   sais que   l'indien mange des   oranges ?
         ESK   you know that the-indian eats art-pl oranges
         'Do you know that the Indian is eating some oranges?'

(19) **Matrix questions**
a.   Qu'est-ce qu'est caché   sous   le chapeau ?
         what-is-it-that-is hidden below the   hat
         'What is hidden below the hat?'

b.   Comment   not'z'amis   rentrent chez eux ?
         How   our-liaison-friends go-back at   them
         'How do our friends go back home?'

(20) **Sequential questions [8]**
a.   Qu'est-ce que tu   penses, Koko ?
         what-is-it-that you think   K.
         'What do you think, Koko?'

---

[7] DE+LE designates a definite article *le* (the) contracted with the preposition *de* (some).
[8] It's the same children who produced both (a) and (b), respectively for the first and the second elicitation. Recall that a sequential question is the simplest way to express long distance dependencies, see (13) in section I.

b.   Qu'est-ce qui est caché   sous   le pot, là ?
        what-is-it-that is hidden   below   the jar there
        'What is hidden below the jar, there?'

(21)   **Unclassified**
        penses a   (hum)   **qui**   va   les   chercher Koko ?
        think   a (*hum* hesitate) who is-going-FUT them looking-for K.
        [Target: **Comment** tu penses que les amis rentrent chez eux.]

2.5   Age results

Table 3: production by age range

	LD adult form	*Wh*-scope marking	Sequential Questions	LD yes-no	Matrix	Others	Total
3 years (n=2)	0	0	0	8	15	1	24
4 years (n=4)	15	19	6	0	5	3	48
5 years (n=3)	8	20	0	4	2	2	36
TOTAL	23	39	6	12	22	6	108

2.5.1   Three-year-olds
                        Table 4: three-year-old production

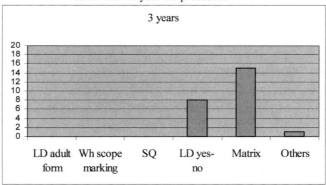

Table 4': production's details

	LD adult form	*Wh*-scope marking	Sequential Questions	LD yes-no	Matrix	Others
3 years (n=2)	0	0	0	8	15	1

The first strategy that was adopted is a non-long-distance strategy: for 3-year-olds, 60% of their total production were matrix questions. They produced no LD *wh*-questions, but some LD dependencies, i.e. yes-no LD questions.

<u>2.5.2   Four-year-olds</u>

Results for the 4-year-olds exhibit a greater contrast in their strategies: they produce predominantly Scope marking strategies, and a lot of LD questions as well.

Table 5: four-year-old production

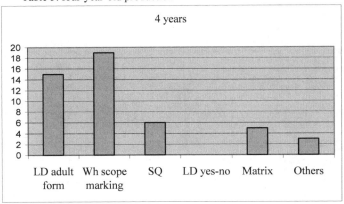

Table 5': production's details

	LD adult form	*Wh*-scope marking	Sequential Questions	LD yes-no	Matrix	Others
4 years (n=4)	15	19	6	0	5	3

The primary strategy for four-year-olds is scope marking, used 40% of the time.

2.5.3   Five-year-olds

Table 6: five-year-olds production

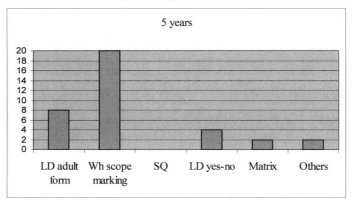

Table 6': production's details

	LD adult form	*Wh*-scope marking	Sequential Questions	LD yes-no	Matrix	Others
5 years (n=3)	8	20	0	4	2	2

The primary strategy for five-year-olds is scope marking, used 56% of the time.

III   Results analysis

These results confirm the existence of *wh*-scope marking strategies in the child grammar.

Along the lines of O&D, I analyse the French data as involving either a direct or an indirect dependency strategy.

3.1   Direct versus indirect dependency

3.1.1   Direct dependency

3.1.1.1 Licensed by a null Q morpheme

In (22), the matrix non-lexical Q morpheme is merged in the matrix clause in an operator/A' position and directly associated with a lower *wh*-phrase *où/where* moved from the adjunct position of *cacher* (hide) to Spec CP2.

(22)   **Q**ᵢ tu penses **où**ᵢ   elle est cachée l'assiette ?[9]
         you think where it-FEM is hidden the-plate
         'Where do you think the plate is hidden?'

3.1.1.2 Licensed by a lexical Q morpheme

The data from Oiry (2005) exhibit a new fact compared to the previous study. We found as in (23) the same partial *wh*-movement, only with a *lexical* scope marker, namely ESK.

(23)   Est-ce que tu penses qu'est-ce qui est caché dans le lit ?
         ESK   you think what-is-it-that is hidden in the bed?
         'What do you think is hidden in the bed?'

      In (23), ESK acts as a counterpart to the null Q morpheme, marking the clause as interrogative, checking the strong Q features of C°, and indicating the matrix scope of the real *wh*-phrase. Children used ESK to license the partially moved *wh*-phrase.

      In the French adult grammar, ESK is usually used as a yes-no question marker. Thus, it seems that children misuse the scope marker ESK in order to mark interrogative *wh*-questions instead of yes-no questions.[10]

3.1.2   Indirect Dependency

Two independent clauses are adjoined, each containing a contentful *wh*-phrase.

(24)   Qu'est-ce que tu penses l'assiette où   elle   est cachée ?
         what-is-it that you think the-plate where it-FEM is hidden
         'Where do you think the plate is hidden?'

(25)   Qu'est-ce que tu   penses, Koko, ce   qui est sous   le tabouret ?
         what-is-it   you think   K.   that who is below the stool
         'What do you think is hidden below the stool?'

IV   Work in progress

4.1   Methodological Issues

Herburger (1994) shows that partial movement and long-distance movement in German don't have the same semantic, so she concludes that they should have a different syntax.

---

[9] Note also that *l'assiette* "the plate" is right dislocated.

[10] We still need an acoustic test to determine whether *est-ce que (ESK)* is not *Qu'est-ce que (what)* with *que* elided. If *Qu'est-ce que* is part of these questions and not *est-ce que* in (22), we should reanalyse the question in (22) as involving an indirect dependency.

(24)

a.   Was glaubt der Georg, wen   die Rosa geküßt hat?
      what believe   G.   whom   R.   kissed has

b.   Wen   glaubt der Georg, daß die Rosa geküßt hat?
      whom believes   G.   that R.   kissed has
      'Whom does Georg believe Rosa kissed?'

In the partial movement structure, the embedded clause has to be understood as *de re*. That is, in (24a), the *wh*-clause cannot be understood as being part of Georg's belief-state. It must be understood as being part of the speaker's *de re* belief (Rosa kissed somebody, who does Georg think it was?).

In contrast, the embedded clause can be interpreted *de re*, though doesn't have to be, in the long distance movement structure. Thus in (24b), it is possible to interpret the proposition that Rosa kissed someone *de re*. But it is equally possible to interpret it as a mere figment of Georg's imagination, that is, *de dicto*.

In the production task illustrated in (14), the target question is *Qu'est-ce que tu penses qui est caché dans le lit? (What do you think is hidden in the bed?)* the subordinate clause has to be interpret as *de re*.
A new experimental design must then be set up where the context makes clear that the subordinate can be interpret *de dicto*.[11] See Demirdache (2005) for more details.

4.2   Comprehension Tasks

Along the lines of O&D, this paper argued for the following steps in the course of the acquisition of long-distance questions: (i) indirect dependency (adjunction), (ii) direct dependency (subordination), and finally (iii) long overt movement, where child grammar matches the adult grammar.

The null hypothesis is such that the syntax of LD questions in French L1 correlates with the acquisition of complementation.[12]

---

[11] I ran a grammatical jugment test with 6 German speakers, offering for each story a choice between partial movement and long movement. Unfortunately, it seems obvious that German speakers do not show a preference for long movement when it involves the complementizer 'dass'.

Herburger's hypothesis seems to be right in one respect: German speakers clearly prefer (i), i.e. long movement, to (ii), i.e. partial movement, in the following context.
"There is gossip about Zoey being involved with someone, and someone claimed she kissed someone, and I don't know who. I doubt there is anything to the rumor; however, I would still like to know who it is about:
(i)   Ich bezweifle dass an der Geschichte irgendwas dran ist, aber wen glaubst du dass sie gekuesst hat?
(ii)   Ich bezweifle an der Geschichte irgendwas dran ist aber
          I   doubt   on the story   anything on-it is but
          was glaubst du wen sie gekuesst hat?"
          what believe you who she kissed has
          'The story seems doubtful to me, but whom do you believe that she kissed?'

I designed and carried out (in tandem with the production task) some comprehension tasks to determine the syntactic status of 'complement' clauses in French L1.

A Bound Variable comprehension task has been conducted to test whether a QP in the matrix question could bind a pronoun in the subordinate clause, where 'every' should be coreferent with 'he' in order to get the distributive reading. A Sequence of Tense task, based on Hollebrandse's dissertation. A task presenting multiple *wh*-questions, based on Weissenborn, Roeper & De Villiers.

V   Conclusion

Oiry (2005) confirms the previous study (O&D), and fits the general idea of two distinct strategies in the child grammar. In the course of acquisition of LD questions, children adopt first an adjunction stage, with a scope marking strategy, and secondly, a subordinate stage with partial movement, then the final stage with overt long-distance movement.

There still remain some open questions that were briefly touched in the last section. These should be addressed in further studies.

References

Abdulkarim, L. 2001. *Complex WH Questions and Universal Grammars: New evidence From the Acquisition of Negative Barriers*. Unpublished Ph.D. Thesis. University of Massachussets, Amherst.

Abdulkarim, L., Roeper, T. and De Villiers J. 1997. "Negative islands in language acquisition." In *New Perspectives on Language Acquisition: Minimalism and Pragmatics*. University of Massachusets, Amherst.

Abdulkarim, L. and Roeper, T. "From universal to language-specific grammars: How do children acquire embedded *Yes/No* questions in English?" Ms. University of Massachusets, Amherst.

Baunaz, L. 2004. "*Un* NPs and *Wh* In Situ: An argument for an indefinite analysis". In *Generative Grammar in Geneva* 4.

Beck, S. 1996. "Quantified structures as barriers for LF movement". *Natural Language Semantics* 4: 1-56.

Beck, S. and Berman, S. 2000. "*Wh*-Scope marking: direct vs. indirect dependency". In *WH- Scope Marking*, Lutz, Müller & v. Stechow (eds), 17-44. John Benjamins Publishing Company.

---

[12] Dayal (2000): Variation in the syntax of scope marking, from juxtaposition to subordination, reflecting diachronic stages in the process of language change.

Roeper (1999) and Abdulkarim & Roeper (2003): sequence in the acquisition of subordination from adjunction, to VP-complement, to subcategorized V°-complement.

Boeckx, C. 1999. "Decomposing French questions." In *University of Pennsylvania Working Papers in Linguistics* 6.1, *Proceedings pf the 23 Annual Penn Linguistics Colloquium*, in J. Alexander, W.R. Han & M. Minnick Fox (eds.). 69-80.

Brandner, E. 2000. "Scope marking and clausal typing". In *WH-Scope Marking*, U. Lutz, G. Müller & A. Von Stechow (eds), 45-76. John Benjamins Publishing Company.

Cheng, L. L.-S. 1997. *On The Typology of Wh- Questions*. Garland publishing, Inc. New York & London.

Cheng, L. L.-S. and Rooryck, J. 2000. "Licensing *Wh*-in-situ". *Syntax* 3: 1-19.

Chomsky, N. 1998. "Minimalist inquiries: the framework". Ms. MIT.

Cole, P. and Hermon, G. 1994. "Is there LF movement?" *Linguistic Inquiry* 25 (2): 239-262. MIT.

Crain, S. and Thornton, R. 1998. *Investigations in Universal Grammar. A guide to experiments on the acquisition of syntax and semantics.* MIT Press.

Dayal, V. 2000. "Scope marking: cross-linguistic variation in indirect dependency". In *WH-Scope Marking*, U. Lutz, G. Müller & A. Von Stechow (eds), 157-193. John Benjamins Publishing Company.

De Villiers, J., Roeper, T. and Vainikka. 1990. "The acquisition of long-distances rules." In *Language Processing and Language Acquisition*, L. Frazier and J. De Villiers (eds), 257-297. Kluwer Academic Publishers.

Demirdache, H. 2005. "Wh-Scope Marking Strategies in L1 French", paper presented at the University of Groningen, october 05.

Demirdache, H. and Oiry M. In progress. "*Wh*-scope marking in child and adult French".

Fanselow, G. To appear. "Partial movement". *SYNCOM (the Syntax Companion): An electronic encyclopedia of syntactic case studies.* In Everaert, M. & H. Van Riemsdijk (in prep). The LingComp Foundation.

Fanselow, G. and Mahajan, A. 2000. "Towards a minimalist theory of *wh*-expletives, *wh*-copying and successive cyclicity." In *WH-Scope Marking*, U. Lutz, G. Müller & A. Von Stechow (eds), 195-230. John Benjamins Publishing Company.

Guttierrez, M. J. In preparation. *The acquisition of English LD wh-questions by Basque/Spanish bilingual subjects in a school context.* PhD dissertation. University of the Basque Country.

Jakubowicz, C. 2004. "Is movement costly?". *Proceedings of the JEL conference.* University of Nantes.

Mathieu, E. 1999. "French *wh*-in situ and the intervention effect". *UCL Working Papers in Linguistics* 11: 441-472.

Mathieu, E. 2002. *The Syntax of Non-Canonical Quantification: A Comparative Study.* PhD Dissertation. UCL.

McDaniel, D. 1989. "Partial *wh*-movement". Kluwer Academic Publishers. *Natural Language Theory* 7: 565-604.

Muriungi, P. K. 2004. "*Wh*-movement in Kitharaka as focus movement". *Proceedings of the Workshop on the Syntax, Semantics and Pragmatics of Questions,* ESSLLI 16.

Nishigauchi, T. 1990. *Quantification in the Theory of Grammar.* Kluwer, Dordrecht.

Oiry, M. and Demirdache, H. In Press. "Evidence from L1 Acquisition for the Syntax of *Wh*- Scope Marking in French", dans Gavarro A., Escobar L. & Wexler K. (éds.), *The Romance Turn: The Acquisition of the Syntax of Romance Languages.* Amsterdam/Philadelphia : John Benjamins Publishing Company.

Oiry, M. 2002. *Acquisition des Questions à Longue Distance.* MA Thesis. University of Nantes.

Oiry, M. 2003. *Acquisition Syntaxique: La Compréhension des Questions à Longue Distance.* DEA Thesis. University of Nantes.

Pesetsky, D. 1987. "*Wh*-in situ: movement and unselective binding." In E. Reuland and A. ter Meulen (eds.), *The Representation of (In)definiteness.* MIT Press, Cambridge.

Reinhardt, T. 1997. "Quantifier scope: how labor is divided between QR and choice functions". *Linguistics and Philosophy* 20, 335-397.

Reis, M. 2000. "On the parenthetical features of German *Was... W*-constructions and how to account for them". In *WH-Scope Marking,* U. Lutz, G. Müller & A. Von Stechow (eds), 359-407. John Benjamins Publishing Company.

Riemsdjik, H. v. 1982. "Correspondance effects and the Empty Category Principle". Tilburg Papers in Language and Litterature.

Rizzi, L. 1991. "Argument/adjunct (a)symmetries". Ms. University of Genève.

Rizzi, L. 1996. Parameters and Functionnal heads: Essays on Comparative Syntax. New York, NY: Oxford.

Strik, N. 2003. Où tu as caché ton sac? Qu'est-ce que tu penses que je lis? Acquisition des Questions Wh- chez les Enfants Francophones de 3 à 6 Ans. DEA Thesis. University of Paris 8.

Thornton, R. 1990. Adventures in Long-Distance Moving: the Acquisition of Complex Wh-Questions. PhD dissertation. University of Connecticut.

Saddy, D.1991. "Wh scope mechanisms in Bahasa Indonesia". MIT Working Papers in Linguistics 15: 183-218.

Weissenborn J., Roeper T. and De Villiers J. 1995. "Wh-acquisition in French and German". Recherches Linguistiques 24: 125-155.

The Acquisition Path of the Determiner Quantifier *Every*: Two Kinds of Spreading[*]

Thomas Roeper, Uri Strauss, and Barbara Zurer Pearson
University of Massachusetts, Amherst

1.0 The determiner quantifier

According to Hale (1985) and Bach et al. (1995), adverbial quantification is universal in the world's languages, while determiner quantification is rare. The unusual status of *every* as a DP quantifier imposes a greater learnability burden for children and thus an opportunity for error as its complex syntax and semantics are analyzed and reanalyzed in the course of acquisition. It is an important step for the learner to see that *every,* unlike many other quantifiers, belongs inside the DP where certain meanings are excluded. This paper is about how the child takes that step.

1.1 The distinction between different types of spreading

In discussions of the acquisition of *every*, the phenomenon we are calling "quantifier spreading" has been reported by many researchers (Roeper & Matthei, 1974/75; Roeper & de Villiers, 1993; Crain et al., 1996; Geurts & vander Sandt, 1999: Philip, 1995, 2004; Drozd 1996, 2001, 2004 among others). The expression refers to the phenomenon, demonstrated in a variety of experiments, of children allowing a quantifier like *every* to apply to two separate noun phrases in a sentence rather than one. For instance, in a scenario like Figure 1, children are asked the test question:

(1)   *Is every girl riding a bike?*

Children, in half a dozen languages, respond "not this bike" pointing to the extra bike. The *every* modifying *girl* seems to have "spread" to modify the mentioned object, *instead*

---

[*] *Acknowledgments: Thanks to Tim Bryant, Jill de Villiers, Lyn Frazier, Bart Hollebrandse, Angelika Kratzer, Bill Philip, Uli Sauerland, and the participants at the UMass Workshop on the Acquisition of Quantification in Spring 2003. Errors of fact or interpretation are ours, not theirs. This work was supported in part by NIDCD Contract N01 DC8 2104 to Harry N. Seymour, P.I. We are indebted to The Psychological Corporation, San Antonio, TX, who undertook gathering the data and the initial analysis of it. The data and example items are used by permission of The Psychological Corporation.*

© 2006 by Tom Roeper, Uri Strauss and Barbara Zurer Pearson
Tanja Heizmann (ed.): Current Issues in Acquisition. University of Massachusetts Occasional Papers in Linguistics 34, 97-128.
GLSA Amherst.

of "a bike," every bike. Using a neutral, descriptive term, we will call this response type "mentioned object spreading" (MOS).

Figure 1. Mentioned Object Spreading (MOS) "Test" item: *Is every girl riding a bike?*

New research highlights a related phenomenon, another kind of spreading that   contrasts with MOS. In the second kind of spreading there is an extra pair of objects – neither mentioned – but involved in a common activity. For the scenario in Figure 2, many children will say "no, not the bunny" referring to the unmentioned eating activity in this scenario:

Figure 2. Un-Mentioned Object Spreading (UMOS) example

(2)   *Is every dog eating a bone* => *no, not the bunny (and/or carrot)*

This kind of spreading, Un-Mentioned Object Spreading (UMOS), appears to involve a quantification over a set of events or situations, rather than over participants in events. (I.e. "Every event is an event of a dog eating a bone.") It can be captured by an adverbial paraphrase: *It is always the case that a dog is eating a bone.*

Philip (1995) observed this kind of response among his subjects, and differentiated a group of "perfectionist" children from a larger group of spreaders of the MOS type (p. 161), but the perfectionist (or UMOS) response was not a focus of his analysis. More recently, Guerts (2001:2-3), calling UMOS his "Type-C" error, noted that "there is little in the way of systematic data on this category," but "such evidence as is available suggests that [these] errors are much rarer and less persistent than others." He calls for more empirical data, and exploration of "the influence of the collective/distributive distinction (*all* versus *every* and *each)*, and the longitudinal dimension of error patterns."

The item development phase for the *Diagnostic Evaluation of Language Variation (DELV,* Seymour, Roeper, & de Villiers, 2003, 2005), provided an opportunity for just such an investigation with a very large and diverse population. Quantifier items based on Philip's experiment were included in the pilot edition of the test. In the analysis of the data from the fieldtesting, the perfectionist response emerged as more widespread than in Philip's work, and it was seen to persist until a later age than previously observed. It seems therefore that it is an important pattern to consider, and it merits an analysis of how it arises and what is required for the child to go beyond it.

In this paper, we provide empirical evidence that bears on the longitudinal dimension of the phenomena and as Guerts suggests, we explore the influence of the collective/distributive distinction on *every* and related quantifiers. Our fundamental claim is that UMO-spreading is distinct from MO-spreading, and that there is an acquisition path involving both syntactic and semantic reanalysis to go from "UMOS+MOS" (where MOS is a subset of the semantic representation needed to capture the broader UMOS), to MOS-only, and to the adult grammar. Our basic question is what shift in representation would exclude UMOS and maintain MOS-only? Then, what further representational shift will exclude MOS as well and allow the child to arrive at the adult construal of the quantifier?

1.2   Overview of the literature

Spreading errors in general have been a topic of great interest since they were brought to our attention by Piaget several decades ago (Inhelder & Piaget, 1964). There has been little agreement, however, about the nature of the explanation best suited for them. Are they a cognitive phenomenon or more narrowly linguistic? Within linguistics, semantic, syntactic, and pragmatic explanations have been pursued.

Initially, children's apparent errors were thought to indicate a failure of their reasoning with conservation, a cognitive deficit (Inhelder and Piaget, 1964), a theme echoed by Donaldson (Donaldson & Lloyd, 1974). Then, Roeper and Matthei (1974/1975) proposed a syntactic analysis. They observed that the quantifiers *all, some,* and *every* behaved like adverbs and proposed that children allow quantifiers to "spread" to two adverb positions in the syntactic tree. They argued that spreading errors arose because of the child's incomplete syntactic analysis. At the time, they had no mechanism within linguistic theory to account for such a proposal, so they did not pursue the argument until many years later (Roeper & de Villiers, 1993) when they included it in discussions of the acquisition of bound variables more generally.

Philip (1995) took up the discussion in a semantic framework. His pioneering empirical and theoretical study was the first to analyze classic quantifier spreading in terms of event semantics. Basically, his account focused on the child's interpretation of the domain of the quantifier with respect to the verb phrase of the sentence. His analysis has since been supported by work in six different languages (Philip, 1996, 1998, 2003, 2004).

Drozd (1996) was one of the first to present a distributivity-based semantic analysis of quantifier spreading. In his Distributivity Hypothesis, MO-spreading can be attributed to children's misidentification of the distributive "key" and distributive "share," the two categories that determine, in sentences with distributive semantics, which element is being distributed, and which is being distributed to. Given sentence (3a), an adult would label the distributive key and share as in (3b), and determine that elephants are being distributed over boys. A child making an MO spreading error would make the determination of key and share in (3c), and derive a semantics in which boys are distributed over elephants (examples are Drozd's).

(3)   a. Every boy is riding an elephant
        b. [Every boy]$_{dist-key}$ is riding [an elephant]$_{dist-share}$
        c. [Every boy]$_{dist-share}$ is riding [an elephant]$_{dist-key}$

Brooks also addresses the role of distributivity in children's heuristics for understanding these quantifiers. Brooks & Braine (1996) showed that children performed better in tasks with collective universal quantifiers, and so in a current study (Brooks & Sekerina, in press) they directly pit distributive uses of the quantifier with collective ones. In fact, they found that children younger than 9 years made numerous errors, with poorer performance in distributive contexts than collective ones. In fact, native English-speaking adults, given a similar task with the distributive quantifier *every*, also made child-like errors. The persistence of quantifier-spreading errors that Brooks finds in adults presages our experimental results (in section 2).

Both syntactic and semantic accounts were rejected by Crain and his colleagues as inadequate explanations of children's errors on these sentences. Crain, Thornton, Boster, Conway, Lillo-Martin and Woodams (1996) claim children's quantifier interpretations are adult-like, but that the pragmatic conditions under which spreading is elicited are not felicitous. In several experiments, they showed that children who made spreading errors in truth-value judgment tasks like Philip's made almost no errors when the pragmatic conditions of the task were varied. They proposed, in particular, that one needed to use scenarios that presented the child with the scene in question and another that differed so the child could plausibly dissent.

There have been several methodological challenges to Crain's concept of Plausible Dissent (see Sugisaki & Isobe, 2001). More recently Brooks and Sekerina (in press) point out that Crain's protocol provides children with information that highlights the people and objects in the domain of the quantifier, so they have lessened the difficulty of determining its proper domain. In a series of experiments, Brooks and colleagues have specifically provided the conditions for plausible dissent and shown spreading effects with them nonetheless (Brooks & Braine, 1996; Brooks et. al., 2001, in press). Drozd's review (2004) also shows internal inconsistencies of the approach.

More recently Philip (2004) re-evaluated his event quantification account and found greater evidence for another pragmatic account, a modified version of the presuppositional accounts of Drozd and van Loosbroek (1999), which he calls the Relevance Account. While Philip specifically excludes the perfectionist response (UMOS) in this comparison (p. 5), he nonetheless leaves the door open for children's partial knowledge of adult grammatical constraints to explain at least some of the facts not captured by Relevance (p. 40).

The syntactic nature of quantifier errors is suggested by Roeper & de Villiers (1993). They showed children two pictures for the sentence in (4):

(4)   *There is a horse that every child is on.*

In one there was one horse with three children on it; in the other, three horses each with a boy on it. Children age 6 chose the pictures equally, whereas for adults only the first reading which does not distribute boys to horses is allowed. If the sentence were "*Every child is on a horse,*" it would be fine to understand it as three horses, one for each boy. Here it is a grammatical barrier, the relative clause, not conceptual development per se, restricting the child's numerical understanding of the situation described by the quantified sentence. The syntactic nature of spreading errors is further highlighted in L2 acquisition studies with adults. Recent work by della Carpini (2003) shows extensively that second-language learners also go through a stage of spreading. This suggests that it is not a factor of child cognition (Inhelder and Piaget, 1964), nor of language-independent child pragmatics (Crain et al, 1996) that lies at the root of these phenomena, but rather the challenge of grammar construction which confronts L1 and L2 learners alike.

Other support for a syntactic account comes from spontaneous production data which indicate that the quantifier may not be properly represented by children. Notably, outside of compounds like *everytime* or *everything*, *every* is not reported in children's early production. A search of five CHILDES corpora (MacWhinney, 2000) involving six children (from Brown [1973], Kuczaj [1976], and MacWhinney [2000]) revealed that children below the age of five years failed to produce forms like "every x" and produced only adverbial forms like "everyday" or misanalyzed forms like "every glasses." In general the children who used *every* + noun seemed to use these constructions only adverbially. That is, they used expressions like *every time* and *every day* in non-argument positions, rather than *every boy* or *every car* in argument position. Of the six children surveyed, only two – Abe (Kuczaj) and Mark (MacWhinney)– had more than two clear instances of *every* + noun not used adverbially, and the total number of these cases in the five corpora did not exceed twenty-five. Moreover, about four of these uses (that is, about 17%) involve agreement errors: *every boys and girls, every cheese, every people,* and *every farm people,* suggesting that the syntactic representation of the quantificational position in DP is not yet well-formed.

For the argument we present here, we draw from syntax, semantics, and pragmatics together to allow for an analysis of the proposed sequence of acquisition and we also suggest the kind of input data that would motivate the child to reanalyze *every* at the different steps. This is the essential question of learnability, which has not been addressed in any purely semantic or pragmatic account —how does the child restrict an overgeneral grammar.

1.3   The components of the analysis

Our claim, based in part on the experimental data presented in Section 2, is that the path to the acquisition of the determiner quantifier involves an added step than has not been taken into account, or has been treated only tangentially, in previous discussions (namely UMOS+MOS).] In Section 3 we develop a confluence of argumentation about how adverbial quantification, floating quantifiers, focus, and distributivity/ collectivity interact under c-command and the theory of Feature Checking (Chomsky, 1995, 2004). Adverbial accounts, we will claim, account best for the UMOS+MOS stage, whereas at the MOS stage, the child uses the analogy of floated quantifiers like *all* and *each* and creates a link between the two positions where the quantifier can float. The syntactic mechanism relating the upper and lower positions is a Focus Phrase in the CP system from which the quantifier in the upper position can c-command the lower one. The move to the adult stage is based on a reanalysis of the distributivity in the *every* sentence as arising from the predicate and not the *every*. When *every* is not involved in feature checking, it can be correctly positioned in the DP. From there, it no longer c-commands the lower NP and so the spreading interpretation is no longer available.

As Guerts (2001) observes, previous work on quantifiers has tended not to include an analysis of UMOS. Indeed, in most small-scale studies, it accounts for only a small number of answers. Even when it has been commented on, it has not been extensively evaluated.   We report, therefore, on a large-scale study which helps establish the importance of UMOS as a significant phenomenon which requires an interpretation independent from MOS'. Then we integrate UMOS into the logic of the acquisition path.

2.0   The Experiment

The experiment which brought UMO-spreading into a new perspective for us was conducted as part of the *DELV* project, investigating developmental milestones for many aspects of children's language development (Seymour, Roeper, de Villiers, de Villiers, & Pearson, 2002; Seymour, Roeper, & de Villiers, 2005). Data collection involved testing over 1450 children ages 4 to 12, including 333 typically developing speakers of mainstream American English (MAE). The data are cross-sectional, so our proposal about a sequence of acquisition is necessarily inferential. Still, they provide empirical support for the move from no demonstrated appreciation of the quantifier to UMOS+MOS → MOS-only → "target" that generally takes place in middle childhood.

2.1   Methods

Design

Children were tested within the context of the piloting for the *DELV*, the *Dialect Sensitive Language Test (DSLT*, Seymour, Roeper, de Villiers, de Villiers & Pearson, 2002), which is comprised of 350 items divided into 14 subtests covering a range of language phenomena. Seven items of *DSLT* Subtest 11, Quantifiers, adopted the format of Philip's (1995) dissertation and tested children's application of the quantifying properties of the universal quantifier *every*. (See Seymour & Pearson, 2004, for more details of the project.) All children received the quantifier questions in the same order, although older children did the whole sequence in one sitting while about a third of the 4- to 6-year-olds were given two sittings to complete the test, with Quantifiers in the second sitting. The outcome measure tallied for each child her response pattern, i.e. whether she showed evidence of spreading interpretations, target (adult) understanding, or some other pattern.

The major independent variable was Age in years with six levels (4, 5, 6, 7-8, 9-10, 11-12) in order to see developmental patterns. Gender, Region, Parent Education, and Ethnicity were included as control variables so their potential effects on the results could be evaluated.

Participants[1]

Table 1 shows the ages of the 333 typically developing-learners of English who participated. The children in the study were identified in their schools as speakers of mainstream American English (MAE). Children were all performing at grade level, and none of the subjects had been identified for speech or language services. Their dialect was confirmed by the Language Variation Status section of the *Dialect Sensitive Language Test* (Seymour et al. 2002).

The participants represent a nationwide U.S. sample with children from the four major regions of the U.S.: Northeast, South, Midwest, and West, with a preponderance (55%) from the South (to match the AAE groups). Three-quarters (72%) of the children were considered to be of "low socio-economic status," measured primarily by Parent

---

[1] It appears from preliminary results that UMOS is even more prevalent among another dialect group that participated in the experiment, the African American English (AAE) learners, but we restrict our analysis to spreading construals in MAE, where there is more guidance from the literature on how to understand the basic syntax and semantics of quantifiers within the MAE dialect. There is no published discussion to our knowledge of the semantics of quantifiers in adult AAE. Without a delineation of the target state, one cannot establish an acquisition sequence.

Education (PED) Level. ("Low-SES" represented parents with high school diplomas or less.) There were 55% females and 45% males. Sixty-eight percent of the children were of Euro-American background, with higher percentages of Hispanics and Blacks among the MAE speakers at the older ages (>6). The effect of the differences by age was evaluated statistically.

Table 1. Subject Demographics

Age	4	5	6	7-8	9-10	11-12	All
N =	60	66	77	38	43	49	333
% Female	52	56	64	53	51	49	55%
% PED </= high school	68	82	80	61	67	61	72%
% from South	54	64	60	58	67	39	57%
% Euro-American	80	70	79	63	47	53	68%

Materials

There were three **Test** questions of the form "Is every girl riding a bike?" like the one in Figure 1. Following Philip, every girl <u>was</u> riding a bike, so a correct answer was "yes" but there was an extra bike in the picture. Also following Philip, there were two kinds of control items: Control-yes items were like the one shown in Figure 2, where in addition to a number of dogs who were eating a bone, there was also a rabbit eating a carrot, an extra pair, not an dog nor a bone, doing the same activity. e.g. *"Is every dog eating a bone?"* The anticipated answer was "yes." A final item type, Control-no (see Figure 3) presented the child with a picture where there was an extra girl, so the answer to "Is every girl sailing a boat" was "no." There were two each of these control item types.

Figure 3. Example of Control-No Item *"Is every girl sailing a boat?"*

Thus there were 3 item types that children could demonstrate mastery of; mastery was defined as answering correctly two of two Control-yes trials, two of two Control-no trials, and two of three Test trials.

Procedure

Children were tested individually in their schools by speech language pathologists. They were shown the seven pictures for the "every" items in the following order: 1. Control-yes, 2. Test, 3. Control-no, 4. Test, 5. Control-no, 6. Control-yes, 7. Test. While looking at the pictures, they were asked the question: "Is someone holding/eating/riding a something?" Whenever a child answered "no," she or he was asked "Why?" and the answer was recorded on the answer sheet.

In Philip (1995) (and other studies), the Control items were used to establish a minimum level of knowledge for the child to be included in the statistical analyses and were not the subject of the inquiry. For this experiment, all responses were entered into the analysis and the analyses were done not just on the Test items, but on the pattern of the child's responses to all items, especially the answers to the follow-up *why*-question.

The seven yes or no answers were scored as correct or incorrect. The classification of the response types (UMOS, MOS, target etc.) was made from the verbatim answers recorded when a child answered "no" and was asked to explain why, or when a child volunteered a "spreading reason" for their "yes" response, for example "Yes, but not the bunny."

1. A special category was made for "Yes-men" (or perseverators) who said "yes" to all questions. They may have known some of the answers (whose answers were in fact "yes") but we determined that we had no way to distinguish true "yes" answers from those which were a set-response, and thus we had no information about their quantifier knowledge.

2. Children who specifically referred to the extra object in a test question ("no, not that bike") in at least one response were counted as "Mentioned-object spreaders" (MOS).

3. Children who referred to the extra participants in the Control-yes questions (i.e., "no, not the rabbit" and/or "no, because of the carrot") were counted "unmentioned-object spreaders" (UMOS), whether or not they also exhibited MO-spreading as well.

4. Those who demonstrated mastery of all the question types AND gave no spreading answers were called target children. (Note: children who answered the Control-yes and the Test questions correctly and only one of the Control-no questions incorrectly exhibited the same overall response pattern as the perseverators, but as they had answered "no" at least once they were not counted as perseverators. They were counted as a subgroup of target children, as long as they did not volunteer any spreading responses.

These four categories accounted for 90% of the answers. All other answer patterns were also tallied to determine if any of them occurred at levels different from what could be expected from random answering. For the chance analysis, a matrix, as in Table 2, was made to tally all 8 possible combinations of mastery (=1) or non-mastery (=0) for the 3 item types. That is, "1-1-1" would stand for Control-no, Control-yes, and Test questions mastered; "1-1-0" would stand for Control-no and Control-yes mastered, but not the Test questions (which is consistent with MO-spreading). Note, though, that the pattern of zeroes and ones did not determine for us whether the child was counted as a spreader or not: that label was given if the child gave a spreading response to at least one test or Control-yes follow-up question.

2.2   Results

The proportions of the response types differed significantly by age. The graph in Figure 4 shows the distribution of the UMOS (i.e. UMOS-only and UMOS+MOS), MOS-only, and target children from ages 4 to 12. (The older ages are aggregated to increase the cell sizes. Percents do not sum to 1 because for clarity, the perseverators and "other uninformative" are not shown in the figure, but are discussed below with Table 2.) UMOS is observed almost throughout the age range, but is less common in children 7-8 and older. MOS was also observed throughout the age range tested, with higher percentages than UMOS among the older children.

Figure 4. Target and Spreading Answer Types by Age (Typically Developing Children)

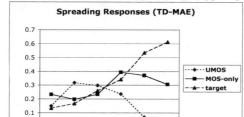

The mean age (and standard deviation) for the Response Type groups, were as follows:

Perseverators:	4.7 (S.D. .8)
UMO spreaders	5.9 (S.D. 1.5)
MO spreaders	7.3 (S.D. 2.6)
target responders	8.4 (S.D. 2.7)

(Note that there were 8 UMOS-only children who averaged 5.9 years old as well, but with a larger S.D., 2.5.) Since all response types were found among the oldest children, it is not strictly speaking a "sequence," but clearly a developmental trend.

The response patterns of interest were the most prevalent, but all eight of the logical possibilities mentioned above were observed. In Table 2, the observed response proportions are compared to the probabilities expected by chance.

Table 2. Occurrence of different response patterns

	CtlNo-CtlYes-Test	Compatibility with Response Type	% of responses expected	% of responses observed
1	0-0-0	no knowledge of qs	.28	.03
2	0-0-1	no consistent response	.28	.039
3	0-1-0	no consistent response	.09	.015
4	0-1-1*	perseveration/ yes-men	.09	.279*
5	1-0-0	UMOS + MOS	.09	.174
6	1-0-1	UMOS-only	.09	.02
7	1-1-0	MOS-only	.03	.12
8	1-1-1	target	.007 to .05	.273
(4b):	*Some 0-1-1 who gave at least one "no" answer were not counted as perseverators	(target)	(.09)	.045

Clearly, some children may have been unreliable responders, but there would be very few among the target children or even the MOS-only children. Getting 7 of 7 items right, as most target children did, is a 1 in 128 (2^7) chance. Some target children got only 6 right but did not offer spreading reasons for their error. There is a 7 in 128 (5%) chance of getting 6 of 7 right with no knowledge of the quantifiers. This is not a high likelihood, but cannot be ignored. Similarly, the 1-1-0 pattern (compatible with MOS-only) would occur by chance 1/32 of the time (1/4 x 1/4 x 1/2), whereas the 1-0-0 (compatible with UMOS+MOS) would occur 1/4 x 3/4 x 1/2 or 3/32 (about 9%) of the time by chance. (With 2 Control-No items, for example, there are 3 ways to get a "zero" mastery score and 1 way to get a "1"; zero = 3/4 probability, 1 = 1/4 probability. The same for Control-Yes. For the 3 Test items, there are 8 possible combinations of correct and incorrect answers. There are 4 ways have at least 2 items correct (4/8, or 1/2) and 4 ways to get fewer than 2 correct.)

In fact both spreading types accounted for much larger portions of the response patterns, 12% and 19% respectively, with higher percentages at some ages. The overall occurrence of the three major response patterns (with the perseverators removed) was significant, chi-square (df 3, n= 244) = 190.04, $p < .0001$. The chance analysis was pursued to understand how much meaning to assign to the "other" categories (#2, 3, and 6), and the conclusion is that no explanation for them seems necessary because chance alone would be sufficient to account for their occurrence. More importantly, we can have confidence that the majority of the other answers truly reflect the child's knowledge and were <u>not</u> just random answering.

Analysis of Variance:
Perseveration declined over the age range, target responding increased, and the two types of spreading rose initially to a peak and then declined, UMOS peaking around 5, and MOS-only not until 7-10.   Multivariate analysis of variance tested whether the developmental trends observed were statistically reliable. It also permitted the testing of the control variables: Gender, Region (southern or not), parent education level (PED, high school or less or not) and Ethnicity (non-Hispanic white or not; also tested for Hispanic and Black). Table 3 reports these results.

Table 3. Effects of Age and other demographic variables.

Age x	F	p
Target response pattern	2.915	.01
Perseveration pattern	2.555	.03
UMOS pattern	2.366	.04
MOS pattern	2.718	.02
Gender (and Region and PED) by		
Target response pattern	.< 1	n.s.
Ethnicity by		
Target response pattern	.< 1	n.s.
MOS-only response pattern	.< 1	n.s.

The most important result was the significant age factor for all four response patterns of interest. By contrast, F-values for the control variables were all < 1 and non-significant, indicating that within this sample, they were no main effects for Gender, Region, Parent Education level or Ethnicity.   Interactions with age for these factors were also not significant.

Pairwise comparisons
In order to investigate where the significant differences were, pairwise comparisons were run for each variable at adjacent ages and at longer intervals. Among the perseverators, the 4 and 5 year olds were not significantly different from each other, but they were different from the 6 year-old and older groups ($p < .05$). The target responders were not significantly different at any adjacent ages except ages 10 and 12, but there were significant differences between the pairs with two intervals (4 and 6, 6 and 9-10, etc.). The two spreading groups showed significant pairwise differences between 5 and 9-10 for the UMOS group and a trend between 6 and 9-10 ($p = .059$) for the MOS group.

2.3   Discussion

These results do not conclusively demonstrate a sequence in the acquisition path: one would need longitudinal data for that. Even then, one would not expect all children to go through all stages. Some go right to the adult interpretation; others may never entertain the spreading interpretations, while others may never reach what we are calling the target response. Nonetheless, the overall timing of the patterns is compatible with the idea that UMOS and MOS-only are steps in a progression from the most general to the most restricted (and adult) interpretations of the quantifier.

This work was motivated initially by the desire to include knowledge of quantifiers as part of the *DELV* (Seymour, Roeper, de Villiers, 2005), a standardized language test for children in the age range from 4 to 9 which was piloted on children up to age 12. Beyond their utility for the development of the *DELV*, the data from such a large sample carefully stratified by age, gender, parent education level, ethnicity, and region provided a rich source of information about developmental patterns in the typical case. Unlike many of the research studies that take place in university communities, this study sampled children in a general population.

It is somewhat surprising to see that even among typically developing children, perseveration and other irrelevant response patterns accounted for about 30% of the 4- to 6-year-olds' responses. Other authors have reported earlier acquisition, but in many cases they did not test children who failed the control questions, so such children are not generally included in their analyses (cf. Philip, 1995; Guerts, 2001). Also, these data are from a lower socio-economic group than is typically sampled, and low SES is generally associated with slower development in many aspects of language (Hart and Riseley, 1995; Oller and Eilers, 2002). Still, there were about 11% of the 5-year-olds who answered correctly, so it is not completely beyond their ability. Nonetheless, it would appear that target performance on these questions is not the most common response among MAE-learners until after age 8 and it is not universal even at 12, the end point of our data collection.

3.0   Toward a formal account of UMO-spreading and MO-spreading

The outline of our argument is as follows:

Step 1. **Always.** At the initial stage, when UMOS and MOS appear together, they can both be captured by the notion of event quantification, a semantic account with relatively little language-specific knowledge of syntactic structure required. We call this the "always" stage.

Step 2. **Each.** To move from the initial adverbial interpretation to MOS-only, we propose the "each" stage, when the child assimilates *every* to NP-determiners *all* and especially, *each*. Both *all* and *each* can "float," and they both can be either in the DP or not. Crucially, the strongly distributive *each* participates in anaphoric and agreement relations between the subject NP and the predicate, which it cannot satisfy from inside the DP. In the account we lay out below, it is the feature [+dist] that motivates the raising of *each* to a Focus Phrase. We assume that the frequency with which *every* behaves distributively leads the child to classify it as distributive as well. It is the child's mis-analysis of *every* as [+dist] that puts it in the FocP and permits MOS spreading.

Step 3. **Every.** To get to the final, adult state, the "DP-every" state, children learn that *every* is in fact a mixed quantifier that is sometimes interpreted as distributive and sometimes as collective, depending on the properties of the predicate that selects it. Using this information, they reanalyze *every* as a quantifier lacking the feature [+dist], and as a consequence can allow it to be in the DP. They also need to realize that two overt instances of the quantifier are different from the floated quantifier (FQ), each applying independently to its own DP, but with one in the scope of the other. When *every* is in the DP, it will not be in a node of the tree from which it can quantify over the predicate, and spreading interpretations will no longer be available.

Thus, the child's grasping of a semantic concept, i.e. collectivity vs. distributivity, is a potential trigger for the syntactic advance that leads to DP-*every*. In its turn, the syntactic shift restricts the child's semantic interpretations, which depend on the quantifier's location in the syntactic tree.

3.1   Step 1 ("Always")

3.1.1   The semantic structure for UMOS

We use Philip's (1995) account as a starting point. According to Philip, structures involving adverbial quantifiers (in this case sentences) are tripartite: they can be divided into quantifier (Q), restrictor and nuclear scope. The events forming the restrictor are the subevents of the contextually relevant event that meet a particular restriction. For MOS, the restriction is that either the subject or the object is a participant in the subevent. To cover UMOS, he introduces a third disjunct to the restrictor, the proposition that a perceived object participates in the subevent (shown in (5)).

(5)   Every boy is riding a pony

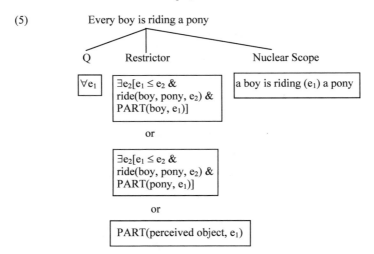

Q   Restrictor   Nuclear Scope

$\forall e_1$ | $\exists e_2[e_1 \leq e_2 \&$ ride(boy, pony, e_2) & PART(boy, e_1)] | a boy is riding (e_1) a pony

or

$\exists e_2[e_1 \leq e_2 \&$ ride(boy, pony, e_2) & PART(pony, e_1)]

or

PART(perceived object, e_1)

Adopting a suggestion from Drozd (p.c.), we suggest that the triple disjunction is unnecessary to account for the judgments of the child in the UMOS stage. The third disjunct is so general that it subsumes the first two as subcases. The effect of the additional option is essentially to make the first two disjuncts in the restrictor vacuous. Without them, the truth condition is as follows:

(6)   All events which are subevents of an event in which x verbs y, and in which x or y
       is a participant, or in which a perceived object is a participant, are events in which
       x verbs y.

Thus we simplify Philip's proposal by removing reference to participants and by simply quantifying over all subevents, as follows:

(7)   Every boy is riding a pony

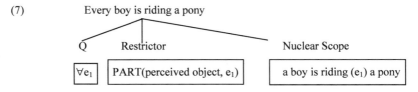

Q   Restrictor   Nuclear Scope

$\forall e_1$ | PART(perceived object, e_1) | a boy is riding (e_1) a pony

This requires the assumption that the child is able to pragmatically fix the set of events appropriately, so that the individual situations depicted in the diagrams in (5) and (7) are considered to be the minimal events, and included in the domain of quantification. In our analysis, a child in the UMOS stage interprets "every x verbs y" as follows:

(8)   All events are events in which x verbs y.

This makes our analysis adverbial in the spirit of event quantificational analyses, as argued for by Philip, while also assuming that children in this stage fix the restrictor to the maximal domain possible, the set of all events, (perhaps because they cannot use subtle contextual and focus cues to limit the restrictor as adults do [de Swart 1993]).

3.1.2 Syntactic representation of UMOS+MOS

Here we argue that *every* at the first stage is like a sentential adverb where it is attached to the CP, as in (9).

(9)

3.2 Step 2 MOS-only ("Each")

The challenge at this point is to find an interpretation that will rule out UMOS but allow MOS. It should also capture the two key properties of this stage, namely that the child's syntax restricts the domain of the quantifier to noun-phrases and that there is an active connection between the NPs in subject and object position. The mechanisms of c-command and Feature Checking (for anaphor and long-distance AGREE), each provide a different piece of the puzzle.

3.2.1 The syntactic argument

The point of departure for our analysis is the floating quantifier (FQ) where a quantifier is separated from the quantified material as in (10b).

(10)   a. Is <u>each</u> rabbit eating a carrot?
       b. Are the rabbits eating <u>each</u> a carrot?
       c. Each of the rabbits is eating two carrots each.

Example (10c) is perhaps redundant, but the meaning is unchanged.

The adverbial properties of FQ have received a good deal of recent attention (Bobaljik, 1998; Brisson, 1999; Terada, 2003; Fitzpatrick, 2005). It has been pointed out that quantifiers can move to all the adverb positions (Terada, 2003; Bobaljik, 1998).

(11)   the children (all) have (all) been (all) going home.

Furthermore, they note that the quantifier can appear even when it could not be a part of the DP:

(12)   a. Susan, Mary, and Sally were all here
        b. *All Susan, Mary, and Sally were here

In addition, one could expand the quantifier to work like an anaphor:

(13)   Susan, Mary, and Sally were all of them here.

French has particularly intricate examples of floated or long-distance quantification of this kind. Labelle & Valois (2001) examine the acquisition path of two of them that can occupy the same adverbial position in the verb phrase: *chacun* and *beaucoup*. The former, which they call an FQ, quantifies over the subject NP (and not the NP in the VP). The latter, which they distinguish from FQ as a "quantifier at a distance" (QAD), is restricted to the object and cannot quantify over the subject.

(14)   Thus   QAD: Les enfants ont beaucoup recu de ballons
                    'the children have a-lot received of balloons'
                    (*beaucoup* quantifies over balloons)

But from the same position,

(15)   FQ: Les enfants ont chacun recu un ballon.
                    'the children have each received a balloon'
                    (*chacun* quantifies over the children).

In acquisition, these floated or floatable elements were difficult for the child to restrict properly. Labelle & Valois (2001) demonstrate a brief period of floating for *beaucoup* with three-year-olds accepting sentences with it quantifying over the subject, but by five, their subjects restricted it properly to the object. However, in their study the syntax of the FQ *chacun* took longer for the children to acquire. Five-year-olds accepted it equally quantifying over object or subject, whereas only the latter is acceptable to adults.

Takahashi (1991) has also shown that children do not appear to distinguish the two sites of the quantifications. When confronted with a sentence with *every* in both subject and object position, children aged 3-6 answered "yes" to the sentence, *is every boy holding every balloon?*, when shown the following scenario:

(16)   balloon   balloon   balloon

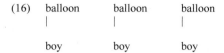

       boy   boy   boy

Similarly, in our diary data, we have a child who said, "each hand is in each glove" and B. Partee (p.c.) reports another: "both rabbits are on both sides of the fence" (with one rabbit on each side). These interpretations appear to be a conjunction for the child of "every boy is holding a balloon" and "a boy is holding every balloon" (or "each hand has a glove" and "each glove has a hand"). For an adult speaker, it would not be a simple conjunction. One quantifier would have to be in the scope of the other. To the balloon question, the adult's answer would have to be "no," since there is no distribution of balloons over children, i.e. each boy holding (a string to) all three balloons.

Drozd (Drozd & von Loosboek, 1999; Drozd 2001) and more recently Geurts (2001) have offered an analysis in terms of *every* being misanalyzed as a weak quantifier whose domain was elastic enough to include an extra element. In particular weak quantifiers on the subject can permit an appraisal of the set marked by the object as in the famous example:

(17)   Many Scandinavians have won the Nobel prize
       where *many* refers to the set of Nobel prize winners, not Scandinavians.[2]

Modern syntactic analyses have moved precisely toward the view that the FQ has a connection to both the subject and the content of the predicate. Sportiche (1988) originally suggested that the FQ was left behind when the subject NP was raised to IP, but since then, analyses have pointed out that the FQ has a relation to the object as well as the subject, and so it is not just a question of moving the subject away.

Terada (2003) uses a Probe-Goal account to capture the dual properties of floated quantifiers. The essence of the account is that a word like <u>each</u> has two features:

---

[2] This shifting of the domain of the quantifier is a very general phenomenon. Roeper and Matthei (1974/75) pointed out that "floatable" expressions like (i) are ambiguous in a similar way, indicating that lexically the class of floatable quantifiers is potentially infinite:

(i)   the committee is 90% behind the proposal

For many adults (i) can mean either 90% of the committee is completely behind the proposal, or 100% of the committee is 90% behind the proposal or behind 90% of the proposal, that is, quantifying over the object. The quantification over the object may be clearer with "The committee was completely behind the proposal" which can be falsified either by a member of the committee objecting or all of the committee objecting to one part of the proposal. Beyond that ambiguity, it can feel "vague" as if a combination of both readings were possible, i.e. that the quantifying expression is not restricted to one syntactic position or the other. Thus interpreting an element modifying the subject of the sentence as if it were also in the predicate does not seem to be excluded in some contexts, even for adults.

(18)   each
              [+anaphoric]
              [+distributive]

The anaphoric feature moves to an NP with an uninterpretable number feature and the Distributive feature is an interpretable Feature that is satisfied by Local Agreement. Therefore it must be adjacent to what it modifies. Terada suggests that the anaphoric feature is an uninterpretable feature [-Num]. Whatever the connection, the critical point is that the adult language requires a dual role for floatable quantifiers.

(19)   anaphoric: NPi   ....each-i
              distributive: each-j X-j

If the FQ is in a Spec position of a predicate phrase, like a small clause, then it can satisfy both of these relations. The agreement relation is what requires that either the FQ position be occupied, as it is for adults, or c-commanded as we will argue that it is for children and possibly second language learners.

Terada's two-pronged analysis, which was developed independently for the syntax of quantifiers, has not been incorporated into an acquisition account. As we argue below, it provides a key transitional element –and also makes distributivity a key concept in explaining spreading and in eventually eliminating the child's spreading interpretations.

As Labelle & Valois (2001) have shown, their subjects (age 5 was the oldest they tested) accepted quantification over the object for *chacun* ('each') as often as over the subject (which is grammatical).   For such a child, (10b) would be equivalent to (20), the spreading interpretation.

(20)   are the rabbits eating each carrot?

or even

(21)   Is each rabbit eating each carrot?
        (as with the child above: "each hand is in each glove").

Thus, for MOS, the quantifier is mis-analyzed as quantifying over both the object and the subject (10b) and (21) (and we have argued above in 1.3.2 this is sometimes possible even for adults). As Bobaljik (1998) has pointed out, there is no known reason why *every* should not float. If *every* floats like *each* for the child, then it too would project a semantic relation to the complement.

In the floated position, the quantifier has a relationship to local elements and in fact loses its potential for a collective interpretation. Bobaljik pointed out the subtle difference in interpretation between (22a) and (22b).

(22)   a. <u>all</u> the contestants can win
        b. the contestants can <u>all</u> win.

In (22a) the contestants could win as a group collectively, or they could win individually. In (22b) the implication is that they can only win separately, distributively, but not that they might collectively win.

Nor, as Terada (2003) points out can the moved quantifier appear by itself. Rather the FQ forms a small clause with the predicate, as in 23.

(23)   a. *the boys came both
        b. the boys came both alone.

He suggests that not only is a further predicated element present, but it must submit to a distributive reading. Consider cases like (24a) and (24b):

(24)   a. John left the two rooms both empty
        b.*John left the two rooms both angry.
        (putatively: he left the two rooms, feeling angry)
Consider also these facts which we have developed to underscore the point:

(25)   a. *the boys arrived each together.
        b. the boys arrived each together with his mother.

It is clear that the moved quantifier requires a distributable element (his mother) to be in a predication relation with it.

A bike (as in Figure 1) can receive this distributive interpretation from the child's floated quantifier, but when distributivity is impossible because of the semantics of the word, as with *cold*, in (26b) it would not be allowed. In example (26b), *cold* does not distribute, though in (26c) distributivity is not required since *each* is not in the Spec of a small clause where it would impose an agreement relation.

(26)   a) the dogs are eating each alone
        b) ?*the dogs are eating each cold
        c) each of the dogs is eating cold

Thus in a structure of this sort (from (23b)), we have these connections:

(27)

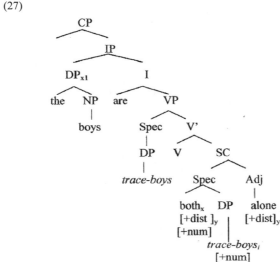

Both is in the Spec of the small clause (and a *trace* is in both possible origins under raising from a small clause or from the VP subject position). The distributive feature functions as a probe seeking an element to which distributivity can apply. Again, it can be linked to the subject (boys) by an anaphoric index, not a Spec-Complement agreement relation. The anaphoric index allows satisfaction of the [+num] agreement and links a [+universal] interpretation to the subject. In effect we have long-distance AGREE. For adults, the traditional FQ position is occupied next to the trace. The child can accomplish the same interpretation with less structure.

What the child needs for this syntactically is to have the quantifier in a higher node, so that it can c-command. Kang (1999) presents an analysis of English child language which argues that *every* is inherently focused in children's speech due to its salience. (See also Hollebrandse, to appear, on Topichood.) Kang additionally assumes that *every* moves to a Focus Phrase (FocP), which immediately dominates the IP layer in the phrase structure. In support, Kang cites Brody's (1990) work on Hungarian, in which he argued that a FocP layer appears optionally, when needed as a target for focus movement. Kang argues that from its position in FocP, *every* has sentential scope. We have assumed movement to a Spec-FocP position dominating IP (following Kang/Brody) which is a general operation on quantifiers. The essential structure is in (28).

(28)

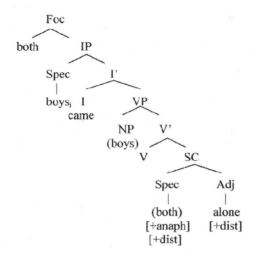

For the bike example (in Figure 1) the analogous structure would be as in (29):

(29)

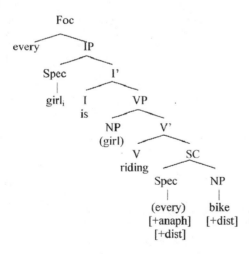

We wish to maintain the part of the analysis that allows movement of the quantifier to FocP, but we argue that this is not the movement of a focused constituent, but rather movement driven by the quantifier's need to check its [+dist(ributive)] feature, which can be checked by the Focus head, (either in the spec or head position, as long as a focus feature is satisfied). The quantifier in the focal position c-commands the FQ in Spec of the Small Clause. Therefore, the invisible FQ behaves like the adult FQ which gives its distributivity to the object and is anaphorically related to the subject.

It is clear that the moved quantifier like *each* or *both* requires a distributable element to be in a predication relation with it.[3] In effect, then, even the initial quantifier can take a distributive modifier (*Each hand has a glove*). In the FQ case, it is obligatory (*a hand has each glove*). It is not clear how to express this obligatoriness, but one could pursue the idea that the quantifier can be in the Spec of the small clause <u>only</u> if it is a licenser with its second feature. In effect the FQ has an agreement feature that must be checked by another feature in a Spec-Head relationship.

The child at this stage can satisfy these relationships if the quantifier is interpreted, not as an adverb applying to events, but as an NP quantifier raised to the FocusP position. The raised *every* now c-commands the VP as well as the subject NP; therefore it can c-command an empty FQ (*every*) position as well which we assume is an adverb position, a default interpretation in that position.

3.2.2 The semantic structure for MOS-only

We argue that, as in the floating quantification syntactic approach that we discussed in 3.2.1, the child associates a single quantifier with two arguments: both the subject and object. But whereas the floating quantifier associated different semantic properties with each argument, we propose that the child in the MOS stage associates the same semantic property - quantificational restriction – with both. We suggest that the way to associate quantificational restriction with two arguments is to make the truth condition **a conjunct**, with one of the verb's arguments constituting the restrictor in each case, as in (30).

---

[3] Gualmini, Meroni, and Crain (2003) hint at intriguing evidence that looks consistent with our account. Like the imposition of distributivity on the Small Clause, they report on a way for distributivity to apply to an OR relation. For a sentence like:

(i)   Every ghostbuster has a pig or a cat

children consistently add an "extra" restriction, much as they say the Drozd (2001) and Philip (1995) accounts do, where either every ghostbuster has the same (collective) or every one has a different (distributive) choice.

To really establish the distributive property we expect one might try:

(ii)   every ghostbuster has a pig or a cat or a dog.

(30)

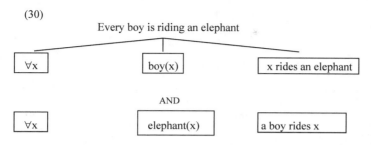

For example, in the sentence "every boy is riding an elephant," the truth condition is

(31)   "every boy is riding an elephant, <u>and</u>
         every elephant is being ridden by a boy".

This approach retains one of the strengths of the adverbial quantification approach - the fact that the quantifier's restriction can be determined beyond just a single NP. It also has one of the strengths of the NP quantifier approach - that restriction of the quantification is connected to the semantic content of specific NPs, not just any part of sentences. In our analysis, the child has advanced from the stage in which quantification ranges over events to the stage in which it ranges over the denotations of NPs, but with the qualification that it is not restricted to a single NP as in the adult grammar. At the MOS stage, the quantifier has elements of both an adverbial quantifier and a nominal quantifier. The adverbial property is that the quantifier takes scope over the entire sentence, enabling it to select the object as well as the subject as its restrictor. The nominal property is that the restrictors are actually determined by the NPs in the sentence, in contrast to adverbial quantification, where the restrictor is determined by other parts of the sentence or by information structure.

To the best of our knowledge, the truth conditions in our approach are equivalent to the truth conditions in Philip (1995) and in Drozd (1996), although each analysis achieves the truth condition using a different semantic mechanism: conjunctive quantification in the case of our analysis, quantification of events coupled with reference to participants in those events in the case of Philip's analysis, and switching of distributive key and distributive share in the case of Drozd's analysis. We nonetheless feel that our solution is preferable. Our analysis relates the development of the child's syntax to the error patterns found with quantification and addresses the learnability problem. The child begins with the adverbial default option for quantification, treating *every* as an adverb. As the child develops, she learns that *every* is a determiner quantifier, but the lack of a DP analysis allows her to analyze *every* as being sentential in scope. Finally, with the development of DPs, the child reaches adult proficiency in the use of quantification, treating it as an NP quantifier, with only its sister NP as its restrictor.

Our second argument applies specifically to Philip's analysis. As noted, we see no semantic difference between our analysis and his. We believe that the conceptual superiority of our analysis is in terms of how the semantic content of the NPs figures into the truth conditions of the sentence. In our analysis, it is done directly: the semantic content of the NP forms the restrictor of the formula. But in Philip's analysis, it is incorporated only indirectly into the truth conditions, through reference to participants in events. Philip's apparatus is set up to capture quantificational statements in this stage as a case of adverbial quantification, when what it looks like is a case of nominal quantification.

3.3 Attaining Adult Competence with Quantifiers

In the MOS-only stage, the child has learned that English has determiner quantifiers, and that projection to the Spec-FocP is motivated by natural focus on the word *every* which now allows it to c-command elements in the VP. This is the stage where children begin to make finer-grained distinctions between quantifiers of different types. Each quantifier has distinct properties of syntactic distribution and there is also cross-linguistic variation in the constraints on sites that host quantifiers, like DP. The child must decide whether his grammar has bare N, NP, or DP, as well as many decisions about the position of quantifiers (and adjectives, possessives, and agreement) within DP, all of which require time and refined experience. In step 2, the child does not distinguish *each* from *every*. This conflation of *each* and *every* is not surprising in light of the mixed properties of *every*, which is highly marked crosslinguistically (Angelika Kratzer, p.c.).

Finally, it is learned that *every* is not inherently distributive and hence does not raise to Spec-FocP. Therefore we do not find the FP-FQ chain with *every* among adults and we do not find the spreading interpretations. But what kind of evidence drives the move to the adult state?[4]

Triggering Collectivity

The restriction to internal DP-*every*---its inability to float—correlates with its having collective as well as distributive readings. Therefore we suggest that situations which force a collective reading are part of the trigger for reanalysis of every as DP-internal. In general, elements that contain complex features producing semantic alternatives tend to be more local (as the complex reflexive *himself* is local, while mono-syllabic reflexives are often not). We can imagine a few different sources of evidence that *every* has a collective reading. One is the ability of *every* to occur under the scope of negation, in which case it necessarily receives the collective interpretation, as in the following sentences from Beghelli and Stowell (1997):

---

[4] The full challenge is for the child to realize three things: a) *every* can be collective; b) *every* cannot float (*the boys had every a hat); and c) *every* is not a partitive (*every of the boys). Classic parametric approaches would suggest that these features are linked in grammar even if there is no logical connection. However, we are not in a position to formulate a full parameter here.

(32)   a. John didn't read every book
         b. ??John didn't read each book

Another case would involve the use of *every* in an argument position that must have a collective interpretation, as in the following:

(33)   The teacher gathered every student
        (compare: *the teacher gathered each student)

In other situations, the argument position is in principle available to both collective and distributive NPs, but the context makes it clear that a collective interpretation is appropriate ((34a) is from Tunstall, 1998).

(34)   a. The waiter lifted every glass
        (where the glasses are all on the same tray and are lifted with one action, whereas for the waiter to lift each glass, separate actions would be required.)

        b. The boy ate every raisin
        (where he gulped them all down in one motion)

Acquiring the details of *every* in this way illustrates how the child's grasping of a semantic distinction can lead to a shift in syntactic representation that in turn causes a restriction of semantic readings.[5]

Triggering Independent Quantifications

Another triggering experience may be found in a situation with unambiguous pragmatics. We suggest that seeing *every* in a situation where there is an overt second *every* which cannot be equivalent to "*a*" may alert the child to the necessity to apply *every* to each DP independently. It must be a circumstance where the conjunctive truth condition we propose for Stage 2 is clearly counter to the facts of the situation. For example, one could imagine that the child is engaged in coloring American flags with his class, a task that requires three colors. He sees that his whole class is busily working, each child with a single crayon. The teacher says: "Oh, every child does not have every color." She may add: "Every child needs every color, but you each have only one color" and then she distributes more crayons so everyone has every color. A case of unambiguous pragmatics such as this one would also be a potential trigger to reanalyze the conjunctive truth conditions presented in (30), or at least to begin the reanalysis, and it would also inform the child that one *every* must be inside the scope of another.

---

[5] Our trigger for DP-*every*, via recognizing collectivity, does not work for the analysis of *all*, but it does not need to since the child receives explicit evidence from expressions like "all the boys" that it can be external to DP.

Discussion and Conclusion

Semantic approaches to quantification have undertaken the important task of discovering exactly what range of interpretations children have for quantifiers, but they have not addressed the learnability question which becomes acute when the child must reject certain interpretations. We claim that the child initially chooses a representation that is closer to unmarked UG choices. We see the shift from a c-commanding position to the position inside a DP as a way to provide a possible route for the acquisition path. No semantic approaches seem to address the issue from the learnability perspective.

Pragmatics and processing accounts also play a valuable role. Previous research in this area has taught us that even the slightest manipulation of the contextual information may affect children's performance (Drozd & van Loosbroek, in press). Great care must be exercised in choosing experimental procedures. Clearly context, hence pragmatics, can elicit different interpretations by children as it does for adults. That does not, however, negate the role of syntax. No matter what pragmatic environment one chooses, the child must have a grammar which allows it. A secure grammar operates with completely anti-pragmatic conclusions. For instance, if a mouse eats cheese and we ask "did the cheese eat the mouse" children will say "no," and we can safely assume that they would say "no" to "is every bone eating a dog." Whatever interpretation of "every dog is eating a bone" they have, it must somehow be compatible with one of the grammatical representations they carry.

There is also a logical "performance" account of child errors which would say that the child ignores the sentence and simply responds to what is salient in the picture. In this case, the "not this one" response should be found for sentences with no quantification at all (Did Johnny eat a hotdog? "not this giant tree"). There have been no reports of children, in other experiments, simply referring to an extra object in the picture as if it were neglected. It is clear that the presence of *every* has an effect, and therefore we must provide a grammar in which it is initially possible to say "not this one" and later reject it.

The goal of an acquisition theory is to explain movement from an initial state to a final grammar. The many subtleties of the syntax of *every*, like the surprising fact that it does not float and has no partitive (*every of the boys) suggest that it is not acquired at once, that there is an acquisition path. The naturalistic data reveal, as expected, that children resist the use of *every*, presumably because they are aware that their partial knowledge does not quite fit the final grammar.

We have argued that the review of the results of a large study suggests an acquisition path with two quite different forms of quantifier spreading in the stage before *every* enters productive use. One is an adverbial projection associated with less mature interpretations, while the other engages sophisticated aspects of syntax, Floated Quantifiers, and continues often until children are 9 years old or older. It is even seen occasionally in production in non-adult sentences like "each hand is in each glove" where both subject and object are marked for the distributive property.

While purely semantic shifts are possible, our model of acquisition growth may reflect a general property of the syntax/semantics interface: shifts in syntax force new limitations on semantics. It is only the syntactic account, where a quantifier is first allowed to be outside the DP, and then restricted to being inside the DP, which predicts the loss of spreading since spreading (or floating) requires c-command.

Our conclusions remain tentative because we do not know enough about how all quantifiers behave. It is clearly the case that collective words like *all* are acquired years before *each* and *every*, which in turn are quite different from each other. Other quantifiers like *both* (Sauerland and Yatsushiro (2003) and *most* (Stickney, 2003) also require a long time before both their syntax and semantics are exactly like those of an adult. Our approach reasserts that it is the subtle properties of language particular variation–*every* cannot float in English but it can in German—that are the essence of the acquisition problem.

References

Bach, E., E. Jelinek, A. Kratzer and B.H. Partee, eds., 1995. *Quantification in Natural Languages*, Dordrecht: Kluwer.

Beghelli, F. and T. Stowell 1997. "Distributivity and negation: The syntax of *each* and *every*". In A. Szabolcsi (ed.), *Ways of Scope Taking*. Dordrecht: Kluwer.

Bobaljik, J. 1998. "Floating quantifiers: Handle with care*". GLOT International* 3.6, pp. 3-10. The Hague: Holland Academic Graphics.

Brisson, C. 2000. "Floating quantifiers as adverbs". In Rebecca Daly and Anastasia Riehl, (eds.), *Proceedings of ESCOL '99*. Ithaca, NY: CLC Publications.

Brody, M. 1990. "Some remarks on the focus field in Hungarian". *UCL Working Papers* 2: 201-225.

Brooks, P. J. and M. Braine. 1996. "What do children know about universal quantifiers 'all' and 'each'? *Cognition, 60(3),* 235-268.

Brooks, P. J., Braine, M. D. S., Jia, G. & Dias, M. G. 2001. Early representations for *all, each,* and their counterparts in Mandarin Chinese and Portuguese. In M. Bowerman & S. C. Levinson (Eds.), *Language acquisition and conceptual development* (pp. 316-339). Cambridge: Cambridge University Press.

Brooks, P. J. and I. Sekerina. (in press). "Shortcuts to quantifier interpretation in children and adults." In K. Drozd, Special issue on quantifier acquisition, *Language Acquisition.*

Brown, R. 1973. *A first language: The early stages.* Cambridge MA: Harvard University Press.

Chomsky, N. 1995. *The minimalist program.* Cambridge MA: MIT Press.

Chomsky, N. 2004. "On Phases." Ms. MIT.

Crain, S. and R. Thornton. 1998. *Investigations in Universal Grammar.* Cambridge, Mass: MIT Press

Crain, S., R. Thornton, C. Boster, L. Conway, D. Lillo-Martin, and E. Woodams. 1996. "Quantification without qualification." *Language Acquisition,* 5(2): 83-153.

DellaCarpini, M. 2003. "Developmental stages in the semantic acquisition of quantification by adult L2 learners of English: A pilot study". In J.M. Liceras, H. Zobl and H. Goodluck (eds.), *Proceedings of the 6th Generative Approaches to Second Language Acquisition Conference (GASLA 2002): L2 Links*. Somerville, MA: Cascadilla Press.

de Swart, H. 1993. *Adverbs of Quantification : A Generalized Quantifier Approach*. New York: Garland.

Donaldson, M. and P. Lloyd. 1974. Sentences and situations: children's judgments of match and mismatch. In Bresson, F. (Ed.). *Current Problems in Psycholinguistics*. Paris: Centre National de la Recherche Scientifique.

Drozd, K. F. 1996. "Quantifier interpretation errors as errors of distributive scope." In A. Stringfellow, D. Cahana-Amitay, E. Hughes, & A. Zukowski (eds.) *Proceedings of the 20th BUCLD* (pp. 177-188). Somerville MA: Cascadilla Press.

Drozd, K.F. and E. von Loosbroek. 1999. "Weak quantification, Plausible Dissent, and the development of children's pragmatic competence". In Greenhill, A., H. Littlefield, and C. Tano (eds.) *Proceedings of the 23rd Annual Boston University Conference on Language Development* (pp. 184-195). Somerville, MA: Cascadilla Press.

Drozd, K.F. 2001. "Children's weak interpretation of universally quantified sentences". In Bowerman, M. and S. Levinson (eds.) *Language Acquisition and Conceptual Development*, p. 340-376. Cambridge: Cambridge University Press.

Drozd, K. F. 2004. Learnability and linguistic performance (Review of Crain & Thornton, 1998). *Journal of Child Language, 31 (2),* 431-457.

Drozd, K. F. and E. van Loosbroek. (in press). The effect of context on children's interpretations of universally quantified sentences. V. van Geenhoven (Ed.), *Semantics Meets Acquisition*. Dordrecht: Kluwer.

Fitzpatrick, J. 2005. "Two types of floating quantifiers and their A/A-bar properties." Talk given at Northeast Linguistic Society 36, October 30, 2005, Amherst, MA.

Geurts, B. 2001. "Quantifying kids". Ms., Humboldt University, Berlin and University of Nijmegen, Nijmegen.

Geurts, B. and R. van der Sandt. 1999. Domain restriction. In P. Bosch and R. van der Sandt (eds.), *Focus: Linguistic, cognitive, and computational perspectives* (pp. 268-292). Cambridge: Cambridge University Press.

Gualmini, A., L. Meroni, and S. Crain. 2003. "An asymmetric universal in child language". In M. Weisberger (ed.), *Proceedings of Sinn und Bedeutung No. 7*. Arbeitspapier Nr. 114, FB Sprachwissenschaft, Universitat Konstanz.

Hale, K. 1985. Lecture on Quantification in Walbiri (UMass).

Hart, B. and T. R. Riseley. 1995. *Meaningful differences in the everyday experience of young American children*. Baltimore: Paul Brookes.

Hollebrandse, B. (to appear). "Topichood and quantification in L1 Dutch". To appear in *International Research in Applied Linguistics* 42.

Inhelder, B. and J. Piaget. 1964. *The Early Growth of Logic in the Child*. London: Routledge, Kegan and Paul.

Kang, H.-K. 1999. "Quantifier spreading by English and Korean children". Ms., University College, London.

Kuczaj, S. 1976. *-ing, -s and -ed: A Study of the Acquisition of Certain Verb Inflections*. Doctoral dissertation, University of Minnesota.

Labelle, M. and D. Valois. 2001. "Functional categories and the acquisition of distance quantification." Ms. Universite du Quebec a Montreal.

MacWhinney, B. 2000. *The CHILDES project: Tools for analyzing talk. Third Edition.* Mahwah, NJ: Lawrence Erlbaum Associates.

Oller, D. K. and Eilers, R. E. 2002. *Language and literacy in bilingual children.* Clevedon, UK: Multilingual Matters.

Philip, W. 1995. *Event quantification in the acquisition of universal quantification,* Doctoral dissertation, UMass Amherst.

Philip, W. 1996. "Symmetrical interpretation and scope ambiguity in child Dutch". In C. Koster and F. Wijnen (eds.), *Proceedings of GALA 1995.* Gröningen, the Netherlands.

Philip, W. 1998. "The wide scope interpretation of postverbal quantifier subjects: QR in the early grammar of Spanish". In *Proceedings of GALA 1997.* The University of Edinburgh, Scotland.

Philip, W. 2003. "Specific indefinites and quantifier scope for children acquiring Dutch and Chinese". Paper presented at the 2002 Meeting of the Linguistic Society of the Netherlands.

Philip, W. 2004. "Two theories of exhaustive pairing." Ms., Utrecht Institute of Linguistics, OTS. Utrecht University, The Netherlands.

Roeper, T. (to appear). "Watching NP Grow". In V. van Geenhoven (ed.), *Semantics Meets Acquisition.* Dordrecht: Kluwer.

Roeper, T. and J. de Villiers 1993. "The emergence of bound variable structures". In E. Reuland and W. Abraham (eds.), *Knowledge and Language: From Orwell's Problem to Plato's Problem.* Dordrecht: Kluwer.

Roeper, T. and E. Matthei. 1974. "On the acquisition of some and all," Presented at the Sixth Child Language Research Forum, Stanford University, April 1974. Appeared in *Papers and reports on child language development* (1975), Stanford University, 63-74.

Sauerland, U. and K. Yatsushiro. 2003. Paper presented at the UMass Workshop on Acquisition of Quantification, May 20, 2003.

Seymour, H. N. and B. Z. Pearson (eds.) 2004. Evaluating language variation: Distinguishing development and dialect from disorder. *Seminars in Speech and Language, 25 (1),* special issue on linguistics and language evaluation.

Seymour, H., T. Roeper, and J. G. de Villiers, with contributions by P.A. de Villiers. 2005. *Diagnostic Evaluation of Language Variation-Norm Referenced (DELV-NR).* San Antonio, TX: The Psychological Corporation, Harcourt Assessments, Inc.

Seymour, H. N., T. Roeper, J. G. de Villiers, P. A. de Villiers, and B. Z. Pearson. April, 2002. Developmental Milestones Report to NIH. Ms., Department of Communication Disorders, University of Massachusetts, Amherst MA.

Sportiche, D. 1988. "A theory of floating quantifiers and its corollaries for constituent structure". *Linguistic Inquiry* 19: 425-449.

Stickney, H. 2003. "Investigations into children's acquisition of 'most.' Ms. University of Massachusetts, Amherst.

Sugisaki, K. and M. Isobe. 2001. "Quantification without Qualification without Plausible Dissent". In J.-Y. Kim and A. Werle (eds.), *The Proceedings of SULA 1*. Amherst, MA: GLSA Publications.

Takahashi, M. 1991. "Children's interpretation of sentences containing *every*". In T.L. Maxfield and B. Plunkett (eds.), *Papers in the Acquisition of WH*. Amherst, MA: GLSA Publications.

Terada, H. 2003. "Floating quantifiers as probes". *English Linguistics* 20(2): 467-493.

Tunstall, S. 1998. *The interpretation of quantifiers: Semantics and processing*. Doctoral dissertation, University of Massachusetts.

Address for Correspondence: Thomas Roeper, Department of Linguistics, University of Massachusetts, Amherst, Amherst MA 01003 USA

Email: roeper@linguist.umass.edu

Uri Strauss, Department of Linguistics, University of Massachusetts, Amherst

uri@linguist.umass.edu

Barbara Zurer Pearson, Dept. of Communication Disorders, University of Massachusetts

bpearson@comdis.umass.edu

Children's Interpretation of Partitive "Most"

Helen Stickney

University of Massachusetts, Amherst

1.   Introduction

Do children have difficulty acquiring the quantifier "most"? And if so, can we approach a characterization of this difficulty? This paper will discuss the possibility that when faced with sentences like (1), children may allow "most" to quantify over *how much was painted in general*, rather than over just how much of the *house* was painted.

(1)   The woman painted most of the house.

I will argue that, indeed, children as old as six have not fully acquired the quantifier "most". This paper will span a broad range of issues involved in the acquisition of the quantifier, discuss them in light of current theories on Quantifier Spreading, introduce a new theory specific to the acquisition of "most," and make suggestions as to the directions in which future research should go. This paper covers topics including acquisition of quantification in general, determiner versus adverbial quantification, partitive versus superlative interpretations, and restricting quantifier domain.

The impetus for this research was a piece of naturalistic data. The following conversation occurred between my (then) five-year-old daughter and myself:

(2)   **Mother:** "If you go to bed right now we can read most of James and the Giant Peach."
       Child: "And what else are we going to read?"
       Mother: "I didn't say anything about reading anything else; I said if you go to bed right now we can read most of *James and the Giant Peach*."
       Child: "Yes, you said we could read *most* of James and the Giant Peach, so what *else* are we going to read?"

After much repetition, it became clear that in this case my daughter was interpreting "most" as if it quantified over *the act of reading*. Why did this misunderstanding occur? The fact that "most" could be so easily misconstrued as something adverb-like here is

© 2006 by Helen Stickney
Tanja Heizmann (ed.): Current Issues in Acquisition. University of Massachusetts Occasional Papers in Linguistics 34, 129-159.
GLSA Amherst.

puzzling and is reminiscent of behavior seen with children's use off "every" (See section 3). In this paper I will explore this potential interpretation in more detail.

In the semantics literature the determiner quantifier (henceforth D-quantifier) "most (of)" has traditionally been classified as a *strong* quantifier. It is usually discussed in conjunction with other strong quantifiers like "every" and "all" (Barwise & Cooper 1981, Partee 1995, Keenan 1996, Matthewson 2001). In the field of acquisition the quantifiers "every" and "all" have been discussed extensively (Philip 1995, Crain et al 1996, Lidz & Musolino 2002, interalia). In experimental research children have exhibited a phenomenon called Quantifier Spreading (Roeper & Matthei 1974, Philip & Aurelio 1991, Takahashi 1991, Philip 1995, Crain et al 1996, Drozd & Loosbroek 1999, Lidz & Musolino 2002). Quantifier Spreading (henceforth Q-Spreading) can be roughly characterized as a D-quantifier behaving as if it takes scope *outside* the DP. Over the past ten years the debate about the nature of Q-Spreading has grown, centering on the D-quantifier "every". The quantifier "most", however, has remained untouched by the acquisition literature. As this paper will show, the reason for this may be based on the complexity of English "most" in general. A detailed look at the acquisition of *all* quantifiers may help more definitively to work out the nature of the patterns already emerging in quantifier acquisition research

The experiments discussed in this paper begin a discussion of the acquisition of "most" and ask whether "most"'s acquisition data can add to and broaden the discussion of Q-Spreading. As "most" is a strong quantifier, children may encounter the same obstacles in its acquisition as they are argued to encounter with the strong quantifier "every." However, "most" is a complicated quantifier that has many features that the child must identify and acquire.

The main experiment discussed in this paper tests whether children interpret "most of DP" as a D-quantifier or as an A-quantifier like "mostly." The results of this experiment will be discussed in light of the prevailing theories on Q-Spreading. I will ultimately make the case that the only existing account that can accommodate the "most" data is the Weak Quantifier Hypothesis (Drozd & Loosbroek 1999) which assumes that children have yet to learn how to appropriately restrict quantifier domains semantically. This hypothesis is plausible because it can also account for the behavior of "every" in child language, but further research needs to be done to show that children's trouble with "most" is not instead due to syntactic error or a preference for the superlative (rather than partitive) reading of "most."

In section 2, I will set the stage for the puzzle regarding the acquisition of "most," defining the basic properties of the quantifier and presenting some naturalistic data. In section 3, I will discuss the phenomenon of Q-Spreading (with "every") and some hypotheses that attempt to account for it. I will then discuss what these various accounts predict for "most" acquisition. In section 4, I will discuss an experiment investigating whether "most of DP" is being interpreted adverbially by children and briefly discuss a second experiment investigating whether children differentiate the partitive and superlative uses of "most." Section 5 will explore possible syntactic reasons for why "most" is being misinterpreted and discuss how the experimental data fits with the existing literature on Quantifier Spreading.

2.   Most

As stated in the introduction, "most" is a complicated quantifier. "Most"[1] can appear as partitive (3) or superlative (4), as an A-quantifier (5), a D-quantifier (6) and possibly even a sentential quantifier (7).

(3)   <u>Most of the boys</u> are at home.
(4)   <u>The most boys</u> are at home.
(5)   James <u>mostly</u> ate apples.
(6)   <u>Most cats</u> like catnip.
(7)   <u>Mostly</u>, tomatoes are red.

As a D-quantifier it can have a comparative feature (8) and/or it can quantify proportionally (9). It can also quantify proportionally as a generic (6).

(8)   Sally ate <u>the most apples, however Jennifer ate a fair amount herself</u>.
(9)   The boys ate <u>most of the pie, the rest of it</u> is still left on the plate.

As an A-quantifier it also can be comparative (10) or proportional (11).

(10)   Everyone threw a bit of garbage on the ground at the fair, but Jim littered <u>the most</u>.
(11)   Jim is a good artist, but subject matter is limited. He <u>mostly</u> draws super heroes.

It must be assumed that children do hear all of the uses in (3-11). The child must then figure out the range of uses allowed, as well as learn to identify what syntactic/morphemic structure goes with each meaning. The child must sort through some confusing data. For example, he might interpret the *-st* part of the root as the superlative morpheme *-st*. Perhaps the partitive "of the" could help pry apart the meanings in (3-11) for the cases where "most" serves as a D-quantifier, but, as this paper will show, this does not appear to be true for children's initial interpretations.

In addition to providing a challenge to the child, this broad range of uses complicates an attempt to compare "most" directly with any one quantifier in particular. In an attempt at simplicity, this paper will only focus on sentences containing "most of DP", but it is important to remain aware of all the different ways in which the morpheme "most" is used, as they are presumably part of the information that the child is sifting through while attempting to acquire an adult-like interpretation.

This paper will investigate whether children initially interpret the D-quantifier

---

[1] I use various morphological forms here, based on the assumption that at a certain point in the quantifier's acquisition children may not be distinguishing anything other than the root.

"most" as if it were quantifying over something larger than the DP. In the adult grammar "most", occurring in D°, only quantifies over DP, its c-command domain.

(12)   The boy kissed most of the girls

In (12), "most" quantifies only over a specific contextually determined set of girls and not over *kissed* or *the boy*. I define "most," following Keenan (1996) as the relation in (13).

(13)   **MOST**$(A)(B) = $ **T** iff $|A \cap B| > |A - B|^2$ [Keenan 1996: 43]

I will use this as the general meaning of "most"[3] (and "mostly") when it quantifies in its strong/proportional/relational sense. Hence, for a sentence like (6), we understand it to mean the amount of *cats-liking-catnip* is greater than the amount of *cats-not-liking-catnip*. (3) can be characterized in the same way: the amount of *boys-at-home* is greater than the amount of *boys-not-at-home*, except that *boys* in this case is a specific set of boys.

As mentioned above, "most" like "every" is a strong quantifier. Barwise & Cooper (1981) provide the following formalization of the definition of strong and weak quantifiers (CN = common noun):

(14)
      (i)   Definition: D is *positive strong* iff whenever $\| D(CN) \|$ is defined, then
           $\| CN \| \in \| D(CN) \|$
      (ii) Definition: D is *negative strong* iff whenever $\| D(CN) \|$ is defined, then
           $\| CN \| \notin \| D(CN) \|$
      (iii) Definition: D is *weak* iff it is neither positive strong nor negative strong.

This definition categorizes definites, universal quantifiers, "most" and "neither" as strong and "a", "some", numerals, "many", "few", etc. as weak. This definition is based on Milsark's observation that strong quantifiers cannot appear in existential *there-sentences*. Strong quantifiers presuppose the existence of the set over which they quantify.

2.1   The Naturalistic Data

In addition to the scenario described in section 1, casual interactions with children in preschools and searches of CHILDES further suggest that "most" is being misinterpreted by young children.

---

[2] This definition implies that "most" means *more than half*, however it must be noted that my daughter (at almost 7 years old) pointed out that the proportion that "most" represents is, for her, greater than 75%, rather than greater than 50%.

[3] Please note that this paper was originally distributed in May 2003. The analysis of the semantics of "most" has not been updated to take account of Nakanishi & Romero's 2004 NELS talk 'Two Constructions with Most and their Semantic Properties.' Their analysis of "most of the NP" begs reanalysis of the "most" acquisition data.

In casual discussions with children I posed scenarios and questions similar to the experiment to be discussed in section 4. The responses were inconsistent, but in follow-up discussion the children seemed to be focusing on the action rather than purely on the object involved.

(15) **Me**: Suppose we were sitting at lunch here and Jane was really thirsty. There were two glasses of water, a glass of milk and one glass of orange juice [*Glasses were set up to illustrate*]. Let's say Jane drank this glass of milk empty, and then her mom said, "You need some vitamin C, drink your orange juice." Jane had a sip of the orange juice but she really wanted water, so she drank this whole glass of water. She was still thirsty so she had a sip from this water, and another sip, and then drank down to here. Then her mother reminded her about the OJ again so she drank until she couldn't drink anymore. She drank the OJ down to here [*almost empty*]. Could I say, "Jane drank most of the orange juice?"
Child: No.
Me: Why?
Child: Well, she drank a lot of water.

Interpretations like these suggest that children are interpreting "most of" as an A-quantifier (similar to "mostly"). This possibility will be discussed in more depth throughout this paper.

Searches of the Brown, MacWhinney, and Kuczaj corpora in the CHILDES database have turned up a large proportion of unusual uses of "most." The number of utterances of "most" was rather small[4], with children first uttering "most" (in either "most", "the most" or "most of" form) late in their third year or early in their fourth. It is hard for CHILDES to give a definitive answer to the question of how children interpret "most" because so little of the utterance context is included in the transcripts. However, it is clear that not all children age 5 and younger are using the quantifier in an adult-like manner. The following transcription, for example, is from the MacWhinney corpus, child aged 4;11. The child's utterance is followed by a comment clarifying his meaning:

(16) **CHI:** They have most of them.
%com: He meant they have the most.

The above data suggests that children might not be getting the superlative/partitive distinction with "most." This possibility will be discussed more in depth in sections 2 and 5.

The search of the Kuczaj, MacWhinney, and Brown corpora for the word "most" revealed the first usage around age 3;8. Many of these uses appeared perfectly grammatical. However, due to lack of contextual information it is hard to tell whether the

---

[4] 33 uses total in longitudinal studies of 7 children.

semantics involved are adult-like. The sentences in (17) and (18), however, are clearly *not* adult-like.

(17)   **MARK (4;5):**   "the most one of the ones upstairs."
(18)   **SARAH (5;1):**   "How come that's most and that's not?"

These examples also add support to the theory that at age 4/5 "most" is not fully acquired. Sarah's comment is interesting. In the situation she is looking at the tape reels on a cassette recorder, and commenting on how there's more tape on one spool than on the other. Here "most" seems to be synonymous with "large amount". Although it could be relational/strong in the sense of "most of", but lacking the syntactic structure.

The data in (15-18) suggest that children are interpreting "most of" as if can take more than just the DP in its scope; analogous to the attested Q-Spreading cases with "every" (see section 3). I claim that indeed, children as old as six appear to allow "most" to take scope outside the DP when it is syntactically part of the DP. This means that for *most(A,B)*, *A* is not defined as the contextually determined set denoted by the DP.

This section has shown how "most" behaves in the adult grammar and looked at some examples of how children use and interpret it. The next section will discuss children's behavior with "every" and tie this in to the discussion of "most."

3.   Quantifier Spreading

The original observations of Q-Spreading are credited to Inhelder & Piaget (1959/64). Experimental linguistic investigation of this behavior began with Roeper & Matthei's (1974) investigation of "some" and "all". In their work they showed that many 3-year-old children were interpreting sentences like (19) as if the quantifier "some" quantified over both noun and verb (roughly like (20)). It seemed that children allowed the quantifier to *spread* across the sentence, quantifying over the predicate as well as the DP.

(19)   Some of the circles are black.
(20)   Some of the circles are some black. [= *some of the circles represented in the drawing are partially black*]

The bulk of the literature since has focused on "every" and centers prominently on examples like (21) in which children reject "every boy is riding a horse" as a description of the picture because there is one horse without a rider.

(21)

> **Experimenter:** Is every boy riding a horse?
> **Child:** No, not that horse.   [Philip 1995: 2]

3.1

The Q-Spreading phenomenon has a few variations (see Philip 1995), but the allowance of the quantifier to quantify outside the domain of the DP is consistent throughout. Below is a description of various hypotheses regarding why Q-Spreading occurs.

3.1.1   D-quantifiers as Adverbial Quantification

Philip & Aurelio (1990) and Takahashi (1991) promote the view that in cases of Q-Spreading "every" is being interpreted adverbially. I will henceforth refer to this hypothesis as the Adverbial Account. Quite simply, this account proposes that in the child's grammar "every" is synonymous with "always". This is supported cross-linguistically, as A-quantifiers are more common in the world's languages than D-quantifiers.[5]

What does it mean for a quantifier to be an adverb? Here I will follow de Swart's (1993) view of the tripartite structure of quantification (Heim 1982). According to de Swart A-quantifiers always quantify over events. This event appears in the left branch of the tripartite structure.[6] How this event is defined depends on focus, and it is focus that will allow different items to appear in the restrictor. For example, focus/emphasis on *dog* in (22) causes an analysis like (22').

(22)   Dogs always chase Felix.

---

[5] All natural languages appear to have quantificational elements that quantify over the domain of the VP or some larger domain. However, some languages, like Mohawk, while having quantificational adverbs, do not appear to have quantificational NPs (see Baker, 1995).

[6] Tripartite structure for quantification: (from left to right) the quantifier, its restrictor (restrictive clause) and the nuclear scope.

(22′) $\forall$e [$\exists$x: x chases Felix in e $\rightarrow$ [$\forall$y: y chases Felix in e $\rightarrow$ y is a dog]]
        =*For all events (e), if there exists an x such that x chases Felix in e then e is an*
        event of a dog chasing Felix.

In de Swart's analysis, the restrictive clause can contain just events of chasing, or events
of chasing with arguments and variables included. Hence, an adverbial quantifier like
"always" has some flexibility the interpretation of its restrictor. Context and focus will
determine which variables and events show up in the restrictor of the tripartite structure.

3.1.2   Event Quantification

In his 1995 dissertation, Philip characterizes "every" in cases like (21) as quantifying
over events of horse-riding (23). I will henceforth refer to this as the Event Quantification
Account.

(23)   'all minimal events in which either a boy or a pony (or both) is a participant are
        events in which a boy is riding a pony'   [Philip 1995: 44]

In his account, it is only the *participants* in the event that appear in the restrictor. For
"every"/"always" this then translates into: Always(if x or y are participants, then they are
both participants in the event).

3.1.4   Quantification Errors are Due to Pragmatics

Crain et al (1996) assert that Q-Spreading is *not* a robust phenomenon and that it
disappears when children are presented with felicitous pragmatic contexts (i.e. the use of
Plausible Dissent in experiments). The condition of Plausible Dissent states that in order
for a yes/no question to be felicitous, the scenario must be set up so that the child
considers both "yes" and "no" answers to be an option. There must be enough
background/contextual knowledge in order for the child to feel that he has two plausible
options from which to choose. Otherwise, the yes/no question might not seem
pragmatically plausible, and the child might attempt to use pragmatics to accommodate
the question that he thinks the experimenter is *really* asking. According to Crain et al's
account, simply showing a picture as in (21) and asking a yes/no question does not give
sufficient information about the quantification domains to be considered. Hence, the child
must make an assumption about what the domain of boys is, and about what question is
really being asked. Crain et al argue that items like (21), which lack Plausible Dissent,
may allow the child to posit another boy who is not riding the horse in question in order
to create a quantification domain that seems appropriate to the question asked.

3.1.5   Weak quantification and domain restriction

Drozd & Loosbroek (1999) put forth the Weak Quantification Hypothesis (henceforth the
WQH) which states that the reason for children's Q-Spreading behavior with "every" is
that they give "every" weak (rather than strong) quantificational force. Weak quantifiers
rely on context/pragmatics, rather than strictly the DP, for determining the domain of

quantification.[7] According to Drozd & Loosbroek, a weak quantificational reading often leads to an adverb-like interpretation of the quantifier, as in (24).

(24)   Many Scandinavians have won the Nobel Prize.   [Westeråhl 1985]

The preferred reading of (24) is the weak quantificational one in which "many Scandinavians" takes as its domain the number of Scandinavians having won the Nobel Prize in light of the number of people expected to win the Nobel Prize from any one country. The strong reading of "many" in (24), where "many" quantifies simply over the set of all Scandinavians, causes the sentence to be false in the world as we know it.

Drozd & Loosbroek assert that children are treating "every" like "many," allowing it both a weak and a strong interpretation. Giving "every" weak quantificational force allows the child to look to context for domain of quantification. In their investigation Drozd & Loosbroek manipulated the presupposition of quantifying domains and were able to show that this had a direct effect on whether or not children exhibited Q-Spreading with "every". The WQH predicts that with careful manipulation of how a story is presented the child could be led to either a weak or a strong interpretation of the quantifier. It assumes that children know the attachment site of the quantifier as internal to the DP, but their grammar, consistent with that of adult English weak quantification allows them to look outside the DP to context for quantificational domain.

3.1.6   Is Syntactic Error a Possibility?

The bulk of the literature on Q-Spreading assumes that the child is misrepresenting the semantics of the quantifier or appealing to pragmatics. Is a syntactic explanation plausible? Lidz & Musolino (2002) propose that four-year-olds' interpretation of quantifier scope relies heavily on surface syntactic representation. When faced with sentences like (25), children seem only to access the reading in which it is the case that for every horse it didn't jump over the fence.

(25)   Every horse didn't jump over the fence.

In their study, children did not accept the reading where "every" is in the scope of negation, the reading in which some but not all the horses jumped over the fence. Hence,

---

[7] For example, in adult English, "many" can have *either* a weak or a strong reading (Partee, 1988). On the weak reading, "many" is cardinal and contextually/subjectively dependent. On the strong reading "many" is proportional and dependent on the contextually relevant set specified by the DP.

(a)   Cardinal/weak: $|\,A \cap B| > n$

(b)   Proportional/strong: $|\,A \cap B\,|\,/\,|A| \geq k$ (k = a fraction or percent)

In (c) the cardinal/weak reading of "many" depends on what might be considered "many" by speaker or hearer --and may depend heavily on the context in which it was uttered. The strong reading requires that "many" be relational, meaning essentially "many of the boxes."

(c)   The man painted many boxes.

the position of the quantifier matters to the child when it comes to determining scope. Could position of the quantifier also affect its attachment site? A syntactic view could be extended to the Adverbial Account (Phillip & Aurelio 1991, Takahashi 1991), which could be explained as an effect of the child misattaching the quantifier to the VP, rather than the DP. In (26), the quantifier is attached correctly, and the domain of quantification is the DP. In (27), the quantifier is instead attached to the VP, and the domain of quantification shifts such that "every" becomes adverbial "always".[8] I will henceforth refer to this as the syntactic account.

(26)

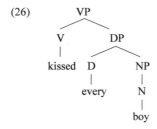

(27)

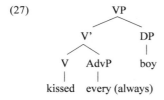

One would have to assume the misattachment was due to DP being dispreferred as a site for quantifiers. A syntactic adverbial account based on misattachment is easily outlined for quantified DPs in object position, but what about subject position? One would have to assume that the quantifier is misattached higher in the tree, possibly quantifying over the entire sentence. This would predict subtle meaning differences between (28) and (29).[9]

(28)   Every girl kissed a boy.
(29)   A girl kissed every boy.

---

[8] This structure raises the question of whether adverbs in English can appear post-verbally (see also footnote 15). In general, it appears that they cannot. However, it is still relevant to question whether English speaking children will accept post-verbal adverbs, and if so, how they interpret them.
[9] Takahashi (1991) does find some difference for "every" in subject versus object position, but whether this is robust needs to be investigated further.

In both cases it would be predicted that a Q-Spreading child would analyze "every" as having a domain larger than the DP. (28) & (29) would be interpreted something like (28') and (29') respectively.

(28')   Always [a girl kissed a boy]
(29')   A girl always [kissed a boy]

This paper focuses solely on quantifiers ("most") in object position. Further research on a syntactic/linear account will have to address whether position in the sentence matters.

3.2   Predictions for "Most"

If Q-Spreading is indeed a robust phenomenon that affects all quantifiers during language acquisition, what do the various theories predict regarding children's acquisition of "most"?

3.2.1   D-Quantifier Interpreted as A-Quantifier: The Adverbial Account

To say that "most" is being interpreted as an adverbial quantifier suggests that the child is interpreting (30) as (31).

(30)   The boy ate most of the kittens.
(31)   The boy mostly ate the kittens.

"Mostly" in this case is assumed to take "events of the boy eating x" as its restrictor clause.[10]

(32)   MOST(events of the boy eating x)(events of the boy eating the kittens)
        =*most events of the boy eating something are events of the boy eating the kittens*

Whether events are quantified by time or by amount was is still an open question.[11]

3.2.2   Event Quantification

The Event Quantification account predicts that (30) will be interpreted as (33).

(33)   'most minimal events in which either the boy or a kitten (or both) is a participant are events in which the boy is eating a kitten'

This differs from the prediction of the Adverbial Account above. Under the Adverbial Account we get the interpretation that most of the time, if the boy was eating something it was one of the kittens that he was eating. Under the Event Quantification hypothesis we get the interpretation that if there were any events involving the boy and/or the kittens,

---

[10] See de Swart's analysis, section 3.1.1

[11] The experiment in section 4.1 takes both possibilities into account but does not attempt to answer this question.

then most of them were events of boy-eating-kitten. This predicts that in a scenario where the kittens spent more time playing than being eaten or in a scenario where the boy spent more time petting the cats than eating them, the child would interpret the sentence in (30) as false.

3.2.3 Plausible Dissent

The claim of Crain et al (1996) asserts that children's errors with quantification are due to the lack of Plausible Dissent within the task. This predicts that if the condition of Plausible Dissent is fulfilled then children will never misinterpret sentences containing the D-quantifier "most."

3.2.4 The Weak Quantification Hypothesis

Drozd & Loosbroek (1999) propose that children interpret strong quantifiers as if they had weak quantificational force. This implies that "most" might be interpreted similar to the weak version of "many" for which (subjective) context is used to restrict the domain of quantification (see footnote 7). Looking to context would allow the possibility of the event(s) denoted by the verb to be part of the domain of quantification.

(34)   Mark is smashing most of the buildings.
(35)   Mary is painting most of the house.

If context allows the domain of quantification to extend beyond the DP, then "most" would be allowed to quantify over the VP or perhaps the entire sentence --allowing a whole array of interpretations. At the very least it would allow for an interpretation similar to the Westeråhl (1985) sentence, such that (34) might be interpreted in light of all the things Mark is smashing.[12]

3.2.5 The Syntactic Account

In this paper I assume the adult syntax of "most of DP" to look roughly like (36). If children make the initial assumption that D-quantifiers are adverbial (perhaps A-quantifiers are the default --see the Adverbial Account above) or if they do not yet know where or how to attach the quantifier in the DP structure, then they might attach the quantifier to the left and allow it to quantify adverbially (37).[13]

---

[12] Note: Westeråhl (1985) and Drozd & Loosbroek (1999) investigate quantifiers in *subject* position.

[13] What is the status of adverbial modifiers that appear between the verb and its direct object? There is a debate in the literature between Partee and Hajicova & Sgall as to whether words like "only" appearing between verb and direct object are attached to the NP or to the VP or if there is some other way of accounting for their behavior. The adverb "mostly" in this position yields similar difficulties. To say "I read mostly the paper" is a marginal construction for some speakers. Discussions between Partee and myself yielded the possibility that the post-verbal "mostly" might be compatible with a superlative/comparative reading. Consider a scenario where during an eight hour period I read the NY Times for two hours, Newsweek for one hour, People for one hour, The Washington Post for one hour, and the LA Times for one hour.

(36)

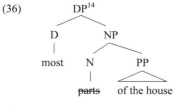

(37)

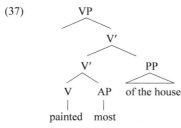

Although the structure is not standard, (37) might be much simpler for the child to project than (36) as it does not need to posit null or elliptical material.[15]

This would predict a subtle difference between "most" in subject position versus object position (as mentioned above). Interpretation of "most" in object position would be consistent with the Adverbial Account (39), or, if children pay attention to the fact that "most" is not "mostly", then they might have a superlative interpretation (40) (see section 3.2.6).

(38)   Sheila painted most of the house.
(39)   Sheila mostly painted the house.
(40)   Sheila painted the house the most.

Subject position would necessitate sentence level interpretation (42) or (43).

(i)   # I mostly read the NY Times.
(ii)   I read the NY Times the most.
(iii)   ? I read mostly the NY Times.

Partee and I have a weak intuition of acceptability for (c), the post verbal "mostly". Regardless of how acceptable it may be, the degree of uncertainty between a reading of "most of what I read" and "what I read the most" in (c) is interesting in its own right. If this issue is difficult for adults, it adds force to the hypothesis that children might be interpreting "most" as a superlative in this position (see section 3.2.6). Certainly it supports the assertion that children might feel ambiguous about how to restrict the domain of quantification.

[14] The prototype for this tree is from Kyle Johnson, p.c.

[15] Nevertheless, children seem to be able to handle ellipsis at a rather young age. For example, "Here are some cookies, do you want some?" (Roeper, p.c.)

(41)   Most of the girls are carrying knives.
(42)   Most of events x are events of girls carrying knives.
(43)   Mostly, girls are carrying knives.

3.2.6   The 'Partitive = Superlative' Hypothesis

Before turning to the experimental data, I want to suggest one more possible explanation for children's misinterpretation of "most." This account is not easily transferable to other quantifiers, but begs mention in light of the different uses of "most" (outlined in section 2) and the discussion of how post-verbal adverbial "most" might be interpreted (section 3.2.5). "Most" has both a partitive and a superlative interpretation (section 2, (3-4) & (8-9)). What if the partitive is initially difficult for the child to acquire[16] and the combination of partitive and multi-faceted "most" is too difficult for the child to interpret or calculate? She might go through a stage where all uses of "most" are interpreted as superlative. One compelling reason to posit a preference for superlative "most" is the cross-linguistic data. English is rather unique in its use of a partitive determiner "most". In the majority of languages that contain a D-quantifier "most" it occurs as a superlative (44). A morphologically separate nominal element is used for the partitive meaning (45) (Partee, p.c.).

(44)   el   más   libros[17]
        the   most books

(45)   la   mayoría   de   los   libros
        the   majority of   the   books   *Spanish*

English uses two separate constructions to convey the meanings in (44) & (45), "the most books" and "most of the books," but it remains true that "most" is phonetically the same in both, which may be confusing to the child. What if the partitive (or specifically partitive "most") is difficult for the child? I propose here the 'Partitive = Superlative' Hypothesis (PSH).

(46)   **PSH**: Children initially lack the partitive feature of "most". Lacking the partitive,
        children interpret "most" as superlative.

This hypothesis has some interesting predictions. It states that, for some reason children are not able to identify the set denoted by the partitive construction. I constrain this hypothesis to "most," but recognize that more work must be done to determine whether

---

[16] For purposes of space, discussion of the acquisition of the partitive in this paper will be brief. For more discussion of the acquisition of the partitive please see the earlier draft of this paper which can be found on my website http://people.umass.edu/hstickne

[17] It must be noted here that "más" (most) is homophonous with "más" (more). Additionally, this word can appear post-verbally, and for certain verbs be a superlative adverb "most," in other cases it appears as comparative adverb "more."

this is a general lack of partitive, or something germane to "most". In essence, if the child is not able to recognize the structure and/or semantics denoted by "most of the x", then he may have no other recourse but to use the superlative construction with which he is already familiar.

The analysis that I propose with the PSH is that if children lack the partitive they may interpret (47) as (48).

(47)   The man painted most of the fence.
(48)   The man painted the fence the most.

How could this be? If children lacked the partitive structure, and only understood "most" as a superlative, they would not be able to process a sentence like (47). An interpretation of a superlative DP in this scenario is ungrammatical (47'). In order for the comparativeness of the superlative to be felicitous, the DP must either be plural or a mass noun (49).

(47')   *The man painted the most fence.
(49)   The man painted the most fences. / The man drank the most milk.

If the superlative reading is the only one available for "most" and the noun following it is singular, then the child may be forced to look outside the DP for something over which to quantify, namely the VP. This could create an interpretation like (48).

Of course, "most" in (47) is between the verb and its object not at the end of the sentence, but in English it is possible to get a bare "most" following the verb and acting as a superlative adverbial quantifier (50). And children do get exposure to sentences like (51).

(50)   The man painted this house most.
(51)   Which one do you like most?

I have outlined six possible analyses of how children might represent "most." The following section presents the experimental data.

4.   Adverbial Quantifier vs. DP Quantifier – The Experiment

The purpose of this experiment (henceforth the Adverbial/DP experiment) was to investigate, specifically, sentences in which "most of" occurred in object position with singular DPs. It was designed as a pilot experiment primarily to show that Q-Spreading with "most" was actually occurring, with the intention that more research will follow to expand upon the results gathered therein. The question: Do children initially interpret the quantifier "most (of)" as strictly an adverbial quantifier, like "mostly" (as outlined in the Adverbial Account --section 3.2.1)?

17 children from the Amherst Montessori School participated in a story comprehension task. The children were aged 3;6-9;8, one 3-yr-old, five 4-yr-olds, three 5-yr-olds, seven 6-yr-olds, and one 9-yr-old. Mean age was 5;7, median age 5;10.

4.1   Procedure

Each child was presented with eight stories. Four of the stories (henceforth MOST stories) contained a scenario in which a character painted/colored *most of* a particular object (but did not *mostly* paint the object) (52). Four of the stories (henceforth MOSTLY stories) contained a scenario in which a character *mostly* painted an object (but did not paint *most of* it) (53). The stories were accompanied by pictures on which the experimenter drew to illustrate the action of painting, coloring, decorating, etc. Filler questions were asked during and after the story (both as fillers and to aid in comprehension). At the end of the story the child was asked a comprehension question that contained "most of DP."

(52)   MostSB-2
       This boy and girl are brother and sister. They always argue. One day they decided to color a picture from their coloring book together. The picture was of a bunch of shapes. **How many shapes do you see here?**
       Because they always argue, they couldn't decide who was going to color which shapes. The girl, who was older, took charge and said, "Okay, you color most of *this* shape, and I'll do the rest." [*experimenter points to particular shape*] The boy didn't think this was quite fair, but he had an idea. He said, "Okay, I'll color most of this shape, but you have to leave the room while I do it, 'cause I don't want you to look over my shoulder." The sister left the room (she decided to get them a snack). And this is what the boy did: He colored this shape like this [*colors majority of identified shape*], and then he colored here, and here…. [*experimenter colors parts of a number of other shapes so that majority of coloring time is spent on other shapes*] When the girl came back, she looked at the picture and said, "Hey! There's hardly anything left for me to color!" Her brother said, "Well, you didn't tell me what I *couldn't* color, you just said I had to color most of this shape." "Well you *didn't* color most of this shape!" said this sister. To which her brother replied, "I *did* color most of this shape!"
       Who is right? **Did the boy color most of this shape?**

(53)   MostlySB-2
       This is Mervo the Magnificent. He owns a big circus. Everybody loves his circus, including those who perform in it. And Mervo loves everybody. As a gift to all those he loves, Mervo has decided to decorate the circus a bit. He found some wonderful rainbow-colored paint with which to decorate, but he only has *one* bucket of it. He knows that one bucket won't be enough to paint *everything* rainbow colored, so he decides to focus on the circus train. Here is the circus train [*four cars are visible in picture*]. It's actually really long, but we're going to look at this part of it, 'cause this is what Mervo is looking at it. **How many cars do you see?** Mervo knows that he probably won't be able to paint the whole train, or

even these four cars, so he has to make a decision. He knows that if he paints *this* car [*experimenter points to car*], the clowns will be really happy, but again, he wants to put paint on *other* cars, too. He thinks to himself, "The clowns are silly folk. I bet they'd be happy if I just painted *most* of this train car." So he spends a lot of time painting and painting this car, but this car is really big and he starts running out of paint [*majority of time spent painting car, but less than half is painted in the end*]. So then he decides to paint here and here and here [*on the other cars --small amount of time spent*] with the last bits of rainbow paint. At this point, one of the clowns walks by. "Do you like what I've done?" Mervo asks. The clown doesn't really notice the paint. Mervo is surprised, "Look! I've painted most of this car, don't you like it?" **Did Mervo paint most of this car?**

The experimental questions were always of the form in (54): "most" in object position as a partitive modifying the DP.

(54)   Did the man paint most of this box?

When the child was asked the experimental question, the specific object in the set was pointed to. Intonation was kept neutral with focus on none of the words in the sentence. Answers to experimental questions were often followed up with "can you show me?" in order to gain insight into how the quantifier was being construed. The stories were randomly ordered for each child.

The purpose of having the experimenter actually act out the verb in the story was to insure that, if the child had a bias toward quantifying over the verb (or events), he would have an easier time understanding the extent of each event in order to calculate proportion/amount. In examples like (53) the experimenter spent the majority of her time/painting-events painting the first box. In examples like (52) the majority of the time was spent in painting the other objects in the picture, and the first box, although more than half was painted, was painted extremely quickly with as little attention given to it as possible.

The MOST/MOSTLY items were further divided by how each set was presented. For both MOST and MOSTLY items, two of the stories contained a set of items that were introduced as being all the same sort of thing (i.e. here are a bunch of shapes/boxes/etc.). I will call these the Set as Background (or SB) items. Both (52) and (53) are type SB. Companion to the SB items were the Individuated Set (or SI) items. In these stories each of the items (which received the verb's action, or were potential receivers) were introduced individually (i.e. here's a tree, a house, a rock, and a dog). Two of each the MOSTLY and MOST items were SI. (55) is an example of an SI Mostly item.

(55)   MostlySI-1
This is Bill. One day Bill was standing on a hill, looking at the view. He saw a tree, a rock, a house, and a sleeping dog. Bill thought, "Wouldn't it be funny if those things were painted different colors?" Suddenly a small elf appeared before him. "Wow!" said Bill. "Hey Bill," said the elf, "how would you like me to grant

you a wish?" "Sure!" said Bill, "I want you to do something really wacky, how about you make that tree blue!" "No problem," said the elf, I happen to have some magic paint." He told Bill to come back in one hour and the tree would be painted. Now you can see that this elf is small. He is also afraid of heights (do you know what that means? It means he's afraid of being up high). This elf looked at that tree and realized that he'd have to *climb* it in order to paint the whole thing. He painted the tree for awhile, starting at the bottom and painting and painting as high as he could reach. He looked at his work. "Hm," he thought, "I really don't want to climb up this tree." He stretched on his tip-toes and painted some more. He looked at his work again. [*elf has painted a relatively thin line along the bottom of the tree*]. He thought, "Maybe if I paint these other things to match, he won't mind so much if I stop." So he painted a thin line of paint around the bottom of the house, the rock, and the pig. Bill came back a little later. "Hey!" he yelled, "I thought you were going to grant my wish! The tree isn't blue!" "Yes it is," said the elf, "I thought you'd like it. I painted most of the tree blue." "No you didn't!" said Bill, "you're trying to trick me!"

Who's right? **Did the elf paint most of the tree?**

SB and SI items were used to explore whether set presentation might have an effect on whether adverbial quantification occurs. If I say "We can read most of a book," is the indefiniteness of "a book" enough to trigger the child to quantify over *events of reading x where x is a book*? Does having a set of identical items encourage quantification over the entire set (appearing adverb-like) rather than just focusing on the one, singled-out object? Conversely, does naming the specific items in a set (i.e. "tree", "box", "dog", "house") encourage DP quantification? In other words, does having a set of similar objects encourage quantification that takes into account the entire set more readily than when a single object is more clearly defined as "different" among a range of objects?

To reiterate, this experiment assumes that if the child is interpreting "the man painted most of this box" as "the man mostly painted this box" she understands "mostly" in a particular way. In effect, "the man mostly painted this box" can be paraphrased either as "for the amount/time of painting done, the majority of the painting was of the particular box indicated" or "for the amount/time of painting-boxes done, the majority of the painting was of the particular box indicated." This is a proportional account where the quantifier picks out the proportion of the painting done (or painting time) in relation to one particular object. As is apparent from section 2, "most" has many other features beyond D- vs. A-quantification that must be acquired. This experiment is a good starting point from which much discussion and hopefully future research will emerge.

The condition of Plausible Dissent can be said to be fulfilled in the experimental items because each story ended with an argument or controversy about whether the desired outcome had been fulfilled.

4.2 Expected Result

For a sentence like (54), repeated below, a number of patterns are predicted based on the factors used in the experiment and the assumption of interpretation possibilities listed above. Remember that this experiment was designed only to test A- versus D-quantification, so only those predictions are listed here. See section 5 for how this experiment bears on the predictions discussed in section 2.

(54)   Did the man paint most of this box?

The chart in (56) outlines the predicted patterns, based on the analysis outlined above. The child either interprets "most of" as an adverb (56a), or the child has the adult DP-quantifier interpretation (56b).

(56)

a) **Most is adverbial in child's grammar:**	
MOST	Reject ("no")
MOSTLY	Accept ("yes")
b) **Most is DP quantifier in child's grammar:**	
MOST	Accept ("yes")
MOSTLY	Reject ("no")

If the SI and SB items have the hypothesized effect, aiding and/or hindering adverbial interpretation, then the pattern in (57a) would be evident. If adverbial quantification is the only option, and SI/SB items have an effect, then the pattern in (57b) would be evident, with only MOSTLY-SB items being accepted.

(57)

a) **introduction of set effects accessibility of adverbial interpretation**	
MOST – SB	Reject ("no")
MOST – SI	Accept ("yes")
MOSTLY – SB	Accept ("yes")
MOSTLY – SI	Reject ("no")
b) **only A-quantification in grammar, introduction of set has effect**	
MOST – SB	Reject ("no")
MOST – SI	Reject ("no")
MOSTLY – SB	Accept ("yes")
MOSTLY – SI	Reject ("no")

4.1.3   Results

In actuality, children did not behave as predicted in *either* (56) or (57). The overall pattern was that children accepted *both* the MOST and MOSTLY items, correctly accepting the object quantification and incorrectly accepting the adverbial quantification reading. This pattern was significant, Univariate ANOVA, MOST versus MOSTLY, $F(1,31) = 13.838$, p = .001. Three children accepted (said "yes" to) every experimental item, while correctly rejecting filler items. Two children exhibited adult-like responses (one 6-year-old and the 9-year-old). All other children fell somewhere in-between.

A Univariate ANOVA including all 17 subjects showed no effect of age. Age was barely significant, $F(1,31) = 4.447$, p = .043. However, when the 9-yr-old was removed from the data set, $(F(1,29) = 2.042)$, the p-value rose to .164. Showing that effectively there is no improvement in performance over time between age 3 and age 6. Hence, 6-yr-olds are making the same errors as the 3-yr-olds. There was no significant difference between SI and SB items across conditions. A Univariate ANOVA of all 17 subjects, SI vs. SB showed $F(1,63) = .032$, p = .859. The p-value actually rises higher when the 9-yr-old is again removed. Additionally, there was no interaction between MOST/MOSTLY conditions and SI/SB, $F(1,63) = 0$, p = 1.000. Whether the child was presented with a MOST or a MOSTLY item first in the experiment had no significant effect. A one-way ANOVA performed on percent correct MOST items results and another on percent correct MOSTLY was not significant. MOST: $F(1,14)=2.14$, p=0.166. MOSTLY: $F(1,14)=0.76$, p=0.399.

To reiterate, the only significant pattern evident in the data is that children overwhelmingly accept *both* MOST and MOSTLY items. This pattern is consistent through age 6. We can assume that somewhere between age 6 and 9 "most of DP" is finally correctly represented in the child's grammar.

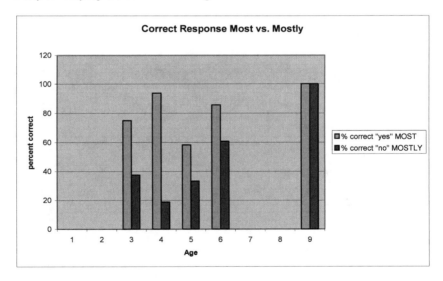

4.2   Superlative v. Partitive Experiment[18]

An earlier study I conducted (unpublished) was designed to investigate whether children distinguished between the partitive and superlative "most". Children aged 5-8 were shown scenarios involving sets and subsets of items. The scenarios used either drawings or toys and were set up roughly like (58) and (59).

(58)   a. Where are *most of the* stars?
        b. Where are *the most* stars?

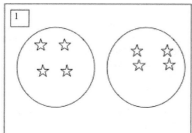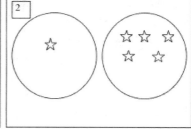

(59)   a. Are *most of the* stars in this oval?
        b. Are *the most* stars in this oval?   -- ["this oval" refers to one on left]

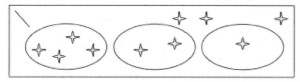

In the scenarios like (58) a story was told as each of the items were set out, making both the possibility of box as set delineator and the possibility of circle as set delineator salient. The subject was then asked either (58a) or (58b). In the adult grammar, the appropriate response to "Where are *the most* stars?" can be either to look at the sets defined by boxes or the sets defined by circles. The correct answer is then either "the box on the left" or "the rightmost circle" respectively. When asked "Where are *most of the* stars?" one must look at *all* of the stars, calculate more than half, and then figure out where this number lies. The answer to this question can only be "in the box on the left." Adult subjects answered accordingly. Nevertheless, *all* of the children answered both of these questions as if "most of" were synonymous with "the most," splitting their

---

[18] For purposes of space I cannot discuss this experiment as thoroughly as I'd like. For more information please see the earlier draft of this paper on my website http://people.umass.edu/hstickne.

responses between rightmost circle and leftmost box, regardless of which question was asked.

A similar pattern was evident with scenarios like (59) where children would be shown a picture (*"here are three sleeping dogs and 10 flies"*), and then asked either "Are *most of the* flies on this dog?" or "Are *the most* flies on this dog?" In the adult grammar, the answer to "most of" must be "no", and the answer to "the most" must be yes. Adult subjects answered accordingly. All child subjects answered "yes" to all questions of this type, regardless of whether superlative or partitive.

I have presented data from two experiments. In the Adverb/DP experiment children allowed "most of DP" to have both D- and A-quantifier interpretations. In the Superlative v. Partitive experiment children treated "most of DP" as if it meant "the most NP." The next section will attempt to integrate the experimental and naturalistic data and discuss them in light of the current theories on Quantifier Spreading.

5. Discussion

The naturalistic data presented in section 2.1 is both interesting and inconclusive. It does serve to support the claim that children at least as old as age 6 are not correctly interpreting the quantifier "most," yet each use seems to point in a slightly different direction. Casual conversation with children aged six and younger showed children focusing on the action/event even when the quantifier "most" should only have quantified over the DP (2) & (15) (repeated below). CHILDES data shows a variety of misuses that are hard to fully account for due to lack of context. One use of most in the MacWhinney corpus contains a comment that explicitly states that the child was intending a superlative meaning when using the partitive "most of DP" (16)

The experimental data from the Adverb/DP experiment show children correctly accepting "most of DP" when the context highlights the object/DP but also incorrectly accepting "most of DP" when the context highlights the verb/action/event. Data from the Superlative v. Partitive experiment show children treating both "most of DP" (partitive) and "the most NP" (superlative) as if they were the superlative "the most NP."

The accounts to be evaluated are Event Quantification, the Adverbial Account, the Syntactic Account, Plausible Dissent, The WQH and the PSH.

5.1 Accounting for the Naturalistic Data

The naturalistic data provides us with three clear cases (portions of which are repeated below). The first case is (2) where "we can read most of James and the Giant Peach" is interpreted as if "most" relates to events of reading something. The second example is the conversation (15) in which the child focuses on drinking events in general and not the amount of milk that has been drunk. The third example involves an explicit statement from the parent explaining that the child intended the superlative when producing the partitive "most" (16).

(2)　**Mother:** "If you go to bed right now we can read most of James and the Giant Peach."

　　　Child:　"And what else are we going to read?"

(15)　**Me:**　　Could I say, "Jane drank most of the orange juice?"

　　　Child:　No.

　　　Me:　　Why?

　　　Child:　Well, she drank a lot of water.

(16)　**CHI:**　　They have most of them.

　　　%com:　He meant they have the most.

5.1.1　Event Quantification and the Naturalistic Data

Philip's (1995) account does not account for the child's interpretation in (2). In this case we are not quantifying over minimal events containing *me* and *JGP* as participants, but purely over events of reading (or events of reading x). Philip's account predicts that the child would interpret (2) as something like (2′).

(2′)　'most minimal events in which either mom or JGP (or both) is a participant are events in which mom is reading JGP.

An interpretation like (2′) would elicit a response like "What else are we going to *do*" rather than "what else are we going to *read*" because it implies that there are some events that don't involve "mom reading JGP," but it does not imply that they are necessarily reading events.

Philip's account can, however, account for the scenario in (15) where in order for "Jane drank most of the OJ" to be true, most of the events involving Jane or the OJ or both must be events of "Jane drinking OJ." In fact, most of the events involving Jane were of "Jane drinking water," so the child would be motivated to say "no."

Philip's account has nothing to say regarding the data in (16).

5.1.2　The Adverbial Account and the Naturalistic Data

The Adverbial Account can account for (2) & (15), but not (16). Interpretations such as (2″) and (15″) account for the data, but the paraphrase in (16″) does not translate into a superlative interpretation.

(2″)　We can mostly read James and the Giant Peach.

(15″)　Jane mostly drank the orange juice.

(16″)　They mostly have them.

5.1.3 The Syntactic Account and the Naturalistic Data

The syntactic account (outlined in section 3.1.6 and section 3.2.5) is compatible with the interpretations in (2) and (15), as in these cases the quantifier is adjacent the verb to which it could be misattached, creating an adverbial interpretation (if indeed post-verbal modifiers can be interpreted in such a way). Additionally this account predicts the possibility of partitive "most" being interpreted as superlative as seen in (16), as a post-verbal adverb may force a superlative interpretation.

5.1.4 Plausible Dissent and the Naturalistic Data

The pragmatic account of Crain et al (1996) does not seem to be able to account for (2) because the child in the scenario was used to situations in which only one book (and often only part of that book) was read at bedtime. Hence, in light of background contextual knowledge available to the child (i.e. the possible scenarios to be considered), her interpretation was infelicitous. Crain et al's account only focused on experimental design flaws and does not seem to be able to take into account naturalistic data in general.[19] It can account for (15) as plausible dissent was not utilized, and it has nothing to say about (16) as not enough context was provided for this particular utterance in the MacWhinney corpus.

5.1.5 The WQH and the Naturalistic Data

The Weak Quantification Hypothesis can account for (15) quite easily by allowing the child to be free in her choice of domain restriction. It has a slightly harder time accounting for the data in (2). Yes, the child is free to restrict the domain how she pleases, but this is done by referring to context, and context would have dictated that only one book was part of the discussion. The WQH has little to say regarding (16), but see section 5.3 for a possible accommodation.

5.1.6 The PSH and the Naturalistic Data

The 'Partitive = Superlative' Hypothesis accounts nicely for the naturalistic data. The PSH predicts that (60) would be interpreted as something like (60') or (60'').

(60)   The monkey decorated most of the kite.

(60')   The monkey painted, (the) most, of the kite.

---

[19] I am unsure that the Plausible Dissent Hypothesis can account for the following piece of naturalistic data with "every". An elementary teacher was explaining to 6-yr-old children about the school play, and about how she wanted some parts to be played specifically by boys, and some parts to be played specifically by girls. She then said, "All the wolves have to be girls." One child in the class started to cry because she did not want to be a wolf, and had interpreted the sentence to mean that "all girls have to be wolves."

(60″)   The monkey painted ~~of~~ the kite, the most.

Both representations (especially the latter) are ambiguous, allowing "most" to be construed as referring to either object or event. This allows the interpretation in (2) to be about the amount of reading and (15) to be about the amount of drinking while also accounting for the superlative interpretation in (16).

5.2   Accounting for the Experimental Data

Two experiments were presented in section 4. One experiment tells us that, depending on the scenario, children accept "most of DP" as quantifying over both DP and VP (event). The other tells us that children treat the partitive "most" as if it were superlative.

5.2.1   Plausible Dissent and the Experimental Data

I will discuss Crain et al (1996) first here, as the other accounts need more careful explanation with respect to the experiments discussed above. The Adverb/DP experiment fulfilled conditions of Plausible Dissent. The pragmatic account would predict that the children behave in an adult-like manner. This was not the case. The second experiment did not satisfy Plausible Dissent. A closer examination of the pragmatics of the experiment is in order.

5.2.2   Event Quantification, the Adverbial Account and the Experimental Data

Event Quantification (Philip 1995) predicts that the child will interpret the experimental questions in (52) and (55) as (52′) and (55′) respectively.

(52′)   Were most minimal events involving the boy, this shape or both events of the boy coloring this shape?

(55′)   Were most minimal events involving the elf, the tree or both events of the elf painting the tree?

In regard to the experiment the predictions of the Event Quantification Account parallel that of the Adverbial Account on which the experiment was based. Children who interpret the D-quantifier as adverbial or event quantification should accept the MOSTLY items and reject the MOST items. In actuality, children accepted both. These accounts have nothing to say about the Partitive v. Superlative experiment that showed children interpreted partitive as superlative.

5.2.3   The Syntactic Account and the Experimental Data

The Syntactic Account suggests that children are attaching "most" to the VP, rather than the DP. Adult interpretations of post-verbal adverbs are shaky (see footnote 16), but may be ambiguous between A- and D-quantification. This would account for the ability to accept both MOST and MOSTLY items in the Adverb/DP experiment.

The ambiguity of "most" in this context is also supported by data from Afrikaans (Andries Coetzee, p.c.). In Afrikaans sentences like (61) (but not *all* sentences with "most" in object position[20]) are ambiguous, allowing both adverbial and determiner interpretation of "most."

(61)   Ons kan die meeste van "Jan en die boontjierank" lees.
        we can the most   of "John and bean stalk"   read.

An ambiguous construction might allow just the sort of acceptance rate for both readings exhibited in the Adverb/DP experiment. However, the quantifier shown in (61) has a slightly different form from the English examples in this paper. In (61) the definite determiner "die" occurs to the left of "meeste" (as in English "the most"). More investigation must be done to see whether "meeste" in Afrikaans is closer to *superlative* "the most" in English rather than strictly the partitive "most" that is being discussed here, but the lack of clarity regarding superlative versus partitive in Afrikaans begs the question of whether partitive and superlative "most" may be hard for the child to distinguish at first. When children see "most of DP" are they initially speaking Afrikaans? Which brings us to the 'Partitive = Superlative' Hypothesis.

5.2.4   The PSH and the Experimental Data

The PSH suggests that the child starts out lacking the partitive feature of "most" and interprets it instead as superlative. A superlative interpretation in this position may promote an adverbial reading (see section 3.2.6). The PSH accounts for data from both the adverbial/DP experiment and the Partitive v. Superlative experiment. The PSH predicts that the child interprets partitive "most" as superlative. If superlative most in object position indeed interpreted as the ambiguous paraphrase in (60″) the child could accept both scenarios in the Adverbial/DP experiment.

Jill de Villiers (p.c.), in regard to the Superlative v. Partitive experiment, points out that young children may not yet be able to do the mathematical calculation needed to accommodate proportions of numbers greater than four. This is not necessarily inconsistent with the PSH, however, as lack of calculation ability may *also* put the partitive interpretation at a disadvantage and promote a superlative interpretation.

5.2.5   The WQH and the Experimental Data

The PSH fits the experimental data in this paper as well as the naturalistic data. However, this is not an account that easily translates to quantifiers other than "most." Ideally we want a theory of quantification that can account for the behavior of *all* quantifiers. The Syntactic Account fares better in this regard, but independent evidence for misattachment is needed. The WQH (Drozd & Loosbroek 1999) may be the best way to think about this. If the quantifier is being interpreted as weak rather than strong, then the child is allowed

---

[20] Coetzee says that it is helpful if the object is a mass noun rather than a count noun. Thus, "the man painted most of the sand" is easier to construe adverbially than "the man painted most of the house."

to appeal to context for domain restriction. This accounts for both the acceptance of A-quantification and the acceptance of D-quantification. It also accounts for the small amount of children who were able to say both "yes" and "no" to a MOSTLY item. For example one child responded to the question in item MOSTLY-SI-1 as follows:

(62)   **Experimenter:** Did the elf paint most of the tree?
        Child: Um. Sort of.
        Experimenter: Can you show me?
        Child: Well, that's just a little bit [*what elf painted*], but that would be a lot of it [*pointing to higher on tree*]. The elf is tiny, to him it's a lot, but to him [*Bill*] it's a little.

In other words, the child felt perfectly comfortable saying that whether the elf painted "most of the tree" was a subjective question and that the answer could be different depending on what one considered to be a large amount of painting. A weak interpretation of "most" may be able to provide just the sort of subjective interpretation required to give the response in (62).

Drozd & Loosbroek manipulated presupposition in their experiments. In the Adverb/DP experiment, presupposition was not controlled in this way. The Adverb/DP experiment controlled only for types of sets. In each story the action ranged over a set of objects ending with a question focusing on one object. However, by focusing on both object and action, and by raising the question at the end of whether or not the claimed action had been accomplished, I may have been promoting domains for *both* weak and strong quantification. This ambiguity may have made it easy for the child to accept either interpretation when asked the experimental question. On Drozd & Loosbroek's account, had I focused more on the one object to be quantified over, and less on the other objects, the child would more naturally restrict the domain of quantification to the one object, rather than taking all objects into consideration and quantifying comparatively.

However, if the WQH is right, then why do some Q-Spreading children spread only occasionally? Studies (e.g. Roeper, Strauss & Pearson, in press) looking at data from the DELV[21] (Seymour, Roeper & de Villiers 2005) show that not all children who exhibit Q-Spreading do so consistently at every given opportunity. All items on the DELV are presented equally and consistently by each test-giver, so one would assume that the behavior of children could be easily categorized by questions asked (and how the test sets them up pragmatically). One way to accommodate this is by taking an approach such as the Multiple Grammars Hypothesis (Roeper 1998) and claim that both semantic representations are available to the child (and/or both syntactic attachment sites are available). One might say that the children who spread inconsistently are transitioning from allowing weak interpretation "every"/"most" to allowing only strong interpretations. It may be interesting to take a closer look at the DELV and how each item is set up presuppositionally --comparing that to Drozd & Loosbroek's experimental items.

---

[21] Data from the DELV- NR (*Diagnostic Evaluation of Language Variation*), the Dialect Sensitive Language Test (DSLT), and earlier versions of the DELV.

5.3   Weak Quantification v. the PSH

Both the 'Partitive = Superlative' Hypothesis and the Weak Quantification Hypothesis seem able to account for the "most" data. The WQH seems optimal because it can account for children's behavior with both "most" and "every," but the data in this paper does not rule out the PSH. Is it possible to combine the two accounts? In answer, let's turn to the partitive construction.

(80) Jim ate half of the cherries.

As generalized in the Partitive Constraint (Ladusaw 1982), the noun in a partitive construction is always a definite (i.e. contextually salient) set. The PSH suggests that children do not know partitive "most", only superlative "most". The WQH suggests that children do not know strong quantification, only weak quantification. One way to combine these accounts would be to say that superlative "most" is weak, i.e. it is the equivalent of weak "many" and may allow the speaker/hearer to appeal to her own knowledge of what is sufficiently "most-like" in the given scenario. Another way to think about this may just be to say that children don't know that the definiteness of the embedded NP in the partitive construction *requires* them to use that definite set as the restrictor of the quantifier. In fact proportional/partitive quantification is necessarily strong quantification. The restrictor of the quantifier is always presupposed in strong quantification and is not as flexible in interpretation as weak quantification. Hence, saying children lack "strong quantification" and saying children "lack the partitive" may be two sides of the same coin.

5.4   A Look Ahead

This paper has given a preliminary analysis of the acquisition of "most", presenting a variety of data, both naturalistic and experimental, but there is still much work to be done. Three theories are able to account for the full range of data, the Syntactic Account, the 'Partitive = Superlative' Hypothesis and the Weak Quantification Hypothesis. The WQH is born out nicely in work with "every." Both the Syntactic Account and the PSH will need to be independently verified. They both predict subtle differences in semantic interpretation for quantifiers in subject versus object position. The adverbial/DP experiment looked only at "most" in object position. It is imperative that experimental research be done looking at the quantifier in subject position as well. Does subject position effect the domain of quantification and the accessibility of the adverbial-like analysis of "most"? Does "most" in subject position elicit and sentential-modifier interpretation?

The Partitive v. Superlative experiment brought interesting data to bear, but it will need to be replicated and expanded. Work must continue to be done regarding children's ability to quantify over sets. It also must be established whether children at this age have acquired the syntax/semantics of the partitive. An experiment with "most" similar to

Drozd & Loosbroek's work manipulating the satisfaction of presupposition is also in order.

The adverbial/DP experiment also only focused on singular objects, in order to minimize the calculation involved in quantification. However, if a simple experiment can be designed, it would be helpful to see if plurality has any effect on this phenomenon, and if sentences with plural DPs pattern as the PSH predicts (see section 3.2.6).

"Most" has additional features that have not been closely addressed in this paper. Do children need to have fully acquired the comparative feature in their grammar? An account of children's acquisition of concepts of cardinality and proportion must also be added to further supplement the "most" acquisition story.

The PSH relies heavily on the assumption that the superlative feature is fully acquired at an early age. Data is needed to support this.

6. Conclusion

This paper has presented the preliminary data necessary to include English "most" in the discussion of Quantifier Spreading. "Most" is perhaps the most complicated of the strong quantifiers, especially as it has many features that may also pose problems for acquisition. These features must each be investigated individually (and ideally experimentally) in order to get a clear picture of the quantifier's acquisition process. It still remains unclear whether children's misinterpretation of "most" is caused by the same factors as Q-Spreading with "every." I have suggested that acquisition of the partitive may play a key role in the difficulty children have acquiring "most". A lack of partitive may force a superlative interpretation that triggers an adverbial analysis. This may or may not set "most" apart from other quantifiers in discussion of quantifier acquisition. Nevertheless the preliminary data regarding the behavior of "most" is compatible with at least one theory put forth concerning "every", namely the Weak Quantification Hypothesis. This suggests that whatever is at the root of Quantifier Spreading is not just particular to "every". I look forward to further research on "most" to help clarify the quantifier acquisition puzzle.

References

Barwise, J., and R. Cooper. 1981. Generalized Quantifiers in Natural Language. *Linguistics and Philosophy, 4:159--220.*

Crain, S., R. Thornton, C. Boster, L. Conway, D. Lillo-Martin, and E. Woodams. 1996. Quantification without Qualification. *Language Acquisition: A Journal of Developmental Linguistics 5(2), pp. 83-153.*

Drozd, K., and E. Loosbroek. 1999. Weak quantification, plausible dissent, and the development of children's pragmatic competence. In *Greenhill,-Annabel (ed. and preface); Littlefield,-Heather (ed. and preface); Tano,-Cheryl (ed. and preface).*

Proceedings of the 23rd Annual Boston University Conference on Language Development, I-II. Somerville, MA: Cascadilla.

Jackendoff, R. 1977. X' Syntax: A Study of Phrase Structure. *Linguistic Inquiry Monograph.* The MIT Press: Cambridge, MA

Keenan, E. 1996. The Semantics of Determiners. In *Lappin, S (ed.) The Handbook of Contemporary Semantic Theory.* Oxford: Blackwell Publishers. pp. 41-63.

Ladusaw, W. 1982. Semantic constraints on the English partitive construction. In *D. Flickinger, et al. (eds.) Proceedings of WCCFL 1.* pp. 231-242

Lidz, J., and J. Musolino. 2002. Children's Command of Quantification. *Cognition 84 (2), pp. 113-154.*

Matthewson, L. 2001. Quantification and the nature of crosslinguistic variation. *Natural Language Semantics 9* pp. 145-189.

Miller, K. and C. Schmitt. 2003. Wide-scope Indefinites in English Child Language. Presented at *Generative Approaches to Language Acquisition 2003.* Michigan State University.

MacWhinney, B. 2000. *The CHILDES project: Tools for analyzing talk. Third Edition.* Mahwah, NJ: Lawrence Erlbaum Associates.

Partee, B. H. 1988. Many Quantifiers. In Powers, J. & de Jong, K. (eds) *Proceedings of the 5th Eastern States Conference on Linguistics.* The Ohio State University. 383-402

Partee, B. H. 1995. Quantificational Structures and Compositionality. In *E. Bach, E. Jelinek, A. Kratzer, and B.H. Partee (eds.), Quantification in Natural Languages,* 541-601. Kluwer Academic Publishers: Netherlands.

Phillip, W. 1995. *Event Quantification in the Acquisition of Universal Quantification.* University of Massachusetts doctoral dissertation. GLSA: Amherst, MA

Philip, W., and S. Aurelio. 1991. Quantifier Spreading: Pilot study of preschooler's "Every". In Maxfield, T., & Plunkett, B. (eds): *UMOP Special Edition, Papers in the Acquisition of WH, Proceedings of Massachusetts Roundtable May 1990.* pp. 267-282. GLSA: Amherst, MA

Roeper, T. 1999. Universal Bilingualism. *Bilingualism: Language and Cognition 2 (3), pp. 169-186.*

Roeper, T. and E. Matthei. 1974. On the acquisition of All and Some. *Proceedings of the Stanford Child Language Conference.*

Roeper, T., Strauss, U. and Pearson, B.Z., in press. The acquisition path of quantifiers: Two kinds of spreading. In *K. Drozd (Guest Editor), Special Issue on Quantifiers, Language Acquisition.*

Seymour, H., T. Roeper, and J. G. de Villiers 2000. *Dialect Sensitive Language Test (DSLT).* San Antonio TX: The Psychological Corporation.

Seymour, H., T. Roeper, and J. G. deVilliers 2005. *DELV-NR (Diagnostic Evaluation of Language Variation) Norm-Referenced Test.* San Antonio TX: The Psychological Corporation.

De Swart, H. 1993. Adverbs of quantification: a generalized quantifier approach. Garland Publications: New York.

Takahashi, M. 1991. Children's interpretation of sentences containing every. In *Maxfield and Plunkett (eds.) Papers in the Acquisition of WH. (1991).* 303-323. GLSA: Amherst, MA

Department of Linguistics
226 South College
University of Massachusetts
Amherst, MA 01003

hstickne@linguist.umass.edu

The Acquisition of Exhaustivity in Wh-Questions

Uri Strauss

University of Massachusetts, Amherst

1.   Introduction

A conventional explanation for the exhaustivity property of wh-questions (e.g. Rullmann 1995) is framed in terms of maximality, a concept familiar from Link's (1983) theory of plurality. In this paper I challenge this view by comparing children's acquisition of definite plurals and exhaustivity. While children master the maximality property of definite plurals at a young age and with few or no exceptions, their acquisition of exhaustivity is less perfect and at a later age. I then show that the acquisition of exhaustivity is much more similar to the acquisition of universal quantification, and that it is typically the same children who make both sorts of errors. Thus, the acquisition evidence suggests that the exhaustivity of wh-questions is related to universal quantification rather than maximality.

The exhaustivity property that I'm referring to can be understood in a couple of different ways. The first is as the property of a question that makes it require an exhaustive answer, that is, an answer that lists all of the relevant individuals that are true as answers to the question. For example, if Dave, Linda and Malcolm are all in the kitchen, and nobody else is in the kitchen, then the exhaustivity property of the question in (1a) guarantees that (1b) is an appropriate answer and (1c) is not.

(1)   a. Who is in the kitchen?
        b. "Dave, Linda and Malcolm"
        c. #"Dave"

The other way that exhaustivity has been presented is in terms of properties of the subject of the matrix clause in a sentence in which the question is embedded. For example, assuming the scenario above, we can embed the question in (1a) under the verb *know*, as in (2a). The fact that (2a) entails (2b) and (2c) is a result of the fact that the question has

© 2006 by Uri Strauss
Tanja Heizmann (ed.): Current Issues in Acquisition. University of Massachusetts Occasional Papers in Linguistics 34, 161-171.
GLSA Amherst.

the property of *strong exhaustivity*, in the terms of Groenendijk and Stokhof (1982, 1984)[1].

(2)   a. Trevor knows who is in the kitchen
        b. For every X who is in the kitchen, Trevor knows that X is in the kitchen
        c. For every X who is not in the kitchen, Trevor knows that X is not in the kitchen

Although the properties are presented in different ways, they appear essentially to be equivalent. It would be possible, for instance, to get exhaustive answers from Groenendijk and Stokhof's strong exhaustivity by requiring that a proper answer name every X for which the predicate holds and none of the X's for which they do not hold. Therefore (1c) would be an inappropriate answer to (1a) because it fails to name individuals that need to be named, and an answer like #"Dave, Linda, Malcolm and Paul" would be inappropriate because it names individuals that ought not to be named[2].

The exhaustivity property, in whatever way we interpret it, is not inherent in all wh- questions. Some questions are understood as requiring an answer consisting of a single individual, and an exhaustive answer is in fact odd. Such questions, known as *mention some* questions (Groenendijk & Stokhof 1984, Beck & Rullmann 1999), are exemplified in (3).

(3)   a. Where can I find a bathroom around here?
        b. "There's one around the corner"
        c. #"There's one around the corner, one on the third floor, one on the fifth floor, and two on the eighth floor"

The same applies to embedded wh-questions.

(4)   a. I know where there is a bathroom around here
        b. There is a place X such that X is around here and a bathroom is in X, I know about X.
        c. #For every place X such that X is around here and a bathroom is in X, I know about X.

This fact does not undermine the notion that wh-questions are exhaustive. But it highlights the fact that exhaustivity is a property of some wh-questions, and not all of them. Explaining the nature of exhaustivity is still necessary.

2.   The Maximality Hypothesis

Rullmann (1995) combined the semantics of questions proposed by Karttunen (1977), in which the meaning of a question in a set of propositions, with the notion of maximality

---

[1] If (2a) had entailed (2b) but not (2c), it would have reflected the property of *weak exhaustivity*.
[2] Strong exhaustivity doesn't assert that there's symmetry between clauses (2b) and (2c). Therefore the fact that the violation of (2c) seems worse than the violation of (2c) is not a problem for this approach, though it does call for an explanation.

that is found in work on plurals. The result is strong exhaustivity of wh-questions, in the sense just discussed. For Karttunen, the meaning of a question is the set of true propositions that correspond to it. For example, on the scenario above, the meaning of *who is in the kitchen* would be as in (5a). Formally, this would be represented as in (5b), where p is a variable over propositions (sets of worlds) and w_0 is the actual world.

(5)   a. {Dave is in the kitchen, Linda is in the kitchen, Malcolm is in the kitchen}
        b. $\lambda p \exists x[p(w_0) \ \& \ p = \lambda w[\text{in-the-kitchen}(w)(x)]]$

Rullmann modifies this proposal by suggesting that instead of a set of several propositions, the meaning of a wh-question is the singleton set, which contains a single proposition with a plural entity that has all of the relevant individuals as atoms. In accordance with Rullmann's modification, the meaning of *who is in the kitchen* would be as in (6a), where *Dave + Linda + Malcolm* indicates the plural individual that has Dave, Linda and Malcolm as its atoms, and nobody else. Formally, this can be accomplished by using the *max* operation in the denotation of wh-questions, as in (6b).

(6)   a. {Dave + Linda + Malcolm is the maximal individual in the kitchen}
        b. $\iota p \exists x[p(w_0) \ \& \ p = \lambda w[x = max(\lambda y[\text{in-the-kitchen}(w)(y)])]]$

To understand what the *max* operator is doing here, and to set the stage for the discussion of acquisition later in the paper, let us take a look at the semantics of plural definites, where maximality is commonly applied.

Link (1983) proposes a theory of plurality that makes use of structured domains of individuals, which are partially related to each other in the part-of relation. The individuals are structured in an atomic join semilattice. For instance, if all of the atomic individuals in the domain we're dealing with are Dave, Linda and Malcolm, the domain is structured as follows:

(7)

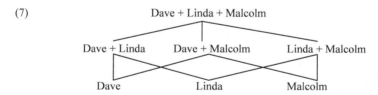

Various sets are defined on the domain. The set of elements is shown in (8a). The set of atomic elements is shown in (8b). The set of plural elements, which equals the set of elements – the set of atomic elements, is shown in (8c).

(8)   a. {Dave, Linda, Malcolm, Dave + Linda, Dave + Malcolm, Linda + Malcolm, Dave + Linda + Malcolm}
        b. {Dave, Linda, Malcolm}
        c. {Dave + Linda, Dave + Malcolm, Linda + Malcolm, Dave + Linda + Malcolm}

The maximal element in the structure can be defined as the element that has every other element as a subpart. Formally, the operator *max* applies to one of the defined sets and returns the maximal element in it. An example is in (9), in which *max* applies to the set of plural elements in our domain.

(9)   *max*({Dave + Linda, Dave + Malcolm, Linda + Malcolm, Dave + Linda + Malcolm}) = Dave + Linda + Malcolm

Link gives the definite article a semantics in terms of maximality. The denotation in (10) is a simplified version due to Rullmann. (Link gives DPs the semantics of generalized quantifiers.)

(10) $[[the\ N]] = max([[N]])$

If N is plural, the definite article applies to it and returns the maximal plural, as in (9). If N is singular, then the article will return the unique element in the set. If there is more than one atomic element, there is a presupposition failure, which nicely derives the fact that *the* has a uniqueness presupposition.

Using this system, we can understand how to get (6a) from (6b). (6b) can be phrased "the unique proposition such that there is an X such that the proposition is a set of worlds in which X is the maximal individual who is in the kitchen, and furthermore the proposition is true in the actual world". This can be simplified to "the unique set of worlds that has the same maximal individual who is in the kitchen as the actual world". If, as in our scenario, the maximal individual who is in the kitchen is *Dave + Linda + Malcolm*, then (6a) is derived.

The point of all this is that there's a plausible theory in which maximality is a central feature of the semantics of wh-questions, and in particular helps to explain the exhaustivity property of wh-questions. If this theory is correct, it makes a prediction about the acquisition of exhastivity: that it is similar to the acquisition of the concept of maximality in definite plurals. Children who have difficulty with maximality should make errors both in interpreting exhaustive wh-questions as exhaustive, and in interpreting definite plurals as maximal. As we see in the next section, this prediction is not supported by acquisition studies.

3.   Acquisition of Maximality and Exhaustivity

Johnson et al (1996) conducted an experiment which shows that children master the maximality property of definite plurals at an early age. They tested 26 children, ages 3 to 5. In the test, the children were given control of the character, Mikey, and his toy car, and told to act out the sentences they were told, which involved Mikey crashing into different things and knocking them over. The sentences were:

(11)   Mikey knocked over two of the trees
         Mikey knocked over one of the signs
         Mikey knocked over the chairs

All the children who were tested succeeded on all of these tasks, knocking over exactly the right objects. In particular, when given the last sentence they drove Mikey into all of the chairs, showing that they understand the definite plural to be maximal. If children by age 3 master maximality, then Rullmann's hypothesis predicts that children should easily acquire exhaustivity in wh-questions by that age. Therefore we expect that when asked wh-questions that call for an exhaustive answer, children should consistently respond with exhaustive answers. In fact, this is not what we find.

On the DSLT test (Seymour et al) there are 9 questions of three types in which nonexhaustive answers can potentially be given, including 6 questions of two types in which the correct answer is exhaustive. Examples of the three types of questions follow.

(12)   i. The child is shown a picture of a boy playing with a train set and a girl playing with a teddy bear. The child is told the following: "Saturday morning my brother and I were playing with toys". After a pause, the child is asked, "What were they *playing* with?" (emphasis on "playing".)   This question targets exhaustive answers. For example, one correct answer to this question would be "a train and teddy bear". An example of a nonexhaustive answer is "a train".

         ii. The child is shown a picture in which the boy is putting on his pants and the girl is putting on a sweater. The story from above continues: "Then Mother said, 'Do you want to go to the zoo?' Tom and I both said yes. So Mother said, 'get ready', and we put on our outdoor clothes." After a pause, the child is asked, "They put on *what*?" (Emphasis on "what".) This question targets echo readings – the correct response is "outdoor clothes". Many children erroneously responses with exhaustive answers like "pants and a sweater", and some even responded with nonexhaustive answers like "a sweater".

         iii. The child is shown a picture of a man eating an apple and a baby eating a banana, and told, "This father and this baby were having lunch together". After a pause, the child is asked, *"Who* ate *what?"* (Emphasis on both wh-words). This question targets answers that are both paired and exhaustive, like "the father ate an apple and the baby ate a banana". Incorrect answers include those that are exhaustive but not paired, paired but not exhaustive, and neither paired nor exhaustive. The last two sorts of answers were counted as nonexhaustive.

I analyzed data from 1295 children, ages 4-12 (mean age roughly 7 years, median between 6 and 7 years), who took the DSLT tryout. I found a significant number of cases among both normal and disordered children in which the children gave nonexhaustive answers to these questions.

(13)   Nonexhaustive answers: normal vs. disordered

# of Errors:	Normal	Disordered	Overall
0	699	269	968
1	135	75	210
2+	55	62	117

The total of nonexhaustive answers was higher at the younger ages, then quickly declined.

(14)   Nonexhaustive answers by age

Age:	4	5	6	7	8	9	10	11	12
Errors/child:	0.93	0.48	0.38	0.37	0.15	0.15	0.02	0.02	0.09

This result shows that unlike the situation with definite plurals, children make a fair number of mistakes of exhaustivity in answering wh-questions, especially younger children. This casts doubt on Rullmann's hypothesis that maximality is the common denominator in the two cases.

If not maximality, then what is it about the semantics of wh-questions that requires answers to be exhaustive? I will suggest that the acquisition data supports an explanation in terms of universal quantification. In the next section I will bring the evidence from acquisition of universal quantification.

4.   Acquisition of the universal quantifier

The DSLT includes a section on quantifiers with several different sorts of questions. There are two questions that test the child's understanding of the most basic use of the universal quantifier. An example is the following:

(15)   The child is shown a picture in which three women are on boats and one woman is on the shore, and is asked, "Is every woman sailing a boat?"

If the child answers yes, this is taken as an indication that she has not achieved basic proficiency in universal quantification. It turns out that a fair number of children make one or more errors of this type. In fact, 39.3% of the normal (non-disordered) children made one or two errors on the two questions. If disordered children are included, the percentage rises to 42.9% of children. The following chart shows the breakdown by category of children and number of errors[3].

---

[3] The DSLT results are inconsistent with the previous findings of Philip (1995), who found a much lower rate of errors. However, even the rate of errors Philip reported (roughly 20%, in preschool children) would be significantly greater in percentage terms than the errors reported by Johnson et al for definite plurals, which is 0% (see section 3). Philip tested 276 monolingual English and monolingual Japanese preschoolers, mean age 4 years 9 months for the 223 English speakers, 5 years 4 months for the 53 Japanese speakers,

(16)

	Normal	Disorder	Overall
0 errors	540 (60.7%)	200 (49.3%)	740 (57.1%)
1 error	128 (14.4%)	74 (18.2%)	202 (15.6%)
2 errors	221 (24.9%)	132 (32.5%)	353 (27.3%)
Total	889	406	1295

So unlike maximality in the definite plural, universal quantification is not something that children acquire easily. This makes it a plausible candidate for the semantics of exhaustivity in wh-questions, where children also make a fair number of mistakes.

There are two more pieces of evidence from the acquisition of universal quantification that support the notion that universality and exhaustivity are acquired together.

The first is the age pattern of the errors. Both in the case of universal quantification and wh-exhaustivity, there is a sharp drop in errors as age progresses, as the following graphs show[4]:

---

and found that 14 (5.1%) consistently made errors on the kind of question I have described, while 46 (16.7%) made one or more errors. That's a total of 60 (21.8%) who have not mastered the basics of universal quantification.

Note that the difference in results cannot be explained by fact that many of the children who took the DSLT were diagnosed as disordered, because the percentage of non-disordered children who failed the quantification part if the DSLT is much higher (39.3% to 21.8%) than in Philip's study. The difference cannot be explained by age bias either, because the mean age for the children in the DSLT study is much higher (about 7 years) than the mean age in Philip's study. I do not have an explanation for the dramatically different results of the two studies.

[4] It shouldn't be taken for granted that this pattern is universal. Many errors show different patterns of resolution. For example, quantifier spreading errors (Roeper & de Villiers 1991, Philip 1995, Crain et al 1996, and many others) remain at their peak until roughly age 7, and decline more gradually, persisting until age 12 for some speakers, and possibly beyond.

(17)   Quantifier errors

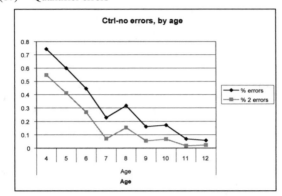

(18)   Exhaustivity errors

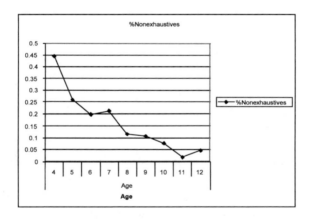

The second piece of evidence is that the children who make errors with universal quantification are frequently the same children who make errors with wh-exhaustiveness. The following table illustrates.

(19)   Wh-exhaustivity errors: 0   1   2+
               Universal errors:

	0	1	2+
0	84.9	11.2	3.9
1	63.9	23.3	12.9
2	59.8	22.4	17.6

The table should be read: out of the children who make N quantifier errors (N from the leftmost column), the percentage who made M errors of wh-exhaustivity (M from the top row) is O (the result from the table). Looking at the table, we can see that making one or two errors of universal quantification is associated with a much higher probability of making one or more errors of exhaustivity.

A chi-squared test on this table was conducted, as follows: assuming independence of the two kinds of errors, we would expect children making one or two errors on the quantifier test to make errors of exhaustivity at the same rate as the children who had no quantifier errors. That is, we expect 84.9% of children making 1 error of universal quantification to make no errors of exhaustivity, 11.2% to make one error of exhaustivity, and 3.9% to make two errors of exhaustivity. The same percentages apply to the children making two errors of universal quantification. The following table gives the predicted results in raw numbers and percentages:

(20)   Predicted results

	Wh-exhaustivity errors: 0	1	2+
Universal errors:			
1	171 (84.9%)	23 (11.2%)	1 (3.9%)
2	300 (84.9%)	40 (11.2%)	2 (3.9%)

The actual results are as follows (percentages are indicated in the table in 19).

(21)   Observed results

	Wh-exhaustivity errors: 0	1	2+
Universal errors:			
1	129	47	26
2	211	80	62

We see that the observed results have a much higher number of errors than what we would expect if the two sorts of errors were independent. The number of children who made one error of exhaustivity is about twice as high as expected, and the number who made two or more errors of exhaustivity is 25-30 times as high as expected. A chi-squared test on the expected vs. actual results reveals that the probability that this discrepancy is due to chance is $p < 0.00000000001$, or less than one in ten billion. We can conclude that there is a relationship between wh-exhaustivity errors and errors of universal quantification.

5.   Conclusion

What the nature of this relationship is cannot be deduced just from statistical analysis. But an obvious hypothesis suggests itself: that exhaustivity in answering wh-questions has to do with universal quantification over the individuals for whom the answer is true. For example, we might say that the question *who is in the kitchen?* is exhaustive because there is a condition like the following on the answer to it:

(22)   For every X, if X is in the kitchen, then X must be mentioned in the answer.

I will not develop such an approach here. What I have done is simply shown that an explanation of the exhaustivity property of wh-questions that uses universal quantification over individuals rather than maximality is better positioned to deal with the acquisition data that I have presented.

References

Beck, Sigrid and Hotze Rullmann (1999). A flexible approach to exhaustivity in questions. *Natural Language Semantics* 7: 249-298.

Crain, Stephen, Rosalind Thornton, Carole Boster, Laura Conway, Diane Lillo-Martin and Elaine Woodams (1996). Quantification without qualification. *Language Acquisition* 5: 83-153.

Groenendijk, Jeroen and Martin Stokhof (1982). Semantic analysis of wh-complements. *Linguistics and Philosophy* 5: 175-233.

Groenendijk, Jeroen and Martin Stokhof (1984). *Studies on the Semantics of Questions and the Pragmatics of Answers*. PhD dissertation, University of Amsterdam.

Johnson, Kyle, Sarah Bateman, Deanna Moore, Tom Roeper and Jill de Villers (1996). On the acquisition of word order in nominals. Pages 397-406 in Andy Stringfellow, Dalia Cahana-Amitay, Elizabeth Hughes and Andrea Zukowski (eds.) *Proceedings of the 20th Annual Boston University Conference on Language Development*. Somervile, MA: Cascadilla Press.

Karttunen, Lauri (1977). Syntax and semantics of questions. *Linguistics and Philosophy* 1: 3-44.

Link, Godehard (1983). The logical analysis of plurals and mass terms. Pages 303-323 in Rainer Bauerle, Cristophe Schwarze, and Arnim on Stechow (eds.), *Meaning, Use and Interpretation of Language*. Berlin: de Gruyter.

Philip, William (1995). *Event Quantification in the Acquisition of Universal Quantification*. PhD dissertation, University of Massachusetts.

Roeper, Tom and Jill de Villiers (1991). The emergence of bound variable structures. pages 225-265 in Thomas Maxfield and Bernadette Plunkett (eds.), *Papers in the Acquisition of Wh*. Amherst, MA: GLSA Publications.

Rullmann, Hotze (1995). *Maximality in the Semantics of Wh-Constructions*. PhD dissertation, University if Massachusetts.

Seymour, Harry, Tom Roeper and Jill de Villiers. *Development and Validation of a Language Test for Children Speaking Non-Standard English: A Study of Children*

Who Speak Black English. National Institute on Deafness and Other Communication Disorders under Contract # N01 DC8-2104 to Harry N. Seymour, P.I.

Department of Linguistics
South College
University of Massachusetts, Amherst
Amherst, MA 01003

uri@linguist.umass.edu

Acquisition of Supplementary Expressions[*]

Anna Verbuk

UMass, Amherst

1.   Introduction

The present experiment was designed in order to investigate the hypothesis that multidimensionality is an innate part of UG. A broader experimental goal was to explore how the acquisition of supplementary expressions that generate conventional implicatures takes place. Prior to the work on conventional implicatures in Bach (1999) and Potts (2003a), expressions such as *therefore, still* and *but* were viewed as giving rise to conventional implicatures. Potts (2003a) demonstrates that supplementary relatives, nominal appositives, and speaker- and utterance-oriented adverbs, inter alia, generate the type of meanings that was originally conceived of by Grice as conventional implicature, and thus give rise to multidimensional meanings. Apart from the experimental question of whether or not multidimensionality is an innate part of UG, the present study will also explore the possibility that certain properties of supplementary expressions, such as the property of being speaker-oriented meanings, are acquired at a later stage. Another issue that will be explored here is children's ability to utilize information from the syntax and phonology modules in interpreting supplementary expressions as generating multidimensional meanings.

The paper is organized as follows. Section 1 is the introduction. In section 2, I discuss Grice's original conception of conventional implicatures (henceforth CIs) and Bach's 1999 discussion of some prevalent misconceptions regarding CIs as a class of meanings. Potts' (2003a) neo-Gricean theory of CIs and his arguments for treating CIs as contributing mutidimensional meanings are introduced in section 3. The present experimental work and its implications are discussed in section 4. It is argued that, while the concept of multidimensionality is not immediately utilized by the younger child for

---

[*] I would like to thank Tom Roeper for many kinds of help with this work that are too numerous to mention here and for encouragement; I would also like to thank Chris Potts for insightful discussion and criticism of this work. I am also grateful to Liane Jeschull and Francesca Foppolo for giving me helpful feedback on this work. Thanks are also due to my fellow students at UMass, Amherst.

Tanja Heizmann (ed.): Current Issues in Acquisition. University of Massachusetts Occasional Papers in Linguistics 34, 173-198.
GLSA Amherst.

syntactically ambiguous constructions, children are able to compute multidimensional meanings when single-dimensional interpretations are excluded by the syntax. Thus the youngest children tested were able to correctly interpret syntactically unambiguous constructions with supplementary relatives in which a Proper Noun was used as a head noun but not the potentially ambiguous constructions in which a Common Noun was used as a head noun.

Section 4.2.1. is devoted to the discussion of the experiment on the acquisition of supplementary relatives; the non-adult stage children go through in acquiring these constructions is discussed in detail. In section 4.2.2., the experiment on the acquisition of speaker- and utterance-oriented adverbs is introduced. It is argued that utterance-oriented adverbs are acquired earlier than speaker-oriented adverbs because only in the case of the former the connection between the VP-modifier uses that are acquired first and the sentential uses is transparent.

In section 5, the results of the present study are summarized. In acquiring supplementary expressions, children go through a stage where they interpret them as contributing single-dimensional meanings. However, when a single-dimensional interpretation is excluded by the syntax, even the youngest children are able to interpret supplementary expressions as contributing multidimensional meanings. On the basis of this evidence, it is argued that the present study provides preliminary support for the experimental hypothesis that multidimensionality is an innate part of UG.

2.   Toward Redefining Conventional Implicatures

In this section, Grice's original definition of conventional implicatures, Karttunen and Peters' (1979) and Bach's (1999) seminal treatments of conventional implicatures are discussed. Prior to the fairly recent work on conventional implicatures in Bach (1999) and Potts (2003a), lexical items like *therefore, even, but, again, yet* and *still* were viewed as giving rise to conventional implicatures (Kempson 1975, Wilson 1975, Karttunen and Peters, 1979, Levinson 1983). Originally, conventional implicatures were identified as a class of meanings by Grice (1975). Grice distinguishes conventional implicatures from conversational implicatures by arguing that, while the meaning of the latter is calculable from the conversational maxims and the Cooperative Principle, the meaning of conventional implicatures is contributed by the lexical meanings of words. Importantly, if the content of a conventional implicature turns out to be false, the proposition as a whole may still be true; this distinguishes conventional implicatures from entailments. Consider the following construction that, according to Grice, gives rise to a conventional implicature.

(1)   She is poor but she is honest

CI: There is some sort of a contrast between being poor and being honest

(Grice, 1961 p. 127).

Karttunen and Peters (1979) identify Grice's notion of conventional implicature with the notion of presupposition. Thus they define conventional implicatures as inferences that belong to the common set of assumptions accepted by the interlocutors. Karttunen and Peters argue that several classes of expressions that were previously viewed as generating presuppositions ought to be classified as giving rise to conventional implicatures, which includes the class of particles, such as *too, either, also, even* and *only* (Karttunen and Peters 1979, p. 11).

Bach (1999) argues that lexical items that were traditionally viewed as giving rise to conventional implicatures, such as *but, still* and *even*, in fact, make truth-conditional contributions to utterances, i.e., contribute to what is said and not to what is implicated. On the view that lexical items like *but* contribute conventional implicatures, the sentence in (2) has a truth-conditional meaning in (3) and a conventional implicature to the effect that there is some sort of a contrast between being huge and being agile.

(2)   Shaq is huge but he is agile

(3)   Shaq is huge and he is agile

(Bach 1999, p. 1).

Bach speculates that the reason why lexical items like *but, still* and *even* were traditionally viewed as contributing non-truth-conditional meanings is that these lexical items contribute meanings that are secondary to the main point of the utterance. Crucially, Bach demonstrates that the lexical items in question make *truth-conditional* contributions to utterances on the basis of the fact that they fail to scope out of embedded clauses.

(4)   Ben, "John said that she was in advertising but that she was poor. # He wasn't suggesting that it's unusual for someone who is advertising to be poor, though."

In (4), *but* is embedded in an indirect quotation of John's utterance. The only possible construal of (4) is that the contrast between her being honest and her being poor is part of the meaning of John's utterance; this is what makes the continuation infelicitous. Bach (1999) argues that conventional implicatures ought to be abolished as a class of meanings on the basis of the fact that no natural language lexical items contribute the type of non-truth-conditional meanings originally conceived of by Grice as conventional implicatures, a view that will be challenged in this paper.

3.   Conventional Implicatures as an Independent Class of Meanings

Section 3 introduces Potts' (2003a) theory of conventional implicatures. In The Logic of Conventional Implicatures (2003a), Potts makes a case for resurrecting Grice's original classification of a certain type of meanings as conventional implicatures. Potts demonstrates that supplementary expressions and expressives give rise to meanings that may be classified as conventional implicatures in Grice's sense of the term, and propounds a formal semantic analysis of conventional implicatures that sharply distinguishes them from other kinds of meanings. First, consider what types of expressions Potts (2003a) classifies as CI-generating.

3.1   Types of Expressions that Give Rise to CIs

The following types of expressions give rise to CIs.
I. Supplemental (appositive) expressions
i. Supplemental clauses
a. As-Clause

(5)   Ames was, as the press reported, a successful spy.

b. Supplementary Relative

(6)   Ames, who stole from the FBI, is now behind bars.

c. Nominal Appositive

(7)   Ames, the former spy, is now behind bars.

ii. Adverbs
a. Topic-oriented

(8)   Wisely, Beck started his descent.

b. Speaker-oriented

(9)   Luckily, Beck survived the descent

c. Utterance-oriented

(10)   Just between you and me, Ames is a dangerous spy

II. Expressives

Next, consider Potts' definition of conventional implicatures.

(i). CIs are part of the conventional (lexical) meaning of words.
(ii). CIs are commitments, and thus give rise to entailments.
(iii). These commitments are made by the speaker of the utterance "by virtue of the meaning of the words that he chooses" (Potts, 2003a, p. 9).
(iv). CIs are logically and compositionally independent of what is "said (in the favored sense)", i.e., independent of the at-issue entailments (Potts, 2003a, p. 9).

In order to explicate why the seemingly disparate classes of expressions listed above are taken in (Potts 2003a) to contribute conventional implicatures, and why conventional implicatures do constitute an independent class of meanings, it will be helpful to spell out the underlying assumptions of each of the statements constituting Potts' definition of conventional implicatures. According to (i), CIs are lexical meanings. All of the CI-generating supplementary expressions listed above are separated from the rest of the sentence by comma intonation. In Potts' (2003a) semantics for the CIs, in case of supplementary expressions, the shift from at-issue to CI content is "achieved by the semantic reflex of the syntactic feature COMMA." Because comma intonation is, in some cases, the only clue to the effect that a supplementary expression should not be interpreted as an integrated phrase but as contributing a CI, in terms of the acquisition of supplementary expressions, it is crucial to investigate whether or not children are able to interpret comma intonation. I will return to this point in the discussion of the acquisition of supplementary relatives.

According to the statement in (ii), "CIs are commitments, and thus give rise to entailments." The purpose of this clause of the definition is to distinguish conventional implicatures from conversational implicatures and presuppositions, both of which are cancelable. Because, as a result of Karttunen and Peters' (1979) seminal paper on presupposition projection, the notions of presupposition and conventional implicature have become interchangeable, here, I will concentrate on contrasting conventional implicatures with presuppositions. Potts argues that, while presuppositions may get filtered out due to semantic properties of constructions they are in, this is not the case with conventional implicatures. Whereas plugs (e.g., verbs of saying) prevent presuppositions from being projected, conventional implicatures always take the widest scope in the sentence. In this respect, conventional implicatures are akin to entailments.

(11)   John told us that Mary, who recently stopped drinking wine for breakfast, has always been a teetotaler. # So Mary never drank wine for breakfast.

>> Mary recently stopped drinking wine for breakfast

The attempt to cancel the conventional implicature contributed by the supplementary relative in (11) makes the discourse incoherent. Note also that the first sentence of (11) is coherent precisely because the content of the supplementary relative is not attributed to John but to the speaker of the sentence.

Conventional implicatures have the status of entailments and the mechanism by which their content may be removed is qualitively different from that by which conversational implicatures and presuppositions are cancelled. The content of conventional implicatures may be removed through the hearer's correction of the speaker; alternatively, the speaker himself may remove through self-correction the content of the implicature that he introduced. Crucially, after the content of the CI has been removed, the content of the at-issue proposition should still be recoverable. Consider an illustration of this in (12).

(12)   A: The woman in the corner, a cat lover, is petting a dog.
        B: Actually, she is not a cat lover.

While the implicature that the woman in the corner is a cat lover has been removed, the at-issue proposition that she is petting a dog can still be recovered.

According to the third clause of Potts' definition, conventional implicatures are "commitments... made by the speaker of the utterance by virtue of the meaning of the words that he chooses." What distinguishes conventional implicatures from conversational implicatures, presuppositions and entailments is that they are the only speaker-oriented type of meanings. Consider an illustration of this.

(13)   Mark said to himself, "Little Julie thought that the animal in the corner, a puppy, was a cat."

        >> Mark thought that the animal in the corner was a puppy

The implicature in (13) is contributed by the content of the nominal appositive *a puppy* and is attributed solely to Mark, who is the speaker of the sentence in which the NA is used.

Crucially, CIs contribute multidimensional meanings that belong to a different plane of meanings than regular entailments. According to the last clause of Potts' definition, conventional implicatures "are logically and compositionally independent of what is "said (in the favored sense)", i.e., independent of the at-issue entailments." What is meant by "at-issue entailments" is the regular asserted content of the sentence that determines its truth conditions. At-issue entailments determine the main themes of a discourse. The content of conventional implicatures provides comments on the at-issue content or guides the discourse in a particular direction. Consider an illustration of this.

(14)   The girl in the blue sandals, who was the youngest, watched the others build the castle.

        At-issue entailment: the girl in the blue sandals watched the others build the castle

        CI: The girl in the blue sandals was the youngest

Because conventional implicatures contribute multidimensional meanings, their content is independent from that of at-issue propositions. Potts' (2003a) rule of CI Application captures this intuition. When a conventional implicature term applies to an at-issue input, the result is a pair of terms – a CI term and an at-issue term – each interpreted independently by parsetree interpretation. Crucially, the at-issue content is passed on unmodified. "If we were to snip off all CI terms from a parsetree, we would find its at-issue value unchanged" (Potts, p. 117).

Next, consider the syntactic assumptions made in (Potts 2003a). Accounting for the special status of supplementary relatives in their semantics, Potts adopts a conservative syntax for nonrestrictive relatives. In case of nonrestrictive relative clauses, a CP that contains the clause is adjoined at the DP level; in case of restrictive relative clauses, a CP containing the relative clause is attached to an NP. Nominal appositives are adjoined at the DP level; the CI-contributing adverbs adjoin to Spec CP.

4.   The Experiment

The present experiment was designed in order to test the hypothesis that multidimensionality is an innate part of UG, which is consistent with the continuity assumption. The concept of continuity was first introduced in Macnamara (1982) and Pinker (1984). Pinker's original argument was that, in view of the learnability problem, the most explanatory theory will posit the fewest developmental changes in the child's cognitive and grammatical mechanisms. The continuity assumption is that, in the absence of evidence to the contrary, the child's grammar should be assumed to be identical with that of an adult. One of the natural consequences of the continuity hypothesis is that child and adult languages differ only in ways in which adult languages differ from each other. While in earlier work in the generative tradition, the system of Principles and Parameters was viewed as constituting the innately available UG, in more recent work, the notion of continuity has also been extended to the pragmatics and discourse modules (Avrutin 1999 and van der Weert 2003, inter alia). This fact is relevant to the present work because the child's success in fulfilling the experimental task depended on his ability to make use of the discourse knowledge. Specifically, the child was to rely on the knowledge that supplementary expressions contribute meanings whose discourse status is that of speaker-oriented comments in order to correctly interpret the experimental scenarios. In accordance with the continuity assumption, the experimental hypothesis is that the concept of multidimensionality is available to the child from the beginning.

It needs to be noted here that the nature of the present experiment is purely exploratory – children were tested on few stories containing each type of a CI-contributing expression; moreover, children of a broad age range took part in the experiment. In view of this, no statistical analysis of the data was performed.

4.1   The Method

A total of 16 children between the ages of 5 and 10 were tested. The experimenter read 9 – 11 scenarios with CI-contributing items to each child. Subsequently, the child was asked questions testing her ability to interpret the supplementary expression in question as a CI-contributing expression. The sessions were audio-taped and the children's responses were subsequently transcribed by the experimenter.

4.2   Types of Expressions Used in the Experiment

In section 4.2, the types of expressions employed in the present experiment and the
specific questions children were asked regarding different types of scenarios are
discussed in brief. Supplementary relatives and speaker- and utterance-oriented adverbs
were the constructions used in the present experiment. While in the case of
supplementary relatives the content of the conventional implicature may be removed
through providing new contextual information, in the case of CI-contributing uses of
adverbs such as *luckily* and *honestly*, this is either implausible or downright impossible.
The scenarios testing the acquisition of supplementary relatives require children to be
able to recover the at-issue content after the content of the conventional implicature has
been removed. The scenarios testing the acquisition of adverbs require children merely to
distinguish between the VP-modifier and the speaker or utterance-oriented uses of the
adverbs; these scenarios are designed to test how children acquire the knowledge that
certain classes of the adverbs may give rise to conventional implicatures.

4.2.1   Supplementary Relatives

In 4.2.1, experimental scenarios with supplementary relatives are discussed in more
detail. Because conventional implicatures have the status of entailments, they cannot be
cancelled through speaker self-correction; attempts to cancel them in this manner raise
issues of speaker credibility. In view of this, I designed my scenarios so that the content
of the conventional implicature was removed as a natural consequence of the events of
the story. Subsequently, children were asked to recover the at-issue proposition once the
content of the implicature had been removed. Children were also asked about the content
of the implicature. As an illustration, consider one of the scenarios in which a
supplementary relative is used.

(15)   The Skiing Competition

Mark and Julie's family moved to a different city and Mark went to a new school. One
day, Mark's new class had a skiing competition. He did his best and came in second.
Mark thought that the winner of the competition had longer skis than everybody else.
When Mark came home, his mother asked him how the competition went. Mark said, "I
came in second. <u>The boy with red hair, who had the longest skis, won the competition</u>."
Later, Mark found out that their coach gave everybody skis of the same length. The boy
with red hair was pretty short, and that's why his skis looked long on him.

(1) Did the boy with red hair win the competition?
The Adult Response: Yes
Why?

(2) Did the boy with red hair have the longest skis?

The Adult Response: No
Why?
I will refer to the Skiing Competition scenario in discussing the acquisition of constructions in which the DP that has the semantics of a definite description is used as a head noun.

4.2.1.1 Common Nouns as Anchors

In 4.2.1.1, the acquisition of constructions in which a Common Noun anchors the relative is discussed. First, it will be useful to define the term "anchor"; this term was introduced in Huddlston and Pullum (2002) and it refers to the syntactic head of the phrase. Thus supplementary relatives and nominal appositives are "anchored" by syntactic heads. The following two types of constructions with supplementary relatives were used in the scenarios. The supplementary relative was anchored either by a Proper Noun or by a Common Noun. Constructions of the second type may have been misconstrued as restrictive relative clauses (16).

(16)   The boy with red hair, who had the longest skis, won the competition.

When a Common Noun anchored the relative, comma intonation was the only clue to the effect that a nonrestrictive rather than a restrictive relative clause interpretation was intended. If children misinterpret these constructions, this may be due to syntactic, semantic or phonological reasons, or due to the interaction of all three. First, it needs to be noted here that comma intonation is not a perfect and unique trigger for CI. On the one hand, comma intonation is used in a variety of constructions that do not give rise to CIs. Comma intonation is complemented with the presence of a low tone (L*) and at the end of the parenthetical. However, the end of an IP is also typically signaled by L* and a pause in English. Adverbs such as *carefully* that do not generate CIs are nonetheless separated by comma intonation from the rest of the sentence when they occur sentence-initially. Conversely, not all classes of CI-generating expressions are separated from the rest of the sentence by comma intonation. For instance, comma intonation does not separate an expressive from the rest of the sentence in English. In view of the fact that the child does need to be able to recognize comma intonation complemented with the presence of a low tone in order to recognize IP boundaries, it is unlikely that the children who participated in the present experiment, aged five to ten, have not learned to recognize this particular intonational pattern. This leaves us with the following two alternatives to consider.

One possibility is that children do recognize comma intonation phonologically but are not aware of the comma-CI connection. Thus the failure to make the comma-CI connection prevents the child from correctly interpreting supplementary relatives modifying DPs that have the semantics of definite descriptions. The child may be at a stage where he has acquired the syntax of restrictive and non-restrictive clauses. It may also be the case that at this stage the child is able to interpret CI-contributing items as such in environments in which he does not have to interpret comma intonation in order to arrive at these meanings. For instance, the child may be able to interpret epithets as contributing conventional implicatures. Thus, at this stage, the child has not acquired the fact that, in case of constructions with the relatives, comma intonation does serve as a clue to the effect that the relative contributes a CI.

Another possibility is that the child is aware of the comma-CI connection but that he has a strong preference for single-dimensional readings. Because comma intonation does not always serve as a clue to the effect that a CI meaning is intended in English, the child reasons that, in constructions with the relatives, comma intonation is not a reliable indicator of whether or not a CI meaning is intended either. My experimental results do not distinguish between these two possibilities because in either case the child will end up misinterpreting nonrestrictive relatives as contributing single-dimensional meanings. However, in the future experimental work, it will be crucial to tease these two possibilities apart.

Syntactically, the child may be at a stage where he has acquired the syntax and semantics of restrictive relative clauses but not those of their nonrestrictive counterparts. Thus the child will assume that nonrestrictive relatives are adjoined at the NP level; semantically, he will analyze nonrestrictive relatives as restrictive as well. In his responses to the questions following the scenarios, he will consistently treat nonrestrictive relatives as restrictive. Thus the child will misconstrue nonrestrictive relatives anchored by Common and Proper Nouns alike as restrictive. It will be demonstrated that 80% of the youngest children tested correctly interpreted nonrestrictive relatives headed by Proper Nouns as such. This result demonstrates that children who were tested did not misanalyze all nonrestrictive relatives as restrictive because they were at a stage where they have not acquired the syntax of nonrestrictive relatives. On the contrary, even the youngest children tested were aware of the syntactic differences between the two types of constructions.

Next, consider another alternative. The child may be at a stage where he has acquired the fact that restrictive relative clauses are adjoined at the NP level and their nonrestrictive counterparts are adjoined at the DP level; at this stage, the child may be unsure whether or not restrictive and nonrestrictive relatives have the same semantics. As a result of this, the child may some of the time analyze nonrestrictive relatives as restrictive and some of the time analyze constructions with nonrestrictive relatives as if the proposition contributed by the supplementary expression as well as the proposition contributed by the at-issue assertion had the status of entailments. At this stage, the child has yet to acquire the fact that nonrestrictive relative clauses always give rise to conventional implicatures. It was found that the majority of the five-year-olds interpreted the construction where a Common Noun anchored the relative precisely in these two ways. None of the five-year-olds provided the target response to the scenario in question. Only 9-10 year-olds had a 100% rate of adult responses. The results are summarized in tables 1 and 2.

Common Noun as an Anchor																
Subject	M	S	N	B1	B2	K	M.O	M.A	J1	P	B3	L	J2	H	C	B4
Age	5	5	5	5	5	6	6	7	7	7	8	8	9	9	10	10
At-Issue	Y	D/K	D/K	Y	N	Y	Y	Y	N	Y	Y	Y	Y	Y	Y	Y
CI	Y	D/K	D/K	Y	N	Y	N	N	N	N	N	Y	N	N	N	N

Table 1. Supplementary Relative Anchored by a Common Noun.

The Key: "Y" stands for "yes"; "N" stands for "no"; "D/K" stands for "don't know."
The target response in tables 1 and 2: At-Issue Proposition: Yes (recovered);
CI: No (canceled).

Common Noun as an Anchor	#	%
Subjects	16	100
Target responses to both questions	8	50
Target responses to the question concerning the at-issue proposition	12	75
Target responses to the question concerning the CI	10	62.5
Children who treat CIs as non-cancelable entailments	4	25
Children who misinterpret nonrestrictive relatives as restrictive	2	12.5
Children who answer "don't know" to both questions	2	12.5

Table 2. Supplementary Relative Anchored by a Common Noun (summary of results).

4.2.1.2 Proper Nouns as Anchors

In 4.2.1.2, the scenario in which the relative is anchored by a Proper Noun is discussed. Consider the construction with a supplementary relative employed in the scenario in question.

(17) Little Julie, who found a pink pencil, drew a pink Barbie doll.

Proper Noun as an Anchor																
Subject	M	S	N	B1	B2	K	M.O.	M.A	J1	P	B3	L	J2	H	C	B4
Age	5	5	5	5	5	6	6	7	7	7	8	8	9	9	10	10
At-Issue	Y	D/K	Y	Y	Y	Y	Y	Y	N	Y	Y	Y	Y	Y	Y	N
CI	N	D/K	N	N	N	N	N	N	Y	N	N	N	N	N	N	N

Table 3. Supplementary Relative Anchored by a Proper Noun.

Proper Noun as an Anchor	#	%
Subjects	16	100
Target responses to both questions	13	81
Target responses to the question concerning the at-issue proposition	13	81
Target responses to the question concerning the CI	14	87.5
Children who treat CIs as non-cancelable entailments	0	0
Children who misinterpret nonrestrictive relatives as restrictive	1	6
Children who answer "don't know" to both questions	1	6

Table 4. Supplementary Relative Anchored by a Proper Noun (summary of results).

The Proper Noun scenario was designed to make it as easy as possible to distinguish between the at-issue and the conventional implicature dimensions of meaning. In this scenario, the only grammatical interpretation of the construction in question was the nonrestrictive relative clause interpretation. This scenario was predicted to be easier than its definite description counterpart also because a proper name functioned as a rigid designator that fixed the referent once and for all; whether or not the person referred to by the proper name possessed certain properties was immaterial. It was found that using a proper noun as an anchor dramatically improved children's performance. Thus the youngest children tested, the five-year-olds, provided 80% of target responses to this scenario. Children aged 6-10 had practically the same rate of target responses to this scenario – 81%, which is additional evidence to the effect that even the youngest children already demonstrate mastery of this construction.

It needs to be noted here that these results reflect children's responses to two experimental scenarios – one of them being the scenario where a Proper Noun was used as an anchor and another one being the scenario where a Common Noun anchors the relative. While the overall difference between children's responses to these scenarios is significant, the present experimental results may not be construed as providing sufficient information regarding individual children's performance on a certain type of a construction.

4.2.1.3 Stage One

In section 4.2.1.3, I discuss the first stage that children go through in acquiring supplementary relatives, during which supplementary relatives are misconstrued either as giving rise to entailments (section 4.2.1.3.1) or as restrictive (section 4.2.1.3.2).

4.2.1.3.1 CIs as Entailments (Yes / Yes Responses)

The proposition contributed by the supplementary expression as well as the proposition contributed by the at-issue assertion are treated as entailments.

(18)   The boy with red hair, who had the longest skis, won the competition.

Entailment One: The boy with red hair won the competition

Entailment Two: The boy with red hair had the longest skis

Five to six-year-olds as well as some seven-year-olds answer positively when inquired about the truth-value of the at-issue proposition as well as about the truth-value of the CI; they ignore the fact that the CI has been cancelled.

Consider again the final part of the Skiing scenario in (15) and five-year-old M's responses to it.

(1)   Did the boy with red hair win the competition?
       M. (5 y. o.): "Yes, cause he liked skiing"

(2)   Did the boy with red hair have the longest skis?
       M. (5 y. o.): "Yes. Cause he wants his skis."

If, syntactically, the child acquires arguments before acquiring adjuncts, it is plausible that the order of semantic acquisition is the same; when the child encounters a challenging construction, he will hypothesize that both clauses of this construction contribute entailments.

4.2.1.3.2 Nonrestrictive Relatives as Restrictive (No / No Responses)

Alternatively, during this stage the child may misconstrue nonrestrictive relatives as restrictive. When this is the case, removing the conventional implicature entails for the child canceling the content of the at-issue proposition. At this stage, children answer negatively when questioned about the truth-value of the at-issue proposition; when questioned about the truth-value of the proposition contributed by the supplementary relative, children answer negatively as well. It will be illustrated below that, in effect, children misinterpret nonrestrictive relatives anchored by definite DPs as restrictive. In the scenario in which the relative was anchored by a Common Noun, a definite DP was employed as an anchor. In and of itself, the use of the definite article contributes an existential presupposition. Thus the sentence in (19) in which a restrictive relative is used has an existential presupposition provided in (20).

(19)   The man who invented television was highly educated.

(20)   Presupposition: A man invented television

Next, consider a version of (19) with a nonrestrictive relative in lieu of the restrictive one.

(21)   The man, who invented television, was highly educated.
        a. At-Issue: The man was highly educated
        b. CI: The man invented television
        c. Presupposition: A man exists

The sentence in (21) has an existential presupposition different from that of (19).
As I have discussed previously, in my scenarios, the child's task was to recover the content of the at-issue proposition once the content of the CI has been removed. Next, consider why the child provides negative responses to both experimental questions if he misconstrues a nonrestrictive relative as restrictive.

(22)   A: The man who invented television was highly educated.
        B: Actually, a woman invented television.

(23)   Was the man highly educated?

In (22), B denies the content of the existential presupposition contributed by A's utterance. As a result of this, the truth-value of, "The man who invented television was highly educated," is undefined. It is for this reason that the question in (23) cannot be answered with certainty. In the present experiment, children provided negative responses rather than expressed uncertainty when the truth-value of a sentence in question was undefined for them. Some children also provided the "don't know" responses to both scenarios. However, it is unclear if these responses were indicative of the restrictive interpretation of the relative or of the child's general inability to interpret the scenario.

Next, consider J1's (7 y. o.) response to the questions following the Skiing scenario, which illustrate that she is treating nonrestrictive relatives as restrictive.

(1)   Did the boy with red hair win the competition?
        J1: "No, the boy with red hair was short. Mark won the competition."

(2)   Did the boy with red hair have the longest skis?
        J1: "No, he didn't have the longest skis. It only looked like it."

J1's response to (1) indicate that, for her, the truth-value of (18) is false; she treats the relative in (18) as restrictive. Next, consider J1's response to the Drawing scenario.

(24) One day, Mark's little sister Julie, who was four, decided to draw a picture of her favorite doll. She wanted Mark to help her but he didn't feel like drawing dolls. He wanted to draw an airplane. Mark and Julie's room was really messy and, at first, they couldn't find any pencils. Mark and Julie started to look for pencils under the table. When they finally found some pencils, they started to draw. Mark drew an airplane in blue pencil. Little Julie, who found a pink pencil, drew a pink Barbie doll. When she was finished, she gave her pencil back to Mark. Oh, wait, she gave her pencil back to Mark because Mark was the one who found both pencils under the table. Julie didn't find the pencil herself.

(1)   Who drew the Barbie doll?
       J1: "Her brother."

(2)   Who found a pink pencil?
       J1: "He did."

Here, J1 is also treating the content of the nonrestrictive relative as restrictive.

Following each scenario with supplementary relatives, children were asked about the truth-value of the at-issue proposition and that of the CI. Four patterns of responses were found:
a) the child provides positive responses to both questions
b) the child provides negative responses to both questions
c) the child provides the "don't know" response to both questions
d) the target response: the child provides a positive response to the question concerning the truth-value of the at-issue proposition and a negatives response to the question concerning the truth-value of the CI.

Importantly, there are no instances in which a child responds negatively to the question concerning the truth-value of the at-issue proposition and positively to the question concerning the truth-value of the CI. This supports the hypothesis that during the first stage of acquisition of supplementary expressions children misanalyze these constructions in the two ways that have been discussed here – either as contributing entailments or as restrictive.

4.2.1.4 The Second (Adult) Stage (CIs as CIs)

At this stage, the content contributed by the conventional implicature is viewed as independent from that contributed by the at-issue proposition. When the content of the implicature is cancelled, the at-issue proposition can still be recovered.

Consider the response to the Skiing scenario of a child who was in the adult stage.

(25)   The boy with red hair, who had the longest skis, won the competition
(1)   Did the boy with red hair win the competition?
       M.O. (6 y. o.) : "Yes."
(2)   Did the boy with red hair have the longest skis?
       M.O.: "No. They looked longer."

4.2.1.5 Supplementary Relatives: Why the Anchor Makes a Difference

Section 4.2.1.5 discusses the question of why using a Proper Noun vs. using a Common Noun as an anchor in constructions with supplementary relatives makes a difference. As it was previously mentioned, two types of constructions with supplementary relatives were used in the present experiment. The supplementary relative was anchored either by a DP that had the semantics of a definite description or by a DP that had the semantics of a proper name. When a definite description is used as an anchor, comma intonation is the only clue to the effect that a nonrestrictive interpretation of the relative is intended. In this condition, 5-year-olds responded either positively to both questions or negatively to both questions; thus they were in the first stage of acquisition of these constructions. 9-10-year-olds had a 100% rate of adult responses. When a proper name is used as an anchor, the sentence does not have a grammatical interpretation if the relative is taken to be restrictive. 80 % of the 5-year-olds provided adult responses when a proper name was used as an anchor for the supplementary relative. One may argue that children misinterpret supplementary relatives anchored by DPs that have the semantics of definite descriptions solely because they fail to interpret the connection between comma intonation and CIs.

4.2.2   The Adverbs

In section 4.2.2, experimental results with speaker- and utterance-oriented adverbs are discussed. In a pilot experiment, it was found that children misconstrued CI-contributing adverbs as VP-modifiers. In order to test if children also misconstrued VP-modifiers as CI-contributing adverbs, a control scenario was used in which the adverb *clearly* was used as a VP-modifier. Potentially, *clearly* may have been misconstrued as a CI-contributing adverb; however, none of the children misconstrued it as such. It appears that the VP-modifier interpretation of the adverb is the default and that the child arrives at the CI interpretation of the adverb only if he discovers that the VP-modifier one is inapplicable.

In the experiment, the CI-contributing adverbs were used in the sentence-initial position, which is the most common position for this type of adverbs. Importantly, both on their VP-modifier and CI interpretations, sentence-initial adverbs are separated from the rest of the sentence by comma intonation. Thus, when a speaker- or utterance-oriented adverb was used sentence-initially in the scenarios employed in the present experiment, comma intonation was not a reliable clue to the effect that a CI interpretation of the adverb was intended. As in the case of scenarios in which supplementary relatives were used, the child's failure to interpret the connection between comma intonation and CI in constructions with CI-contributing adverbs could not be the only stumbling block.

In The Acquisition of Adverbs (1999), Alvarez provides experimental evidence demonstrating that in acquiring different uses of manner adverbs (*quickly, foolishly, well, carefully, loudly*, etc), both English-speaking and Spanish-speaking children go through the following stages. Initially, all manner adverbs are construed as VP-modifiers;

subsequently, children acquire subject-oriented uses of manner adverbs; utterance-oriented uses of *well* are acquired at a significantly later stage. In view of these experimental results, in the present experiment, my prediction was that, in the initial stage, children construed all adverbs as VP-modifiers. In addition, I expected children to find utterance-oriented uses of adverbs more challenging than their speaker-oriented uses. The first prediction was confirmed; initially, children construed CI-contributing adverbs as VP-modifiers.

It needs to be noted here that only three adverbs – *honestly, frankly* and *luckily* -- were employed in the present experiment; assuming that the adverbs in question are representative of their adverb classes, the present experimental results may be construed as indicative of the differences in the acquisition of speaker- vs. utterance-oriented adverbs.

4.2.2.1 Stage One

In section 4.2.2.1, the VP-modifier stage of the acquisition of speaker- and utterance-oriented adverbs is discussed. First, consider a scenario in which the speaker-oriented interpretation of the adverb *luckily* was intended.

(26)   Hide-and-Seek

Mark and Julie were playing hide-and-seek one day in the garden. It was Mark's turn to hide and Julie's turn to look for him. Mark wanted to hide really well. He climbed on top of a big apple tree. It was taking Julie a very long time to find Mark. Julie was getting hungry. But she made up her mind to find Mark and wasn't going to quit. Julie was not going to leave anything to chance. She thought about it carefully and decided that the only place where she hasn't looked was the big apple tree. Luckily, Julie found Mark after all.
Did Julie find Mark because she was lucky?
The Adult Response: No
Why?

All of the five-year-olds responded affirmatively to the question following the scenario. The affirmative response is indicative of the VP-modifier reading of the adverb; children take *luckily* to modify the verb *found*. This interpretation of the adverb is clearly ruled out by the context. Adult controls respond negatively to the question following the scenario.

(1)   Did Julie find Mark because she was lucky?
J2 (9 y. o.): "Yes, because she said at the end she was lucky to find Mark."

Next, consider the scenario in which the utterance-oriented interpretation of the adverb *honestly* was intended.

(27)   Fishing

One day Mark and Julie went fishing. When they were about to start fishing, a fisherman saw them. The fisherman knew that there was plenty of fish in the pond and he wanted all of the fish for himself. The fisherman told Mark, "there are no fish in this pond." Julie didn't hear what the fisherman said, so she asked Mark to tell her what it was. Mark told Julie, "<u>Honestly, the fisherman said that there are no fish in this pond.</u>"

(1)   Was Mark honest with Julie?
        The Adult Response: Yes
        Why?

(2)   Was the fisherman honest with Mark?
        The Adult Response: No
        Why?

With one exception, all of the five-year-olds interpreted *honestly* on the VP-modifier reading in this scenario. On the VP-modifier reading of *honestly*, the adverb modifies the verb *said*; if a child takes *honestly* to modify the verb, he will answer positively to question (2) above. As in the Hide-and-Seek scenario, the context rules out the VP-modifier reading of the adverb. Consider M. O.'s (6 y. o.) response.

(2)   Was the fisherman honest with Mark?
        M.O.: "Yes. Cause, like, most grown-ups are honest with kids and he believed him."

4.2.2.2 Stage Two (Adult)

At this stage, speaker- and utterance-oriented adverbs are construed as contributing conventional implicatures. The youngest child who got the speaker-oriented reading of *luckily* was the seven-year-old M.A.

(1)   Did Julie find Mark because she was lucky?
        M.A. (7 y. o.) "No... She saw a big apple tree and said, 'Why don't I eat some of them?' When she, like, picked an apple, she saw Mark up there."

The youngest child who computed the target utterance-oriented reading of *honestly* in his response to the Fishing scenario was five.

(1)   Was the fisherman honest with Mark?
        B1 (5 y. o.): "No. Because he wanted the fish for himself."

(2)   Was Mark honest with his sister?
        B1: "Yeah."

Children's responses to scenarios with the two types of adverbs are summarized in tables 5 through 8.

Speaker-Oriented Adverbs																
Subject	M	S	N	B1	B2	K	M.O.	M.A	J1	P	B3	L	J2	H	C	B4
Age	5	5	5	5	5	6	6	7	7	7	8	8	9	9	10	10
VP-Modifier	√	√	√	√	√	√	√		#			√	√			
CI								√	#	√	√			√	√	√

Table 5. Constructions with Speaker-Oriented Adverbs.

The Key for tables 5 and 6: "√" indicates the child's response; "#" indicates that the experimenter could not interpret the child's response as indicative of either the VP-modifier or the CI readings.

Speaker-Oriented Adverbs	#	%
Subjects	16	100
VP-Modifier reading	9	56.2
The target CI-reading	6	37.5
Uninterpretable response	1	6.25

Table 6. Constructions with Speaker-Oriented Adverbs (summary of results).

Utterance-Oriented Adverbs																
Subject	M	S	N	B1	B2	K	M.O.	M.A	J1	P	B3	L	J2	H	C	B4
Age	5	5	5	5	5	6	6	7	7	7	8	8	9	9	10	10
VP-Modifier		√	√		√	√		#	√							
CI	√		√			√	#			√	√	√	√	√	√	√

Table 7. Constructions with Utterance-Oriented Adverbs.

Utterance-Oriented Adverbs	#	%
Subjects	16	100
VP-Modifier reading	5	31.25
The target CI-reading	10	62.5
Uninterpretable response	1	6.25

Table 8. Constructions with Utterance-Oriented Adverbs (summary of results).

Interestingly, all of the children who misinterpret utterance-oriented adverbs also misinterpret speaker-oriented adverbs (S, N, B2, K, J1). Five more children correctly interpret utterance-oriented adverbs but misinterpret speaker-oriented adverbs (M, B1, M.O., L, J2). Children who provided target responses to the scenarios with speaker-oriented adverbs provided target responses to scenarios with other types of supplementary expressions as well (M.A., P, B3, H, C, B4). The experimental results indicate that, contrary to my prediction, speaker-oriented adverbs are acquired at a later stage than utterance-oriented adverbs. The answer to why this is the case lies in the semantics of the two types of adverbs, which will be discussed below.

4.2.2.3 Speaker-Oriented Adverbs

In section 4.2.2.3, the semantics of speaker-oriented adverbs is discussed. Following Jackendoff's (1972) earlier intuition, Bellert argues that sentences with evaluative adverbs express two asserted propositions. Evaluative adverbs (*luckily, happily, surprisingly,* etc.) give rise to a second proposition "whose predicate (the adverb) evaluates the fact, event, state of affairs denoted by S..." (Bellert, p. 342). Bellert further argues that sentences with evaluative adverbs express two propositions each of which can be negated independently ((28), (29)), an observation which is particularly relevant for the present work because in the experimental scenarios with supplementary relatives and nominal appositives children were asked to recover the at-issue proposition after the content of the CI has been negated.

(28)   Unfortunately, John has come

(29)   John has not come, fortunately

Semantically, Bellert treats constructions in which evaluative adverbs are used as multidimensional. In (28), the negative adverb negates the proposition evaluating the fact denoted by S, not S itself. In (29), negation does not take scope over the adverb. Potts (2003a) formalizes the intuition that evaluative adverbs give rise to multidimensional meanings.

4.2.2.4 Utterance-Oriented Adverbs

In section 4.2.2.4, the semantics of utterance-oriented adverbs is discussed. Bellert (1977) argues that pragmatic adverbs, such as *frankly, sincerely, honestly,* etc., "are predicates with two arguments: one is the speaker, the other one is the proposition... The speaker characterizes his attitude toward *what* he is saying" (Bellert, p. 349). As in the case of constructions with the evaluatives, Bellert treats pragmatic adverbs as contributing multidimensional meanings. She further points out that, as distinct from evaluatives, utterance-oriented adverbs enable speakers to contribute something to the specification of how the sentence is uttered. It is for this reason that all pragmatic adverbs may be used with the participle *speaking*.

Formalizing this earlier intuition, Potts (2003b) proposes the following semantics for utterance-oriented adverbs. He builds his analysis around a two-place relation termed 'utter', which is a relation between individuals and natural language objects. It holds of a pair <a, S> just in case the individual a uttered the sentence S. In turn, Potts defines *frankly* as a modifier of the 'utter' relation. In brief, the pair <a, S> is in the relation picked out by 'utter frankly' just in case a uttered S in a frank manner. Potts defines 'utter' so that the first member of any pair in the relation must be the speaker. This achieves speaker-orientation for both 'utter' and any modifier of it. In case of speaker-oriented adverbs, speaker-orientation is built into the semantics of the adverb itself; when the adverb takes the at-issue proposition as its argument, a speaker-oriented CI meaning is generated.

4.2.2.5 Why Speaker-Oriented Adverbs are More Challenging than Utterance-Oriented Adverbs

On a purely syntactic account of how the acquisition of speaker- and utterance-oriented adverbs takes place, one may not predict that speaker-oriented adverbs (*luckily, unfortunately, surprisingly* etc.) would be acquired earlier than utterance-oriented adverbs (*frankly, honestly* etc.). In Cinque's hierarchy of adverb phrases, utterance-oriented adverbs are located in the Spec of the highest "speech act" functional projection, while speaker-oriented adverbs are located in a lower functional projection.

(30)   [*Frankly* speech act [*surprisingly* evaluative...]]

Cinque argues that the fully articulated structure of the clause is provided by UG. The child "will only need to recognize and locate in the appropriate structural places made available by UG the morphological and lexical material provided by his / her language" (Cinque 1999, p. 107).

Considering the semantics of speaker- vs. utterance-oriented adverbs in more detail will provide an insight into why the former are acquired at a later stage than the latter. McConnell-Ginet (1982) and Ernst (1984) draw the following distinction between evaluatives (speaker-oriented adverbs) and pragmatic adverbs (utterance-oriented adverbs); while pragmatic adverbs "include" the meaning of the VP-readings, in case of the evaluatives, the connection between the VP-readings and sentential readings is not transparent. Consider the semantics that McConnell-Ginet proposes for pragmatic adverbs.

"Let ε be a member of Ad-V (*i.e., VP-modifiers* A.V.) such that the translation of speak ε is defined. Then it is possible to define ε', (*i.e., pragmatic adverbs* A.V.) a member of the syntactic category t/t... such that for φ, a member of t, ε'φ is equivalent to the discourse sequence *In making the following assertion, I speak* ε:φ" (McConnell-Ginet, p. 175).

(31)   John spoke frankly

(32)   Frankly, John doesn't care

If *frankly* is a member of Ad-V such that the translation of "speak frankly" is defined, then it is possible to define a pragmatic adverb *frankly* such that for φ, *frankly* (φ) is equivalent to the discourse sequence *In making the following assertion, I speak frankly*:φ.

McConnell-Ginet argues that, in the case of pragmatic adverbs, sentential readings are derived by adding the higher verb *speak*. In Potts' terminology, an utterance modifier like *frankly* is a function that restricts the utterance relation [[utter]]. McConnell-Ginet (1982) and Ernst (1984) argue that, in the case of evaluative adverbs, the connection between the VP-modifier uses and sentential uses is semantically opaque. Consider an illustration of this.

(33)   Sam sucks lemons happily

(34)   Happily, Sam sucks lemons

        (selective citations from McConnell-Ginet, p. 148).

In (33), the adverb *happily* is used as a manner modifier indicating how Sam sucks lemons; in (34), *happily* contributes "some sort of positive evaluation (by the speaker) of the fact that Sam sucks lemons" with no indication of the manner in which he does it (McConnell-Ginet, p. 148).

The acquisition of utterance-oriented uses of the adverbs in question is facilitated by the fact that, on their VP-modifying uses, which are acquired first, these adverbs frequently modify the verbs of saying. For instance, the VP-modifier use of *frankly* is the one where it has the subject whose referent is the speaker as its second (agentive) argument. The utterance-modifier use of *frankly* is also the one where it has the speaker as its second (agentive) argument. In the case of speaker-oriented adverbs, children cannot derive the fact that adverbs like *luckily* are speaker-oriented on the basis of their VP-modifier uses, which makes the acquisition of speaker-oriented uses of adverbs more challenging than that of their utterance-oriented counterparts.

5.   Conclusion

In section 5, the results and implications of the present study are discussed. Prior to the fairly recent work on conventional implicatures by Bach (1999) and Potts (2003a), conventional implicatures were conceived of in terms of meanings given rise to by lexical items like *therefore, even, but, again, yet* and *still* (Kempson 1975, Wilson 1975, Karttunen and Peters, 1979, Levinson 1983). Bach (1999) convincingly argues that lexical items that were traditionally viewed as giving rise to conventional implicatures, in fact, make truth-conditional contributions to utterances, i.e., contribute to what is said and not to what is implicated. Potts (2003a) demonstrates that supplementary expressions, such as supplementary relatives, 'as clauses', and speaker- and utterance-oriented adverbs, among others, give rise to meanings that conform to Grice's original conception of conventional implicatures. According to Potts (2003a), one of the main distinguishing characteristics of the CI is that it has the status of an entailment that belongs to a different plane of meaning than the regular entailment generated by the at-issue proposition of the sentence. It is in this sense that CI-generating supplementary expressions give rise to multidimensional meanings.

The present experiment was designed in order to test the hypothesis that multidimensionality is an innate part of UG. Another experimental goal was to explore how the acquisition of CI-generating supplementary expressions takes place in English. While, as a class of meanings, CIs are universal, their instantiation in the child's grammar takes place through the acquisition of complex lexical items that generate CIs in a target language. The factor that complicates matters is the syntactic complexity of expressions that give rise to CIs. Supplementary expressions are acquired relatively late for independent syntactic reasons. In view of this, the present experiment was designed so that in certain types of scenarios additional syntactic challenges were removed in order to facilitate the child's task of interpreting the constructions in question as multidimensional. The youngest children tested were able to interpret syntactically unambiguous constructions as multidimensional.

The following two classes of constructions were used in the present experiment: supplementary relatives and speaker- and utterance-oriented adverbs. The scenarios in which supplementary relatives were used elicited the most enlightening results. 80% of the youngest children tested, the five-year-olds, correctly interpreted these as giving rise to CIs if a DP that had the semantics of a proper name was used as an anchor. English relatives anchored by Proper Nouns do not have a grammatical interpretation on which they can be construed as restrictive.

In contrast, 100% of the five-year-olds failed to provide the target response to scenarios in which a Common Noun anchored the relative; only 60% of the 6-7-year-olds provided the target response to these scenarios; 100% of the 9-10 year-olds provided target responses. Constructions with supplementary relatives were misconstrued in the following two ways. The content of the supplementary expression was construed as giving rise to an entailment that had the same status as the entailment given rise to by the at-issue proposition; alternatively, the content of the relative was misconstrued as restrictive. Experimental results with constructions in which a Proper Noun was used as an anchor provided evidence supporting the hypothesis that the concept of multidimensionality is innate. However, this concept is not immediately utilized by children for syntactically ambiguous constructions. While being able to compute multidimensional meanings, younger children still have a preference for single-dimensional interpretations.

As far as the acquisition of speaker- and utterance-oriented uses of adverbs is concerned, it was found that only the older children, the 8-10-year-olds, were able to consistently interpret constructions in which these adverbs were used as multidimensional. One reason for the fact that interpreting CI-contributing adverbs proved to be more challenging than interpreting constructions in which other types of CI-contributing expressions were used is that sentential uses of the adverbs in question are rarely in the input that children are exposed to. Thus no occurrences of speaker- and utterance-oriented adverbs were found as a result of some extensive searches in CHILDES.

There is also a theoretical reason why the adverbs in question are more challenging than other types of CI-contributing expressions. Thus the child will fail to correctly construe one of the adverbs in question as sentential unless he is aware of the fact that it contributes a speaker-oriented meaning. Utterance-oriented adverbs are inherently speaker-oriented because they restrict the two-place utterance relation [[utter]] that has the speaker of the sentence as one of its arguments; a speaker-oriented adverb takes an at-issue proposition as its argument, which gives rise to a CI meaning that is the speaker's comment on the at-issue proposition.

However, in the case of scenarios in which constructions with supplementary relatives were used, the child may have been able to recover the content of the at-issue proposition once the content of the implicature has been removed without ever realizing that the implicature had the property of being a speaker-oriented comment. The child may realize that the implicature has the status of an entailment that belongs to a different dimension of meaning than the entailment given rise to by the at-issue proposition, and, at the same time, view the content of the CI as a kind of an impersonal comment on the at-issue proposition. In all of the experimental scenarios, supplementary relatives occurred in the matrix clauses, whereby the speaker of the matrix clause was the same as the speaker of the parenthetical. If it turns out that younger children do misinterpret CIs contributed by supplementary expressions as impersonal comments, then it is only to be expected that they would misinterpret sentential adverbs at this stage. In terms of the semantics of CIs, at this stage children have not acquired the fact that CIs are speaker-oriented meanings. In terms of the Point of View theory, at this stage, children fail to attach POV to functional categories (CP in case of the adverbs and supplementary relatives). Hollebrandse (2000) proposes that every CP has a representation for Point of View in the form of a formal feature. A given Point of View domain can be associated with a speaker, a hearer or a matrix subject, depending on the reference of the feature. In case of the adverbs, alternatively, children may need to acquire the fact that POV is attached to the lexical items themselves (Roeper, 2004 UUSLAW handout). As it was previously discussed, speaker-oriented adverbs proved to be more challenging than utterance-oriented adverbs. In case of the former, eight to ten-year-olds provided 100% of the target responses. In case of latter, only the ten-year-olds demonstrated a mastery of constructions in which these adverbs were used. These data are accounted for in terms of McConnell-Ginet's insight that, while in case of utterance-oriented adverbs there is a direct connection between the VP-modifier and utterance-modifier uses of the adverbs, in case of speaker-oriented adverbs, there is no transparent connection between the two uses of the adverbs. There is a further way to test McConnell-Ginet's account. When an utterance-oriented adverb modifies an interrogative, the dominant reading is the one on which the speaker implores his addressee to answer in a manner specified by the adverb.

(38)   Frankly, who was nominated to give a colloquium in the Fall?

On McConnell-Ginet's account, the prediction is that utterance-oriented adverbs modifying interrogatives should be more challenging because in these constructions there is no way to derive the target interpretation directly from the VP-meaning of the adverb, while in the case of the declaratives the child may straightforwardly do so.

To summarize, the fact that 80% of the five-year-olds were able to correctly interpret supplementary relatives anchored by Proper Nouns as contributing multidimensional meanings suggests that the concept of multidimensionality is available to children from the start. The experimental results also suggest that, when faced with syntactically ambiguous constructions, children exhibit a preference for single-dimensional interpretations. Also, there remains a possibility that children acquire the fact that CIs are speaker-oriented meanings only at a later stage. Overall, the present experiment has provided evidence in support of the view that the concept of multidimensionality is an innate part of UG and, thus, provided support for the continuity hypothesis.

References

Alvarez, I. 1999. *The Acquisition of Adverbs*. UMass dissertation

Bach, K. 1999. The Myth of Conventional Implicature. *Linguistics and Philosophy* 22(4): 367-421.

Bellert, I. 1977. On Semantic and Distributional Properties of Sentential Adverbs. *Linguistic Inquiry* 8(2): 337-351.

Cinque, G. 1999. *Adverbs and Functional Heads*. Oxford University Press.

de Villiers J. & de Villiers P. 1986. *The Acquisition of English*. Lawrence Erlbaum Associates.

Ernst, T. 1984. *Towards and Integrated Theory of Adverb Position in English*. Indiana University dissertation.

Grice, P. 1975. *Logic and Conversation*. In Cole and Morgan 1975: 41-58

Horn, L. 1996. *Presupposition and Implicature*. In Lappin 1996: 299-320

Karttunen L. & Peters, S. 1979. *Conventional Implicature*. In Oh & Dinneen 1979: 1-56

Loetscher A. 1973. On the Role of Nonrestrictive Relative Clauses in Discourse. *Papers from the Ninth Regional Meeting of the Chicago Linguistic Society*. 356-368. Chicago: CLS.

McConnell-Ginet S. 1982. Adverbs and Logical Form: A Linguistically Realistic Theory. *Language* 58:1, 144-184.

O'Grady W. 1997. *Syntactic Development*. The University of Chicago Press.

Pinker, S. 1984. *Language Learnability and Language Development*. Cambridge, MA: Harvard University Press.

Potts, C. 2003 (a) *The Logic of Conventional Implicatures*. UC Santa Cruz dissertation.

Potts, C. 2003 (b) A Layered Semantics for Utterance Modifiers, Talk presented at the Workshop on Direct Compositionality, Brown University, June 19-21, 2003.

Roeper, T. 2004. UUSLAW handout

Anna Verbuk

Anna Verbuk

Department of Linguistics
University of Massachusetts
226 South College
150 Hicks way
Amherst, MA 01003-9274
USA

averbuk@linguist.umass.edu

Made in the USA